I Walk Through the Valley

To each of the millions of Americans who served their country in time of war as a combat infantryman.

Your unselfish, Herculean efforts were responsible for America's glorious victories.

May your deeds of valor be remembered forever.

I Walk Through the Valley

*A World War II
Infantryman's Memoir of
War, Imprisonment and Love*

by
Bruce C. Zorns

McFarland & Company, Inc., Publishers
Jefferson, North Carolina, and London

Publisher's Note: Bruce C. Zorns died on October 27, 1990 (he was born on July 20, 1913), two months after sending us his manuscript, along with his Purple Heart, his dog tags, his Combat Infantry Badge, his escape map of France and a number of other documents, telegrams, and pictures.

Mr. Zorns wrote us in September of 1990 that "The story is true—it occurred on the dates, at the times and in the places mentioned—the characters are real, none is fictitious."

He wrote that it was quite a traumatic experience both for him and for the family he left at home ("I participated in some of the most bitter combat engagements in Europe" and was wounded, captured, and "endured endless days of misery in a prisoner of war camp"); at war's end he began a long rehabilitation in a succession of American military hospitals.

"Ever since my discharge from the Army in 1945 I had wanted to write of my experiences as a combat infantryman in World War II but I was too busy trying to make a living," he wrote us (he retired in 1980 as chairman of the board of the Brownfield State Bank and Trust Company, Brownfield, Texas). "I began my book in 1987, the year I moved to Kerrville, Texas. I completed the book in early 1990."

British Library Cataloguing-in-Publication data are available

Library of Congress Cataloguing-in-Publication Data

Zorns, Bruce C., 1913–1990.
I walk through the valley : a World War II infantryman's memoir of war, imprisonment and love / by Bruce C. Zorns.
p. cm.
ISBN 0-89950-607-0 (lib. bdg. : 50# alk. paper) ∞
1. Zorns, Bruce C., 1913–1990. 2. World War, 1939–1945—Personal narratives, American. 3. Soldiers—United States—Biography. 4. United States. Army—Biography. I. Title.
D811.Z663 1991
940.54'8173—dc20 90-53607
CIP

Manufactured in the United States of America

McFarland & Company, Inc., Publishers
Box 611, Jefferson, North Carolina 28640

Foreword

Millions of Americans served as combat infantrymen in World War II. This is one of the many stories of their participation in this war—a war that was to become the biggest and deadliest in the history of mankind.

It produced the biggest armies, the longest battle lines, and the most devastating weaponry of any war to date. It inflicted more suffering, it destroyed more, and it cost more than any other war. (Actually, it cost more than all the previous wars in the history of mankind combined!) It put 70,000,000 people in uniform and killed 35,000,000—most of whom were not in uniform—and it slaughtered more people indiscriminately than any other war.

There was never any doubt about what we were fighting for or whether the victory was worth the price. Few wars have had such a clear-cut purpose and conclusion. We fought to *win* and *win* we did! But when peace came it was a different world than the one we had known before—and it would never be the same again. World War II was a vast, earth-convulsing revolution, the after-effects of which are still going on.

One hopes and prays that such a monumental massing of men and material will never occur again. Perhaps the probing eyes of the satellites in the skies will prevent it.

—B.C.Z., 1990

Contents

Cast of Characters

Real People — Real Names

Bailey, C. W., Jr. (Bill)
Bailey, C. W., Sr. (Bill)
Bailey, Mrs. C. W., Sr.
Bailey, Lieutenant
Baker, Sergeant
Barber, John
Ballard, Rebecca
Benedict, Paul L.
Cunningham, Natalie (Nat)
Day, Mrs.
Freeman, Charley H.
Friedeburg, Hans von
Gearheart, Oscar W.
Gearheart, Mrs. Oscar W.
Gifford, Ernest
Good, Richard L.
Harris, Pete
Hawes, Richard W.
Herrera, Ernest
Ianella, Daniel R.
Jones, Captain
Kelley, Lawrence E.
Lewis, Bill

Lewis, Reuben G.
May, Ida May
May, Tom (Big Boy)
May, Tom, Mrs. (Granny)
Oxenius, Wilhelm
Parker, Melvin T.
Patch, Alexander M.
Percival, Arthur
Shigemitsu, Mamoru
Somer, John
Sowers, Captain
Stewart, Eva Jo
Stewart, Todd
Swan, Herman Arthur
Swan, Leila May
Tandy, Emily May
  (Cunningham)
Tibbets, Paul W., Jr.
Tinder, Private
Umezu, Yoshijiro
Zeigler, Major
Zorns, Thomas Bruce
Zorns, Virginia May

Real People — Pseudonyms

Holmes, Charles M.
Jones, Captain
Kenney, Bobby
Mohr, Captain
Moore, Marvin

Schmidt, Eva
Schmidt, Frau
Schmidt, Herman von
Slim, Sergeant
Turner, Major

"Yea, though
I walk through the valley
of the shadow of death,
I will fear no evil;
for thou art with me . . ."

Introduction

This is the story of me and my family caught up in the tragic winds of World War II, and it is similar to the stories millions of others in these United States who suffered through this great war can tell. Yet each of these stories will be different. So is this story different.

When I received my draft notice I was thirty-one years old and my family consisted of me, my wife Virginia May (whom I called "Ginny" most of our married life — a carryover from our courting days), and our eighteen-month-old son, Thomas Bruce.

Ginny and I were married shortly after I came to Brownfield from Texas Technological College in Lubbock where I had been working on a degree in Architectural Engineering. It was in the mid-1930s and I finally finagled a job as clerk at one of the local banks. Not because I wanted to be a banker, but because brand-new architects were not in demand during the depth of the Great Depression.

When the war started, we didn't own a house or a car, but we did own a bicycle equipped with two baskets — one on the handlebars and the other behind the seat. In my mind's eye I can still see Ginny pedaling that bicycle wherever she wanted to go around town with Thomas Bruce in the front basket and packages or groceries in the other. Our home was a small, three-room apartment with a handful of our own furniture.

Even though we were short on the material things, we were rich — rich because we were extremely happy and very, very much in love. And then the bubble burst! It came in the form of a letter I never expected to receive because I was a father and thirty-one years old.

ORDER TO REPORT FOR INDUCTION

The President of the United States,

To Bruce Cunningham Zorns

Order No. 828

GREETING:
. . . .

You will, therefore, report to the local board named above at Court House, Brownfield, Texas at 9:30 A.M., on the 24th day of March 1944.
. . . .
. . . .

R. A. *Simms*
Clerk of the local board

I had been drafted!

In three short weeks I was sent to Fort Sill, Oklahoma, for induction and then shipped on to Camp Hood, Texas, an Infantry Replacement Training Center, where I graduated from basic training and eventually wound up at Camp Campbell, Kentucky, assigned to the 62nd Armored Infantry Battalion, 14th Armored Division. My new division was ready to be shipped overseas for combat duty.

From the very beginning, I had hoped I wouldn't be put in the infantry or sent overseas. I managed to do both. I became a combat infantryman like one of the cartoon characters Bill Mauldin drew for *The Stars and Stripes*.

Willie and Joe were two mythical soldiers whose situations were always heartrending and, at the same time, hilariously funny. They did more to immortalize the combat infantryman than anything to come out of the war — with the exception of Ernie Pyle's writings.

In his book *Up Front*, Bill Mauldin describes the principles he used in creating Willie and Joe to portray the combat infantryman.

> I don't make the infantryman look noble, because he couldn't look noble even if he tried. Still there is a certain nobility and dignity in combat soldiers and medical aid men with dirt in their ears. They are rough and their language gets coarse because they live a life stripped of convention and niceties. Their nobility and dignity come from the way they live unselfishly and risk their lives to help each other. They

are normal people who have been put where they are, and whose actions and feelings have been molded by their circumstances. There are gentlemen and boors; intelligent ones and stupid ones; talented ones and inefficient ones. But when they are all together and they are fighting, despite their bitching and griping and goldbricking and mortal fear, they are facing cold steel and screaming lead and hard enemies, and they are advancing and beating the hell out of the opposition.

They wish to hell they were someplace else, and they wish to hell they would get relief. They wish to hell the mud was dry and they wish to hell their coffee was hot. They want to go home. But they stay in their wet holes and fight, and then they climb out and crawl through minefields and fight some more.

War correspondent Ernie Pyle wrote:

> In their eyes, as they pass, is not hatred, not excitement, not despair, not the tonic of their victory. There is just the simple expression of being there as if they had been doing that forever and nothing else.
>
> A soldier who has been a long time in the line does have a look in his eyes that anyone who knows about it can discern — it is a look that is a display room for what lies behind it: Exhaustion, lack of sleep, tension for too long, weariness that is too great, fear beyond fear, misery to a point of numbness, and a look of surpassing indifference to anything anybody can do.

I can relate to Willie and Joe — and to the soldiers Ernie Pyle wrote about. I was one of them.

The events described in this story are true; they occurred on the dates and in the places named. All of the people mentioned are real — none are fictitious. I have taken the liberty of supplying names for those I can't recall after forty-four years. (See cast of characters.)

From the day I boarded the bus for the induction center until the day I was discharged from McCloskey General Hospital in Temple, Texas, I wrote Ginny. I wrote letters from my foxhole, from my barracks, from recreational areas, during rest periods, and even while pulling KP! Whenever possible I wrote — 121 in all.

In one of her letters to me Ginny wrote that when she received a letter from me she read it, numbered it, and filed it in chronological order with the others so she could get it out and reread it when she didn't hear regularly.

Ten years after Ginny died in 1977, I was rummaging around in the storage room in the garage, and came across this box. It was on the floor and in addition to being covered with dust and cobwebs, it had begun to mildew. I cleaned the box as best I could and opened it. Much to my surprise I found two bundles of letters—one contained all of the letters I had written to her; the other contained all the letters she had written to me that had been returned to her with the notation, "Missing in Action," written on the face of the envelope.

I took these letters into my den, sat at my desk, and began to read them. As I read her letters to me and mine to her, I had vivid memories of the events and the impact this monumental war had on the lives of not only my family but on the lives of all of the people in this battered old world.

As I read and reread these letters I asked myself: "Why don't you write a story of this war? Use these letters to present a one-man view of some of the events in this war—events you saw take place in one small geographic area of embattled Europe."

I read some more, and ran across one from Ginny:

> My darling: I am worried about you more than ever since you have been committed to combat. Your letters all tell of your closeness to death and God. One of the songs of David keeps running through my mind—the Twenty-Third Psalm. You remember it, don't you?

Do I remember it? I repeat it to myself day after day. Yes, I will write the story! Its title will come from this beautiful song of the shepherd boy: "I Walk Through the Valley."

Chapter One

"You'll Never Get Rich, You Son-of-a-Bitch, You're in the Army Now"*

Ginny and I always slept late on Sunday mornings, till about noon, but this morning she woke me early, about ten o'clock, shoving me away from her.

"What's the matter?"

"I want you to get up and make some coffee. Remember? I made it last Sunday."

"Just one more time?" I ask her.

"No, it's late and I want some coffee."

"OK, stingy," and I sat up and turned on the radio just in time to hear the announcer say:

". . . the President of the United States."

The voice of Franklin Delano Roosevelt came in loud and clear as he made this startling announcement that was to affect the lives of every human being in the United States and over half of those in the world. Simply, and with controlled emotion, he said: "The naval and air forces of the Empire of Japan have attacked the United States of America at Pearl Harbor in Honolulu, on the island of Oahu, Hawaii. Tomorrow, I will ask Congress to declare war on the Empire of Japan."

We both got up and went into the kitchen. I got the coffee perking, and we sat down at the table and looked at each other in silent bewilderment. We didn't say anything, but we both knew our lives would never be the same, and I would take some part in the war that had just begun. There was no great burst of patriotism on my part, it was just knowing there was something that had to be done, so let's get on with it.

The President got on with it Monday morning. We managed to

*From a very popular little ditty of the time.

5

pick up his address to Congress, broadcast direct from this joint session. He began:

"Yesterday, December 7, 1941 — a day which will live in infamy — the United States of America was suddenly and deliberately attacked by the naval and air forces of the Empire of Japan."

There was only one negative vote.

Three days later the Germans and Italians declared war on us. Overnight, our country became united more strongly and with more singleness of purpose than had ever happened in our history. The cry, "Beat the hell outa' the Japs and the Krauts — only *unconditional surrender!*" became nationwide.

I was assistant cashier of one of the local banks when I was drafted. My *Greeting* from the President ordered me to report to local draft board number one at the courthouse in Brownfield at 9:30 A.M. on 24 March 1944 — which I did — and was inducted into the United States Army on 25 March 1944, at Fort Sill, Oklahoma.

And thus began the metamorphosis: the transformation of a normal, intelligent, healthy, religious, fun-loving, and, most of the time, law-abiding, young American male into a destructive machine trained in the art of fighting, killing, and survival. This was quite a change!

My first military assignment came at the draft board before we boarded the bus. I was appointed leader of the consignment of draftees on that bus to Fort Sill and charged with enforcing Selective Service Regulations while we were en route. My major responsibility was to find an eating place that would honor the voucher issued by the draft board for the noon meal.

It was nearly eleven o'clock when we got loaded and the bus pulled away from the station. There were the goodbyes, and these were hard. Virginia had brought me to the courthouse and had waited for the bus to take off. Saying goodbye to her was very difficult. I tried to be brave as I held her and said:

"*Don't Sit Under the Apple Tree....*"

I was trying to be funny, but when I looked down at her she was crying, and I broke down and cried with her.

When I climbed on the bus my eyes were full of tears. I never looked back at Virginia. When I looked around at the other draftees, I saw tears in their eyes too. I broke the silence:

"Well, we could float the ark with these tears."

That broke the ice, and everyone leaned back, relaxed, and talked as our bus headed for Lubbock — thirty-eight miles northeast.

APPOINTMENT OF LEADER OR ASSISTANT LEADER

OFFICE OF THE DIRECTOR OF SELECTIVE SERVICE
WASHINGTON

To Whom It May Concern:

Special confidence being placed in the integrity and ability of

BRUCE   CUNNINGHAM   LOWIS

he is hereby appointed $\left\{\begin{array}{l}\text{leader}\\\text{assistant leader}\end{array}\right\}$ of a contingent of selected men from Local

Board No. _____ ONE _____ of _____ TERRY _____ County, in the State

of _____ TEXAS _____

He is, therefore, charged with the enforcement of the Selective Service Regulations governing selected men enroute to Induction Stations during the journey from

_____ BROWNFIELD , TEXAS _____ to _____ FORT SILL OKLAHOMA _____ .

and all men included within the contingent are directed to obey his lawful orders during the journey.

By Order of the Director of Selective Service

Date_____ MARCH 24 , 1944 _____ _____ *O B Knight* _____
Chairman of Local Board

D. S. S. Form 158

Order appointing me leader of contingent of draftees to Fort Sill, Oklahoma.

"You guys want to stop and have lunch in Lubbock?" I asked.

"There's no other place between Lubbock and Fort Sill that will honor our meal voucher," observed one of the fellows.

"Let's start looking for a place as soon as we get in Lubbock," and I leaned over and told the driver our plans.

"I've been making this run for several years. The only places that will honor your voucher are the larger hotels. I suggest you try the Lubbock Hotel."

I looked around at my fellow draftees, and they indicated they thought this would be fine. I told the driver to stop at the hotel and I went in to see what I could do. The manager listened to my problem and called the coffee shop operator.

Their problem was whether or not they had enough food cooked so they could serve our group (about fifty) for the amount of the Selective Service voucher. The cafe man told me what he could serve for the money. It wasn't very fancy but there was a lot of it. I said OK and motioned to the guys to come in. They dug in and put away the grub. I paid for the meal; we boarded and took off for Fort Sill — several hundred miles away.

We woke the place up when we got there. It was nearly midnight, but there was an officer there to welcome us. He asked the group's leader to step forward. I did. I handed him the envelope and stepped back in formation.

There is an old army saying, "The Army travels on its stomach" — well, so do draftees. Before we were dismissed someone said he was hungry and then the whole group of fifty joined in. The officer said he would do what he could and led us to the mess hall. The mess sergeant had a room there, and waking him up did not help our cause. He finally said he would fix something. He served us hot coffee and sandwiches.

"I want you brand-new bastards to enjoy this. When you're through, clean off your table, throw the paper plates and cups and any other trash in the garbage can by the door as you go out."

The officers told the sergeant he would see it was done. The sergeant mumbled a few more obscenities and slammed the door of his room.

I remarked:

"Hey guys, this is your first Army meal."

"Don't get too damn excited about it until you see what's on your plate," said one of the draftees.

I looked down at my plate and there was a sandwich. I took the lid off, and there was a thin slice of Spam — two thick slices of Army-baked bread and a tiny slice of Spam.

I had gotten a cup of coffee before I sat down and had put a little milk in it. I looked at it, and it was a greenish color. I tasted it, and it was bitter, so I took it back to the serving counter and put lots of sugar in it. When I took another sip, it tasted like sugar syrup — better than that greenish, bitter taste.

It was close to 1:30 A.M. when we finished eating. The officer led us to the infirmary for a quick physical examination: height, weight, stick-out-your-tongue, spread-your-cheeks — and we had been examined. When we had finished dressing, the young officer gave us a five-minute talk on the Army — how great it was. Someone in the group yelled out:

"Bull-shit!"

"Who said that?" asked the officer but there were no confessions so he led us to our barracks and turned us over to our orderly. Little did we know what a misadventure this was to become. To describe briefly: horse's ass comes closest to the truth but that doesn't do him justice. However, considering the output, I suppose it fits him.

The "little corporal," as he was quickly named, took us to the supply room and issued bedding. Then back to the barracks and assigned bunks. Never have I met a more negative, ugly, and despicable person. He was convinced his mission in the U.S. Army was to insult, harass, belittle, and intimidate draftees. He took pride in the fact that his inductees were the most miserable on post! It was probably the first time in his life he had any authority over another human being, and he was going to make sure we knew it and didn't forget it. It was 2:30 A.M. by the time the little corporal got around to showing us how to make up a bunk, Army-style, and left. I was asleep before I finished undressing.

My induction began on 25 March 1944. I was assigned my Army serial number — I have never forgotten it, nor have I forgotten the importance of my dog tags. We stood in line while a detail of GIs manufactured our tags. Mine said:

BRUCE C. ZORNS
38693068
O
P

O was my blood type, P was my religious preference — Protestant.

The tags were two oblong, stainless steel plates, about the size of an elongated fifty-cent piece, connected with two stainless steel chains. One of these chains was much longer than the other. It threaded through a hole in the top of one of the plates and fastened around my neck. The short chain was fastened to the other plate in a like manner and attached to the longer chain for easy, quick removal. If I were killed, this tag would be left on my body for the Graves Registration team so my body could be properly identified.

After the dog tags came another physical, more shots, vaccinations, issuance of some of our uniforms and lectures — Sex Hygiene, Military Courtesy, and Army Regulations — and finally, evening chow.

This first evening was free, so several of us went to the base movie *Heavenly Bodies* starring William Powell and Hedy Lamar. Leaving the movie, we passed the Service Club, and I heard the jukebox playing, *I'll Walk Alone.* It was one of mine and Ginny's favorites. Right then and there the events of the past two days hit me right in the heart, and the bottom seemed to drop out of my life.

We all slept late on Sunday. We were just dressing when a tornado hit. It was the little corporal — and he was a cocky little fart. All he needed to make him a complete dictator was a little square mustache. He had a date last night, and apparently his girlfriend didn't let him have any because he was mean as hell this morning and determined to take it out on everybody.

He assembled the men and began a lecture and demonstration on the fine art of making up a bunk — Army way. He threw the sheet on the mattress and pulled it tight as he tucked it under. He worked until the sheet was so taut it didn't touch the mattress in the middle. Then he pulled a quarter from his pocket and threw it on the bed. It bounced up and down three or four times.

"I want you shitheads to make up your bunks every day with the sheet this tight. I will personally inspect each bunk every morning, and if my quarter doesn't bounce this high the bastard responsible will find his ass on KP, guard duty, latrine duty, or picking up butts the rest of the time he is on this post. Do you understand me? You son-of-a-bitch over by the window, did you hear what I said?"

He pointed to me. I wanted to kill him and tell God he died, but I didn't and instead said:

"Yes."

He kept on and on — yak, yak, yak, until he finally ran out of steam and left.

I dressed and went to church. It was the fifth Sunday in Lent. The nondenominational service opened with the words of welcome from Colonel Reuben G. Lewis, CO of the induction station. The sermon, *Our Duties to Fellow-Men,* was delivered by Chaplin Paul L. Benedict. It was excellent, and the music by the base choir was very good. I left feeling much better than the night before. Much of the loneliness and emptiness was gone — at least for a while.

RECEPTION CENTER RELIGIOUS SERVICE

26 MARCH 1944

FIFTH SUNDAY IN LENT

TEN FORTY-FIVE

MUSICAL PRELUDE: Private Jack W. Hoffman, Song Leader
                   Corporal Earl R. McCandless at the piano

CALL TO WORSHIP:

    Chaplain: O sing unto the Lord a new song;
                Sing unto the Lord, all the earth.
    Response: Sing unto the Lord, bless his name;
                Show forth his salvation from day to day.
    Chaplain: Declare his glory among the nations,
                His marvelous works among all the peoples.
    Response: For great is the Lord, and greatly to be praised:
                He is to be feared above all gods;
    Chaplain: Honor and majesty are before him:
                Strength and beauty are in his sanctuary.

INVOCATION PRAYER IN UNISON: "Almighty God, unto whom all hearts are
                open, all desires known, and from whom no secrets are
                hid, cleanse the thoughts of our hearts by the in-
                spiration of thy holy spirit, that we may perfectly
                love Thee, and worthily magnify Thy Holy Name. Amen."

HYMN 252, "The Doxology"

HYMN 26, "God Will Take Care of You"

GREETINGS FROM COLONEL REUBEN G. LEWIS, COMMANDING OFFICER

SCRIPTURE READING

PRAYER - THE LORD'S PRAYER

RESPONSIVE READING: "Confidence in God"
                      Hymnal with music : Selection 21, Page 360
                      Hymnal, words only: Selection 4, Page 145

ANNOUNCEMENTS

VOCAL SOLO: Private Hoffman

SERMON: "Our Duties to Follow-men"
         Chaplain Paul L. Benedict

BENEDICTION

POSTLUDE

Order of worship, Fort Sill, Oklahoma, 26 Mar. 1944.

After lunch I laid around the barracks, read, and napped all
afternoon, then back to the mess hall for dinner. Afterward, having
nothing to do, I strolled around the area and then stopped at the PX
for a beer. While drinking a bottle of Lone Star I happened to look

across the bar and saw a guy I graduated with from Abilene High School fourteen years before. We both jumped up and grabbed each other. It was great to discover an old friend in this hellhole. His name was Bobby Kenney, and it happened he was billeted in the barracks next to mine. It was just like a family reunion. We sat there and drank bottle after bottle of Lone Star and reminisced about school and people and things in Abilene. It was getting late and we were pretty well boozed up when the little corporal walked through the PX on his way to the barracks. Bobby and I were about broke, but we stayed and drank until all of our money was gone.

While we were sitting there I told Bobby about the little corporal.

"We have one just like him in our barracks. I think they are all alike — maybe trained that way. The talk around our barracks is a corporal is trained to be negative, ugly, and despicable — to the extent he is so sour on the world he smiles only when someone salutes him."

The beer didn't run out at the end of our money, so we left the PX and walked back to my barracks and sat on the steps and lit a cigarette. The little corporal walked out of the barracks, right between us, and down the walk toward Bobby's barracks. As we watched the cocky little fart, Bobby said to me:

"Bruce, you know how castrating an animal changes its personality and attitude?"

"Yeah, so what?"

"If we caught the little corporal, tied a rope around the bastard's right leg and hung him upside down to that rafter up there and let the other leg hang loose and cut his balls off, do you think his personality and attitude would change?"

"It sure couldn't get any worse. Let's try and see what happens."

It's hard to believe we actually got up and went inside Bobby's barracks to get him when *Tattoo* sounded and that meant *Taps* in fifteen minutes. We went to the latrine instead. I wonder what would have happened if that bugler hadn't intervened?

We were marched to supply early the next morning and were issued all those things new soldiers are always issued.

Brand-new inductees are very easy to spot, especially when they are marching in formation for the very first time. Every time a platoon of inductees that had been in the Army three or four days longer than we had passed us they sang out loudly:

> You're in the Army Now
> You're Not Behind the Plough,
> You'll Never Get Rich
> You Son-of-a-Bitch
> You're in the Army Now.

Someone in our group began to sing the little ditty, and before long everyone had joined in. By the time we got to the mess hall we were as good as any other unit. After lunch there was time to write Ginny a quick note:

> You should see me now, I'm GI Joe in person! We were issued the rest of our uniforms this morning. We had heard the Army just shoved something at you and told you to take it and wear it and like it. Well, I found out differently. They took us to supply and very carefully measured us for everything we would wear. Then they gave us a complete issue of everything. I had to try on everything and was inspected twice to see if everything fit according to Fort Sill's standards. Two different officers, independently of the other, made inspections before I could take anything out. My dress uniform looks good — and so do my fatigues.
>
> This morning the group I arrived with sat through three training films: *Military Courtesy, The Articles of War,* and *Sex Hygiene.*
>
> We have been on the go since 0545 hours, and I am tired. I can see there's not going to be much rest in the Army. Tomorrow, when we take our classification tests, we are through with the induction process. After that we begin the waiting game to see where we have been assigned and to what kind of duty.

The induction process was over. Assignments were slow in coming. Time hung heavily on our hands. In the Army — or in any other military service — the less the GI has to do the thicker the scuttlebutt flows. Speculation as to where we would be assigned and when was rampant. One of the newer inductees was a bull-shit artist from way back. He convinced many of the guys that he had actually seen a report lying on the first sergeant's desk listing everyone's assignment. More important, no one, he said, was assigned to infantry! Most were assigned to ordinance or the quartermaster corps — and a small contingent were slated for MP duty in Hawaii. And later another artist said he had seen a classified document lying on the seat of the CO's jeep. It said all new inductees were on hold because of a significant decrease in offensive pressure from the Germans, and if the decrease held, unassigned inductees would be released and sent home!

"Tenn ... *shun!*"

It was the gravel voice of our drill sergeant. Our company commander had just come in.

"At ease, men. Colonel Lewis has just told me he has received orders to prepare for an inspection team from Washington. He wants all troops to assemble on the parade ground and police the area thoroughly. Your drill sergeant has been told what the colonel wants and will see that his orders are carried out. Carry on sergeant."

"Tenn ... *shun!*"

After the lieutenant left the sergeant said:

"At ease, men. You men are to put on your helmet liners. Buckle the chin-strap of your helmet. Now grab hold of the chin-strap, and carry your helmet like you would a bucket. Follow me!"

He led us to the south end of the parade ground and spaced us evenly and far enough apart so we covered the width of the parade ground. We were facing north.

"You privates are going to get this parade ground as clean and smooth as a basketball court. Walk slowly. When you see something: If it moves, salute it; if it doesn't, pick it up; if you can't, paint it.

"Hold your helmet in your left hand by the strap. Bend over from the waist with your arms away from your body and your butt high in the air. All I want to see as you move north is ass-holes and elbows and a little cloud of dust. Move out and pick this parade ground clean. Private Zorns, get your butt up and your elbows out and start filling that helmet. Let's go — hut two. Get those heads down and those asses high."

We made the trip up and down the parade ground three times. At the end of each trip we deposited our helmet-full of debris in a ditch at the north end as our drill sergeant told us.

The next afternoon the sergeant assembled us again:

"The Corps of Engineers jumped on Colonel Lewis and told him filling the ditch at the north end of the parade ground would cause serious flooding in the area. They want the rocks out of that ditch and stacked in a neat pile on the west side of the ground so Army trucks can pick them up at a later date. Put on your helmet liner. Fasten the chin-strap of your helmet; hold it in your left hand and follow me."

I thought the first rocks I picked up were awfully smooth, like those you find in a stream that have been washed smooth by flowing water over the ages, or by constant handling by the tens of thousands of soldiers passing through Fort Sill. I still wonder who takes the rocks stacked on the west side of the parade ground and scatters them evenly over the parade ground so the next contingent of troops can pick them up, put them in the ditch, and then. . . .

Saturday afternoon I decided to call Ginny. The lines of waiting soldiers were long and telephone lines were busy, but I waited and kept trying. It took five hours fo finally get through. It was worth the wait. After noon chow on Sunday I wrote her:

> It was so good to hear your voice after all this time. I couldn't help it but I cried a little after we hung up. I know it's silly for a 31 year old man to cry but I was — and still am — so lonesome.
>
> As tough as things are we do have a lot to be thankful for. It's hard on both of us to be apart like this, but when you think about it that's about the only hardship we have. Some of the fellows in the barracks really have problems. There's one guy whose wife died two months ago today. He sure is blue. I've been talking to him most of this afternoon and I think I did cheer him up a little. His wife was about eight months pregnant and was doing fine until she got sick one night. The doctor told him it was kidney poisoning. She died the next day. I really feel sorry for him having to go through all this Army crap with no one to back him up.
>
> This will come as a shocker but there are men here, some of whom were leaders in their towns, that flunked the short-arm inspection. They have a venereal disease. They were immediately put in another barrack and isolated from the other troops.
>
> Then there are the guys who worry constantly about the faithfulness of their wives or sweethearts. Some say they have private detectives spying on them and get weekly reports.
>
> A lot of them have financial worries — some have families who are sick and in poor health.
>
> Gotta go. There's shipping call. I'll finish this when I get back. Sure hope my call is there. . . .
>
> No luck — guess I'll hang around a little longer and pick up more rocks. Some of the guys, including Bobby Kenney, got their orders and are taking off early in the morning. Guess I'll get mine eventually.
>
> Will try to call you when I do. I would like to know where I'm going for basic. Wherever it is I'll be restricted for two weeks. After that I can get off on passes, and we can live together for a little while.

Instead of picking up rocks on Monday, I caught guard duty, black wooden rifle and all. I was relieved at 1800 hours on Tuesday — just in time to answer shipping call and write Ginny a quickie post card:

My orders came! I'm leaving at 0130 tomorrow for parts unknown, but it looks like we are going a long way — chartered troop train, kitchen, and sleeping cars. Duty rosters have been posted for the trip. I have been assigned KP for however long we are enroute. The Army must think I'm a good hand; they keep giving me such good assignments! Will write or phone you when I can. Love, Bruce.

Chapter Two

Of Guns and Men

The KP duty I pulled wasn't very hard, but it sure was steady work. The train was late getting off, and it was 0300 hours when I climbed into my upper berth. It was 0530 when I was called to the kitchen to prepare breakfast. About the time we had cleaned up after breakfast, it was time to begin preparing for lunch — after lunch, dinner — after dinner I got to bed about 2300 hours — and then it began all over. Mine was a kitchen-sink view of the country, but for the some thirty hours on the train we seemed to be going around in circles. The countryside looked the same — and it all looked like Texas.

On the third afternoon, a captain, who was CO of this shipment of troops, came into the dining-car kitchen and told us we were approaching Camp Hood, Texas. He said finish in the kitchen as soon as we could and go to our berth, pack our gear, and be ready to disembark within an hour.

Army transport trucks, engines running, were waiting to take us to our barracks area. There, Corporal Bailey was waiting to welcome us to our new post. He assigned us our barracks and bunks, took us to quartermaster for bedding and then to the mess hall for evening chow. After dinner we were free for the rest of the day. We were reminded of *Tattoo* at 2215 and *Taps* at 2230.

I was one of the first out of the mess hall and made a beeline for the recreational center and a telephone. A strange voice on the phone in Brownfield accepted my call but Ginny wasn't there! She had gone to the store. I was told to call back in an hour. One hour later the call went through. I don't know which of us was more excited, but there's not too much we didn't talk about for the next forty minutes. We finally said our goodbyes and hung up after reminding ourselves how high the telephone bill would be that month.

The next day was Saturday, so I spent most of the afternoon writing Ginny a long letter.

My darling Ginny:

. . . so great to talk to you last night . . . am at Camp Hood, Texas
. . . 38 miles from Temple and 60 miles from Waco . . . the largest
Army post in the U.S.A. . . . 160,000 acres . . . can train 160,000
troops at one time . . . also one of the best in the nation . . . now an
Infantry Replacement Training Center (IRTC).

I have been placed in a clerk company. Out of 10,000 soldiers who
came here last week only 240 were chosen for this training—lucky
to be one of them! We will have seven weeks of basic infantry training and ten weeks of special training in typing, accounting, and
allied subjects. The entire clerk company is made up of college
men—bankers, accountants, insurance men, etc. They are a nice
bunch of fellows, and I know I'm going to like everything.

The training is going to be extremely hard—we will be working
night and day. Only the most physically-fit are sent to the Infantry.
The limited service men are sent to places like quartermaster,
finance, hospital corp, and other non-combat assignments. After six
physical exams I've been told—after each of them—that I'm in A-1
physical shape.

I've gained some weight and am much stronger than when I left
home. The chow is really good, and there is plenty of it. Wish I could
share some of the things we eat every day that are rigidly rationed
to you civilians.

Here the war is taken very seriously. We live, talk, and sleep war.
We study war—learning to defend ourselves, learning to survive.
Army records show the largest percentage of casualties come from
those who goofed off in basic training—I'm not going to be one of
them.

Tomorrow is Easter Sunday—I would like to be with you and
Thomas Bruce. Being separated is the biggest and most heartbreak-
ing part of the war. It is agony. We are not the only ones who feel
this way.

I love you so very much, Bruce.

Basic training held no surprises for most of us. We had heard
tales of those who had been through it before us, and we had seen
all kinds of movies about war and training for war.

The stories we heard, and the movies we saw were glamorous.
There was nothing glamorous about being a private in the Infantry
undergoing basic training process!

A typical day began at 0530 when we fell out of bed and stood
reveille at 0545; 0600 to 0630 made bunks, swept and mopped barracks floor, washed our hands and face, brushed teeth, combed hair;
0630 breakfast; 0700 began the day's training, sometimes with a lecture and sometimes with a drill but wherever it started, it was
intense!

Rush to the drill field; rush to the lecture hall; rush everywhere!

"Tenn . . . *shun!* Fall . . . *in!* Right . . . *face!* Left . . . *face!* About
. . . *face!* Present . . . *arms!* Forward . . . *haarch!* Platoon . . . *halt!*
To the rear . . . *haarch!* About . . . *face!* Order . . . *arms!* Parade . . .
rest! Fall . . . *out!*

It was that way all day long. We thought we were through for
the day when we were dismissed, then Corporal Bailey got a call to
take us to a lecture until 1700, then bathed, changed on the double;
retreat 1730; supper. After supper we undressed, climbed in our
bunks, and tried to get a little rest—but not for long. Corporal
Bailey came in and told us to get dressed again—we were going to
a lecture on "ORGANIZATION OF AN ARMY." We sat there like good
soldiers and pretended we were listening. We were dismissed at 2200
hours; marched back to our barracks; jumped into our bunks—
asleep for the second time, then we would fall out and start over at
0530.

I never got too tired to think of Ginny and Thomas Bruce. After
two hard weeks of basic training, I asked the first sergeant for a
weekend pass—and got it. When I called Ginny she was ecstatic—
but had anticipated my call. She had already borrowed her mother's
car, been to the ration board for extra gasoline ration stamps, asked
her mother and sister, Ida May, to come along and help with the
driving—and to take care of Thomas Bruce so she and I could have
some time alone. She had even reserved two connecting rooms at the
Kyle Hotel.

When they got to Temple, they drove straight to camp. By
some hook or crook they gained admittance at the front gate—
drove past all check points to my barracks area—right up behind my
platoon which was marching, and honked the horn. The whole platoon jumped in fright—some troops broke and ran. Our platoon
leader looked around and saw what had happened and issued this
quick command:

"Platoon . . . *halt!* Order . . . *arms!* Private Zorns, Fall *out!* Fall
back in for retreat at 1700 hours.

"Platoon . . . Right shoulder . . . *arms!* Forward . . . *haarch!*"
And they marched off without me.

I ran to the car, leaned in the open window, and kissed
Virginia. I was sweaty, filthy, and smelled worse than a goat. I was
in full uniform with all of my equipment, including my helmet.
Thomas Bruce finally made himself heard. I dragged him out of the

Left: Author and son Thomas Bruce during first leave from Camp Hood in front of Kyle Hotel. Right: Ginny Zorns.

back of the car and held him very tight. He broke loose a little and looked me up and down and said:

"Da, Da, 'ook 'ike 'oldier."

"I'm training to be one."

"You c'othes wet."

"That's perspiration. It's very hot here and when you're marching you perspire a lot," I answered him.

"Can me be 'oldier when me get big? 'ooks 'ike 'un."

"We'll wait and see," and I handed him back to Mrs. May.

I spoke to Mrs. May and Ida May, and they both commented on how hard training looked. I didn't have any time to give them much of an answer; I wanted to talk to Ginny—we had so much to say to each other.

The platoon marched in front of company headquarters, halted, and did a right face. I excused myself and fell into formation for retreat. After we were dismissed, I went into the barracks, showered, dressed in Class A uniform, and reported to company headquarters for my pass.

Virginia and I headed for Temple for a rendezvous with heaven. The weekend was our honeymoon relived. We found a new

Private First Class Bruce C. Zorns in Class A uniform.

dimension, a new splendor, a new animation in our lives caused by the demands of war — separation for long periods of time, uncertainty, and anxiety. These demands heightened our desires.

I described this new dimension in the letter I wrote Ginny on Wednesday:

> Darling, I shall always keep, in my memories, the beautiful weekend we had together. I would not take anything for it. Just seeing you and Thomas Bruce, even for such a short time, was a shot-in-the-arm for me. I have really been on-the-ball this week. So you see, my darling, you are everything to me. You are what makes me tick! The thought of your being mine makes everything bright and beautiful; makes everything go as it should; makes everything easy and makes me rested when I am tired.
>
> If anyone should ask me about this new dimension we have found in our love, I will tell them it is a trophy-of-war and can only be won by participants.
>
> I love you so very much, Bruce.

On Thursday we went on maneuvers. It was a twenty-mile hike with full equipment. A hard rain was falling, and we were instructed to put on our raincoats. The night was hot; the humidity was high; the plastic raincoats caused us to perspire heavily, and our clothes got wet — even with raincoats. Off they came at the first five-minute break. This wasn't an easy job. We were wearing all of our equipment over the coats — backpack, bed roll, ammunition belt with all of its attachments, gas masks, shovel, canteen and canteen cup, first-aid pack, and suspenders to hold it all up. We were determined to get rid of the coats. We worked on the double and completed the change in time to respond to the command:

"Tenn . . . *shun!*"

We stepped off briskly on the order:

"Forward . . . *haarch!*"

Everyone was singing *Sing-in' in the Rain.* We marched along for a long time continuing to sing. Finally we began to wonder if it wasn't time to turn around and head back. At the next five-minute break, I asked our squad leader.

"We're taking the short-cut back," he told me.

It turned out there was one big booby-trap in the short-cut back. While we were on our break he told us:

"We're going to have to cross a little creek on this short-cut, but it doesn't amount to anything — about six feet across and not over six inches deep. This way will save us a lot of time.

"OK, on your feet. Tenn ... *shun!* Right shoulder ... *arms!* Right ... *face!* Forward ... *haarch!* Hut, two, three, four; hut, hut, three, four!"

The little creek may have been six feet wide and six inches deep during the dry season, but during this monsoon it had spread out and looked more like the mighty Mississippi. Before we crossed, we did a little scouting. The creek turned out to be about three hundred feet wide and about five feet deep in the middle. We all thought:

"What-the-hell? We are already as wet as we can get. Let's wade in and slosh across."

We marched and marched in the rain, in more rain, and in downpours. We finally halted in front of company headquarters at 0300 hours. Captain Sowers told us to clean our equipment before going to bed. We would have inspection at 0545 hours.

Training got more rigorous and more combat oriented. We went to North Camp Hood for a week of training with the M-1 rifle. This was the first time to fire our rifles. We fired on the range and were scored for accuracy. Out of a possible 210 points I got 147 and qualified as a marksman — not very good, but passing. The rifle frightened me at first, and I missed the first shot I squeezed off. The men working in the trench at the other end of the field signaled the scores by running up a flag. After my first shot, they didn't run up a flag but instead raised a pair of white drawers. Everyone looking — and I think the whole company was — yelled out:

"You got yourself a pair of Maggie's Drawers. You're not supposed to play around with them. Now don't be naughty."

Every time I missed, up came the drawers.

My score was low because I got too many pairs of Maggie's Drawers.

North Camp Hood was way out in the boondocks — twenty-eight miles from our barracks area at South Camp Hood. Accommodations were primitive and the weather unbearably hot.

We finished work on the range late Saturday — about 220 hours — strapped on all of our equipment, and began the long twenty-eight-mile march back to our barracks. No one griped about beginning this long march so late — everyone was glad to get out of this hellhole.

About midmorning Sunday we got home. We showered, cleaned up, and fell into our bunks where we stayed until dinner. Then we had to clean our equipment for inspection at reveille Monday.

At 0630 hours Monday we began our march to the field to practice throwing grenades. Next to our M-1 rifle, the grenade was our most important weapon. It was a traumatic experience — throwing the grenade the first time. Our cadre demonstrated the procedure, then handed one to me to throw. I pulled the pin, threw the thing as far as I could, fell flat on my face, and while lying there waiting for it to explode, prayed that the fragments would not zoom in on us and blow an arm or leg off. The cadre gave each man in our platoon a grenade to throw. Every time one was thrown, we all fell on our faces. We each threw six in all, and this took all day. We marched back to our barracks and had dinner at a table. We had been introduced to C ration for lunch, which we ate out of a can while sitting on the ground — not bad when you're hungry.

We left again the next day at 0630 for field maneuvers. We threw grenades again — on orders and in unison. Our platoon was lined up in front of a cliff with a three-feet high fence along the edge. Each of us was given a grenade and told to hold it in our right hand. The platoon leader gave the command:

"Pull . . . *pin!*"

Every one executed. Then we got the command:

"Throw . . . *grenade!*"

It appeared that everyone threw his grenade. I glanced at the soldier next to me — he had been acting like he was frightened throughout this maneuver. I could not believe what I saw. There, in the palm of his right hand, was his grenade — pin pulled, handle released — ready to explode.

Instinctively I gave the order:

"Platoon . . . *down!*"

I grabbed the grenade out of his hand and threw it over the fence and down the cliff. With all the power I could generate, I lunged toward him with my head down and hit him in the stomach with my steel helmeted head. He hit the ground like a chunk of lead and I was on top of him — and the grenade exploded. I raised up and looked around — no one was hurt — the fragments had behaved themselves. I noticed our platoon leader motioning for me. I walked over to him. He wanted me to tell him exactly what had happened. He had the walkie-talkie operator contact Captain Sowers. After a brief conversation with the captain he told me:

"The captain told me to keep the platoon together in this location. He will be here within thirty minutes. He wants to talk to you before he talks to the soldier."

In about twenty-five minutes the first sergeant drove the captain to where the lieutenant and I were sitting. We stood up and when the captain got near the lieutenant said:

"Tenn . . . *shun!*" We came to attention and saluted. He returned the salute and said:

"At ease men. Now Private Zorns, tell me exactly what happened."

I gave him a very detailed account. He asked me a number of specific questions about the incident and finally said:

"Thank you, that's all."

He turned to walk away and the lieutenant said:

"Tenn . . . *shun!*" We saluted as he walked off.

That was the end of the incident. We never heard what happened to the soldier. However, at retreat Captain Sowers commended me highly on the way I performed in a dangerous situation.

After training with grenades we took up the bazooka. This weapon looked very much like a long piece of stove-pipe. It was named after the gadget comedian Burns played in his movie skits and on his radio shows. It was actually a rocket launcher — and anti-tank weapon. The rocket it fired could burn through more than three inches of the hardest steel. It took two men to fire it, but these two men, if their aim was accurate, could knock out a multimillion dollar tank and cremate the crew. It was a devastating weapon.

We had a lot of fun with enemy aircraft defense. First we practiced firing our M-1 rifles at moving aerial targets. Some were little self-propelled planes controlled by radio, while others were target planes pulled by Air Force planes. This was great sport. I stuck my chest way out whenever I knocked one of the target planes out of the sky.

Next we fired the .30-caliber machine gun at the planes. The most deadly and accurate weapon, the one we depended on for enemy aircraft protection, was the .50-caliber machine gun. One was mounted on each half-track. Every man in our company was taught to fire it. It would really reach out and bring them down.

Our seven-week infantry tactical training ended with shooting these target planes out of the sky. To celebrate, I went to the PX with some of the fellows for a few longneck Pearl beers. During this celebration, I was notified I had been appointed acting platoon sergeant. This was the highest position a trainee could hold. It was not a permanent rank — I was a private acting in the capacity of a sergeant. I would be in command of my platoon — giving all of the orders. I thought this was quite an honor to have been chosen for this position — maybe my work had been satisfactory.

I called Virginia and told her the good news. She was very happy about this. Then I asked her:

"Do you know what day next Sunday is?"

"Of course I do. It's 4 June 1944, and that is our fourth wedding anniversary. You did remember it, didn't you?" she replied

"I was wondering if you and Thomas Bruce could come here, and we could spend it together — we've spent the other three together. I'm through with my basic infantry tactical training and during my special training I can get off every night and every weekend I am not on duty. I sure do want you to come."

"I'm so happy you said that! I have already made plans to come out if you thought it would be OK, and we would not interfere with your training. I have made reservations for a week at the Keystone Hotel in Lampasas. This time I thought we would come on the bus and not have to worry about borrowing a car. We will arrive there Saturday morning, 3 June."

"Ginny, the trip will be very hard on you since you're bringing Thomas Bruce. Besides, the weather is very, very hot."

"I don't care about all of that. These are my plans and this is what I want to do."

"You've done a great job planning all of this. I can hardly wait for you to get here — see you about 1700 hours 3 June. Bye, darling, I love you so very much."

We began our technical training Monday, and that evening I wrote Virginia and told her all about it.

> We have finished our first day of technical training, and it's a snap. It's just like going to college — all classroom work — no marching, no rifles, no field packs, no ammunition belts. We do have one hour of physical training each day, but I enjoy that.
>
> We reported to class at 0700 and broke for lunch at 1130. We reported back to class at 1300 and off for the day at 1700. I can't believe this is the infantry. Our first seven weeks were hell, so I guess we deserve a little easy life for a while.
>
> I'm like the little boy waiting for Christmas. Seems like time will never pass so Saturday can get here and I can be with you. I know we will have a wonderful time. One we can look back on in the future and say, "What a Wonderful Fourth Anniversary!"
>
> Good night, darling, sweet dreams. I know mine will be sweet, for they will be of you. I love you so very much. Bruce.

Time did pass, and Saturday at 1715 I stood in front of the door to Ginny's room and knocked. She opened it and stood there – the most beautiful, the most inviting person I had ever seen. Neither of us made a move for a moment. Then we reached out and embraced and kissed each other passionately – time and time again. Thomas Bruce thought enough was enough. I felt him pulling at my pants leg and saying:

"Daddy! Daddy!"

I let go of Ginny, picked him up, hugged, and kissed him. He began talking so fast no one could understand what he was saying, so I set him down.

We were all nervous for a little while. This prompted Ginny to pull a quart of bourbon out of her suitcase and ask:

"Drink, anyone?"

"Cote, Mommy. I want a cote," Thomas Bruce yelled out.

Virginia poured some Coke over ice and handed it to him. He took it and sat by the window with a funny book and entertained himself.

She mixed each of us a drink – bourbon and Coke; we sipped on them and began to talk about all of the things we'd saved to tell each other. As she talked, I looked at her and thought:

How beautiful she is! Much prettier than I remembered. Her hair is gorgeous – a natural auburn – red more predominant than brown – hangs down to her shoulders – turns outward at the ends. Her dress defines her figure – full breasts, small waist, shapely hips, beautiful legs. I wonder how I got her to marry me.

We talked and talked and she mixed us a second drink. About the time we finished this she said:

"It's later than I thought. We had better get something to eat before the coffee shop closes."

Thomas Bruce agreed:

"Eat, Mommy; eat, Mommy."

We ordered a large meal. It was delicious. As we ate, we talked and talked. We couldn't catch up with our talking. The place began to clear out, and Thomas Bruce got sleepy, so we went to our room.

She put Thomas Bruce to bed and went into the bathroom to dress. Framed in the doorway, as she came out, was the most alluring sight I have ever seen. She had on a beautiful black lace nightgown – what a seductive sight! She walked over to the side of the bed where I was sitting. I stood up and we embraced. As we stood there so close to each other, I placed my hands on her shoulders and slid them under the straps of her gown and pushed them off. The gown slithered down her body to the floor. I pulled her onto the bed and pulled the sheet over us. All of the stars in the blue sky of Texas fell upon us.

It was nearly noon when Thomas Bruce came in our room saying:

"Eat, Mommy. Eat, Mommy."

Ginny was still in my arms — more seductive than last night. She told him to get his clothes while she drew his bath. When he went into his room she broke away from me, jumped up, and put on a robe.

It was a little after 1300 hours when we left our room. The dining room was nearly full, but the hostess told us to start through the buffet; she would have us a table ready when we got through the line. They were serving turkey and dressing and baked ham and all of the goodies that go with them. We loaded our plates, picked up our dessert, and headed to our table. We ate and talked and talked.

It was a beautiful central Texas spring day. We walked out onto the streets of Lampasas — to walk off some of the lunch — and to look around the city. We saw a lot of soldiers up and down the street — all dressed in their crisply ironed khaki Class A uniforms. Various insignia indicated many branches of the military were represented here. There were some Army nurses among them. All ranks were mingled together. I asked one of the nurses where these men were from.

"All of these soldiers have been wounded in either Africa or Italy — they are all amputees. They are from McCloskey General Hospital in Temple. We have them out as part of their therapy. When we take them out on Sunday we have them dress in their best. They seem to enjoy wearing their Class A uniforms.

"At McCloskey they are undergoing their rehabilitation training — being fitted with prostheses, trained in their use — and discharged. These men have served their country; they have made their sacrifice; we can never do enough for them."

"We appreciate the information, thank you," I told her.

We continued down the street. I asked Ginny:

"See that infantry sergeant ahead of us?"

"How do you know he's in the infantry?" she replied.

"By the blue braid on his cap and the Combat Infantry Badge

above his empty left sleeve. I wonder how he feels about the badge and all those ribbons he's wearing?"

I turned and asked the nurse the same question. She looked questionably at me and said:

"These men are all proud of their service to their country. They carry no bitterness or resentment for the sacrifice they have made."

We spoke to the sergeant as we passed. He responded courteously. There was a look in his eyes that sparkled with joy because he had served honorably in this war.

We saw a distinguished looking soldier in a wheelchair propelling himself across the street — something he would have to do for the rest of his life. We could tell that both of his legs were off at the hip. As he got closer, we noticed his hair was beginning to grey — it was beautiful. Suddenly, as he turned the chair toward us, the reflected rays of the sun blinded us, and we noticed the brightly polished silver eagle on each shoulder — a full colonel!

When he got a little closer, I saluted him. He returned my salute.

"Private, where are you taking your basic training?"

"Sir, how did you know I was in training?"

"When you have been in the service as long as I, it's easy to spot a trainee."

"Oh. I'm in training at Camp Hood."

"That's only thirty-eight miles from Temple. We're neighbors, soldier. I was with the Seventh Army in Sicily. General Patton was commander then. I was commander of an artillery unit. One morning, a German artillery shell landed in the middle of us — killed many of my men, wounded many others, including me. There's not much of me left, but this little bit is happy to be back in the United States."

He began to talk to Virginia. I noticed a small soldier go into a nearby drug store. He was an infantryman, and from his back he looked as healthy as I. He sat at the bar — both of his hands were missing. I could not tell what he ordered, but when the soda-jerk set it in front of him he looked around for the nurse that came in behind him and nodded to her. She reached across the bar and got two straws — put them in his mouth. He bent his head and drank his drink. Again, he looked for his nurse — spotted her — stuck out his left chest. She came over and got the cigarettes out of his pocket, put one in his mouth, held a lighted match to it; he puffed two or three times, she took it out of his mouth, and dusted it in the ashtray.

When he finished, she snuffed it out in the ashtray, reached in his right shirt pocket, got money out of a coin purse, and paid the soda-jerk. He got up and left. When he came out, I could tell he was a private and was wearing the Combat Infantry Badge. He spotted the colonel and yelled something to him. The colonel motioned him over. When he got close, the colonel put out his right hand — palm up — the private laid the stump of his right arm in it; the colonel gently closed his hand around the stump and they looked at each other and smiled. There was no saluting here — the colonel and the private were equal now in rank.

Virginia began to walk off. I saluted the colonel and joined her. We noticed a soldier on crutches coming toward us. His right pants leg hung loosely and flopped back and forth with each step. Thomas Bruce noticed him and pointed to him as he yelled:

"Mommy, Mommy, thee that . . ."

She grabbed him and put her hand over his mouth. She knew he was fixing to say:

" . . . man has just one leg!"

She told him never to point or say anything about a handi-capped person if they could see or hear him.

As the soldier got nearer, I saw two gold bars on his shoulders and the Silver Wings on his left chest. As we passed, I saluted. He had to stop — balance himself with both crutches under his left arm — to return my salute.

We continued to walk down the streets of Lampasas on that beautiful Sunday afternoon of our fourth wedding anniversary. I glanced at Ginny, and she looked disturbed. I asked her:

"Have you ever thought of my coming home from war with missing parts?"

"No, I had only thought of two possibilities. Your being killed in one piece, or your coming home in one piece. I had never thought of just a part of you coming home."

We walked along in silence for a while. Then I asked her:

"Do you think death is the supreme sacrifice in war?"

She did not answer this question. She looked at me, and I did not answer it. Neither has ever attempted to answer it.

The sun was getting low. We had spent all afternoon on the streets of Lampasas with the wounded who were home from war. I needed to get back to camp soon to continue my training. I had a feeling I would be called to continue the fighting that had taken so much of these men.

We stopped for a sandwich and a Coke. Thomas Bruce was getting tired. I needed to get my shaving kit from the hotel. She did not go to the bus depot with me — she had to put Thomas Bruce to bed. We said goodbye at her door. As I was leaving, she grabbed me, kissed me, and said:

"Darling, I don't want you to go overseas to fight in this war."

"I don't either," I answered her.

Plans were made for a sitter to stay with Thomas Bruce while Ginny came to the base tomorrow night. We would go to the service club, have dinner, and dance to the music of the juke box.

Our anniversary had been wonderful. One we would never forget, but yet I was disturbed. What I had seen this afternoon would stick in my mind for a long, long time.

Technical training continued as usual on Monday. We were dismissed at 1700 hours promptly. I showered, changed to Class A uniform, and walked to the bus station to meet her.

We walked arm in arm toward the service club. We were sublimely happy to be together again. We walked and talked and walked and talked. We stopped and kissed — we wanted each other so badly. We kissed and kissed, walked and walked, talked and talked ourselves to the service club, and out on the patio.

All of the furniture had been painted — each piece a different color — red, blue, yellow, brown, orange, white, black, and green. The color added charm and romance to the atmosphere already punctuated by the brilliant central Texas sunset. We were two wartime lovers who had found our haven.

Ginny selected us a table. Throughout dinner the juke box was playing many of our favorites — *I'll Walk Alone, It Had to Be You, Don't Get Around Much Anymore.* It was a beautiful dinner.

I walked over to the box, dropped a nickel in, and selected the song dearest to us — *I'll Get By as Long as I Have You.* I asked her to dance with me. I held her so very close to me as we danced and danced under all of the twinkling stars in heaven — suddenly heaven was shattered by a shrill whistle — the club would close in fifteen minutes.

We left as we came in — arm in arm. I showed her the short-cut to the bus station. We walked and talked and kissed, then we came to a little stream. We crossed it, and I really kissed her and wanted her so much I could hardly stand it. She said no, and we continued to walk arm in arm to the bus station.

She got on the bus and we waved goodbye. My heart was sad

as I headed for my barracks. I got there in time for *Tattoo* — I had fifteen minutes before lights out and *Taps*. I hoped my dreams would be of seeing her tomorrow.

Tomorrow was Tuesday, 6 June 1944. It began as usual, but the routine changed when we broke for lunch at 1130. My platoon fell in with all of the others of Company A, and it fell in with all of the other companies of the 175th Training Battalion in front of battalion headquarters. Company commanders gave the order:

"Order . . . *arms!*"

The entire battalion was standing at attention when its commander appeared.

"At ease, men," the colonel ordered.

"I have an important announcement. The invasion of Europe began this morning. As of now — 1200 hours — the time on the Normandy beaches is 1800 hours. Approximately 150,000 Allied troops are ashore occupying nearly eighty square miles of France."

A thunderous roar broke out with this electrifying announcement, although the invasion had been anticipated for a long time. The colonel did not try to stop this emotional outbreak — instead he became cheerleader and whooped it up as loud as anyone.

When everyone calmed down he continued:

"The invasion achieved complete surprise. Our losses have been staggering. General Eisenhower's *Hortatory Message* says, 'The tide has turned! The free men of the world are marching together to victory!' I expect a heavy demand for all available infantrymen. Thank you, men — that's all."

As the colonel left, company commanders ordered:

"Ten . . . *shun!* Right shoulder . . . *arms!* Forward . . . *haarch!*"

As we marched back to our company area, there was complete silence except for the sound of marching feet — each man's mind was spinning like a windmill in a sandstorm trying to comprehend the effect on his life of this stunning news.

As Virginia got off the bus, I noticed she was concerned. After we kissed, she said:

"I heard about the invasion over the radio this morning. What have you been told about it?"

I told her what the colonel had said and emphasized his remark about a heavy demand for infantrymen. She replied:

"Now I know you will be shipped to Europe. I talked to the hotel manager about my staying another week, if it was alright with you. What do you think?"

"It's a great idea! I'll have the time since I'm in the middle of my technical training. I doubt we'll see each other after I leave Camp Hood. You are very smart, sweetheart, to think of this. We will have two more weekends together; I'll come to Lampasas and spend them with you and Thomas Bruce, you come into camp on week-days; we'll have a marvelous time. Come on, let's head for the ser-vice club — dinner and dancing under the stars. OK?"

She responded by squeezing my arm. She picked out a table and we ordered. After dinner, I went over to the juke box, put my nickel in the slot, scanned the directory, and selected, *I'll Be Seeing You.*

I walked her to the dance floor, and as the music began I put my arm around her and held her tight.

"Why did you play that record?" she asked.

"Because we both like it. When I leave this place, we won't see each other for a long, long time — if ever again. If you want to know what I'm doing, get this record and play it. I'll say the words while we dance."

We danced in each other's arms to this beautiful music under the stars up in heaven. We needed to enjoy each other as much, and as often, as we could — the rest of our life together was one big, blurred question mark.

Once again the whistle shattered this interlude. We walked out arm in arm, across the little stream to the bus depot; another good-bye, *Tattoo,* and *Taps.*

On Wednesday, 7 June, the news media were crammed full of the news of the invasion. The most startling account was written by America's most respected war correspondent — the lovable little man with the worm's eye view — Ernie Pyle.

> The wreckage was vast and startling. The awful waste and destruction of war, even aside from the loss of human life, has always been one of its outstanding features to those who are in it. Anything and everything is expendable. And we did expend on our beachhead in Normandy during those first few hours.
>
> For a mile out from the beach there were scores of tanks, and trucks, and boats that were not visible, for they were at the bottom of the water — swamped by overloading, or hit by shells, or sunk by mines. Most of their crew were lost.
>
> There were trucks tipped half over and swamped, partly sunken barges, and the angled-up corners of jeeps, and small landing craft half submerged. . . .
>
> On the beach itself, high and dry, were all kinds of wrecked vehicles. There were tanks that had only just made the beach before

being knocked out. There were jeeps that had burned to a dull gray. There were big derricks on caterpillar treads that didn't quite make it. There were half-tracks carrying office equipment that had been made into shambles by a single shell hit, their interiors still holding the useless equipage of smashed typewriters, telephones, office files. . . .

In this shore-line museum of carnage, there were abandoned rolls of barbed wire and smashed bulldozers and big stacks of throw-away life belts and piles of shells still waiting to be moved. In the water, floated empty life rafts and soldiers' packs and ration boxes, and mysterious oranges. On the beach lay snarled rolls of telephone wire and big rolls of steel matting and stacks of broken, rusting rifles.

On the beach lay, expended, sufficient men and mechanism for a small war. They were gone forever now. And yet, we could afford it.

We could afford it because we were on, and we had our toehold, and behind us there were such enormous replacements for the wreckage on the beach that you could hardly conceive of the sum total. Men and equipment were flowing in from England in such a gigantic stream that it made the waste on the beachhead seem like nothing at all, really nothing at all.

Ginny came into camp every night during the week and I went into Lampasas and spent the weekends with her and Thomas Bruce. These two weeks were the happiest and most wonderful of my entire life. They passed so fast. Now I had to say another goodbye to her Sunday night — awfully hard to do. I felt so alone on the bus back to camp.

After I left, she wrote me a letter.

I'm just so blue I can hardly stand myself. Seems like I've been saying goodbye to you for years and years. Every time I do, it simply cuts me to pieces. I love you with all of my heart, and I never want to be anywhere except with you.

I have been hoping and hoping you would never go overseas. Now it seems certain you will go soon.

This war is creating uncertainties unlimited. I'm going home and get everything cleared up so, if you do call me, I can come to you without anything hanging over my head. I hope it won't be too long before I can see you again — one can't go too long without one's heart, can one?

It seems as if I have grown up a lot these past two weeks, and I'm a lot older, if you please, because there simply isn't anything worthwhile except the three of us and our lives together. A lot of things I've thought about — just things in general — just don't matter anymore. You fill my thoughts constantly, and I'm forever thinking of ways and means to be with you. More than anything, I want us three to be together — somehow — somewhere — just anywhere — it doesn't matter as long as we're all together.

This was one of the happiest anniversaries and Father's Day I've ever had — and it was one of the saddest — my darling, as I know it was with you. But we were together, weren't we?

That night on June 4, 1940, when I placed my heart, my confidence, and myself in your hands, was the happiest moment of my life. And how well you have cherished these things! And I, in turn, accepted these things from you. Now we are so much a part of each other we are just one, only one. My darling, I want us together for years, and years, and years to come. I wouldn't be me without you. I would be a person — just any person — without you ever again.

This damn war! But some day it will end and we can be together again and time will stretch on and on into years and years. We will have all of the time we want and hours won't seem like seconds. We can go on with our plans — work — and play.

I need you so much, and I miss you constantly. But, there is going to be a next time, and someday the one we have been looking for — All of the Time. You have my love, my life; we have Thomas Bruce; we have ourselves. Ginny.

The summer at Camp Hood was miserably hot. On 19 June, 120 new men were attached to our company. Fifty-two were hauled in from the field in ambulances their first day of training — heat prostration. Only half this number required ambulance service the next day. It was hot, hot, hot, but training went on — hot weather — cold weather — wet weather — dry weather — its routine basis.

During the last week of our technical training, we were tested to see if we had learned anything. We were assigned to various companies of the battalion as company clerks — I got Company D.

We did all of the clerical work at company headquarters including making the payroll. The work was interesting and pleasant, but it passed in a hurry, and we came face to face with two weeks of bivouac in the terrific midsummer heat of Central Texas.

Our company was scheduled to move out at 1900 hours Sunday, July 16. I had to go out early on the trucks loaded with equipment for the bivouac area. I came back to march my platoon in company formation to the area. We carried full field equipment — steel helmet, gas mask, rifle, full field pack. It all weighed seventy-four pounds. It was twenty miles to the area. Estimated arrival time was 0100 Monday. We arrived fifteen minutes ahead of this time, pitched our tents, slept until 0400, and began our problem for the day.

This was intensive battlefield training — and to make it warlike, it was hell. The terrific heat took its toll — men fell to the ground, out cold with heat prostration. I came close to joining these victims of the heat, but I took everything thrown my way. We changed locations to finish bivouac. We were moved to the Battle Conditioning Course. We quickly changed its name to Killer Kollege.

We completed bivouac with a trip through the Infiltration Course. The course was about the size of a football field. On either end was a deep trench. At the finishing end, there were two .30-caliber machine guns on either side. Each could be swiveled from one side of the course to the other and were set to spray bullets eighteen inches above the ground toward the beginning end.

We were lined up in the trench at the beginning end — spaced evenly so we covered the entire width of the course. Our assignment was to slither up the side of the trench, onto the course, keep our butts and our heads down, creep the entire length of the course under the screaming hot lead just inches above us, and slide into the trench at the finishing end without getting shot.

The rain had been pouring for two days — the course was covered with over two inches of liquid mud. In unexpected places throughout the course were tangles of barbed wire. We crept into one of these, our clothes got snagged, and it was hard to get untangled, and in doing so, we triggered an explosive charge that scared the hell out of us and made us want to jump straight up — but there was the hot lead — so we stayed down and let the explosion blow liquid mud all over us and into the barrel of our rifle.

As we crept through the mud, we gradually became mudpies — rifles were clogged, mud was leaking into our gas masks, mud was scooped into the inside of our field packs. We were one big muddy mess from head to toes. But we made it — no one was even scratched — and slid head-on into the finishing trench at 2200 hours, completely exhausted, but extremely happy. We had finished the basic training required to become combat infantrymen.

We shook off as much mud as we could and began the long march back to camp. Exhausted as we were, no one complained about this late start. We marched the rest of the night and on into the morning. Sunday at 0400 hours, we stacked our equipment by our bunks, stepped out of our stiff, muddy clothes, left them standing where they were, showered as much of the mud off as we could, climbed into our bunks, dreamed the sweetest dream in the world — *we're through with basic training!*

Sandwiched in between clothing and equipment inspections

and physical fitness tests for overseas duty, I got my orders. I stole enough time out of clothing inspections that night to write Virginia:

> Here it is — just like a bombshell. I'm getting a furlough effective Monday, 7 August 1944, for 12 days, plus travel time, to report to Fort Meade, Maryland for overseas assignment — something I thought I would never get.
>
> I have never been so blue in all of my life. The thought of leaving you and our baby and going so far away is more than I can stand. I know it is going to be as hard on you — perhaps worse. But, after all precious, we are two young, intelligent Americans doing our duty as God has shown us how to do this duty. This we are doing without faltering or hesitation — we are both proud of this — we hold our heads high and bow to no one.
>
> There is one thing to be excited about in all of this, and that is we have 12 days of our own — to be together and do exactly what we want. I want this to be our second honeymoon — to go places and do things together.
>
> We had both thought I would be assigned as a cadre here at Hood. You and Thomas Bruce would move either to Temple or Lampasas and set up housekeeping for the duration — but then, "The best laid plans of mice and men. . . ."
>
> Just bring your and the baby's clothes and enough money for us to have a glorious time together for twelve days. Please bring my suitcase. I'll use it instead of my B bag.
>
> I'm really looking forward to seeing you Saturday at 1930 hours. It will be better for you and Thomas Bruce to come to the base Saturday and Sunday — will go to the service club — eat — dance — and have a great time. Monday pick me up at 0800 — we will take off on my furlough. By-the-way, Monday, 7 August, is Thomas Bruce's second birthday. We will all three celebrate.
>
> I'll be seeing you Saturday — just drive to the bus depot — we'll walk to the Service Club. I do love you so much, Bruce.

There was plenty for me to do to get ready to leave Camp Hood — inspection after inspection — and checking in equipment to quartermaster. The clocks ticked off the time to Saturday and at 1800 hours chimed an end to the rigors of basic training at Camp Hood. I took a shower, dressed in my Class A outfit, and ran practically all the way to the bus station. I got there about fifteen minutes early — she was already there, waiting. Her sister, Mrs. Rebecca Ballard, had driven her and the baby to be with me — and in her car. They had just gotten out of the car and were locking it when I got there. I grabbed Ginny and hugged and kissed her, picked up

Thomas Bruce and hugged and kissed him. I kissed Rebecca and thanked her for bringing them. She was excited about getting to come — had heard a lot about Army life and glad to get a first-hand peek-in.

We took the short-cut — across the little stream — everyone talked at the same time, and before we knew it we were on the patio. Wowee! There had been some changes — brightly colored umbrellas had been placed over each table. These were as varicolored as the tables and chairs. Rebecca could hardly believe what she saw — a patio as beautiful as any at the finest country club in the country. Thomas Bruce was beside himself, and we let him select our table. He was in his chair, on his knees, with a fork in one hand and a knife in the other, ready to eat before we got seated.

Just as I sat down, the juke box began to play the beautiful and very popular *What's New?* The gorgeous red afterglow of a mid-Texas sunset, the delectable and enchanting music, the bright colors of the patio, the uncertain sensation of our love and our lives being sacrificed to the hungers of war, all combined to create an atmosphere that encouraged us to drink heavily from the Silver Chalice — and look for divine guidance through the hell that lay before us.

The menu offered tasty items. Each ordered something different and each enjoyed what they ordered. Even before we had finished, a bunch of the fellows from A Company dropped by and spoke to Ginny. I introduced them to Rebecca, and she immediately got a date for dancing. A couple of guys asked Thomas Bruce if he would like to be a soldier — his answer, of course, was yes — and we were left to ourselves. I asked her:

"What are the plans for our furlough?"

"I thought when we picked you up Monday we would head for Austin — it's not very far, about sixty miles — get two rooms at a nice motel, spend a couple of days or as long as you want, and take off to Brownfield. When you get through visiting your friends, we can go to Ruidoso some, to Lubbock some, just do what we feel like doing. The whole idea is for us to be together. What do you think?"

"I think it is all great. We must remember, however, 7 August, is Thomas Bruce's second birthday. We need to get him a present and have some kind of a party for him, don't we?"

"I have a present for him in Rebecca's car. It's not very much, but it's what he wanted — an Army uniform with ammunition belt, canteen, and holster with toy Colt .45. My plans are to go to a restaurant that serves Mexican food — it has been a long time since we have eaten any, and we all love it. I will make reservations first thing when we get there — ask them to have a small birthday cake with two candles and serve it for dessert. When we finish the cake, I plan to give him his present. Don't you think he will enjoy this?"

"You bet he will. I might have known you would think of everything, darling. There is something of a rather serious nature we need to talk about. I don't know how to say this delicately, so I'll go ahead and say it crudely. Being apart from each other is going to be hard on each of us. We will be tempted many times. There is only one answer — be constantly true to each other. Some day, hopefully before too long, this war will be over and we can pick up our happiness where we left off and keep it for a lifetime. We have both seen so many people in a moment of loneliness and boredom — and for a brief moment of promised joy — throw away a lifetime of happiness. I know we will keep our happiness for ourselves — and forever."

The juke box began to play *Do You Miss Me Tonight.* I held her very close to me as we danced to this beautiful tune. Next up was, *You'll Never Know.* As we began to dance to this one, I looked down at Virginia. She was looking up at me, and when our eyes met she began to sing the words to this enchanting song.

As she sang, there was a look in her eyes that displayed the thoughts in her mind:

"This can't be happening to us — this is all a dream — someday we'll be together again — you won't get killed — you'll come back to me — one day it will all be over — we can start all over again — you do love me, don't you?"

She finished her song, and the whistle blew.

We walked back to the table and sat down.

"Bruce, nothing bad is going to happen to us, is it? You won't let it, will you?"

"We'll have to ask God to help us. I'll pray to Him tonight."

"Will you, please?"

Rebecca's boyfriend brought her back to our table. I could tell she was having a wonderful time. I have never seen her so happy since her husband had been killed a few years before in a pickup and truck collision. Thomas Bruce was missing.

"I bet I know where he is," I told them, and got up and went upstairs to the Reading and Writing Room. There he was, marching up and down the room to the orders of my buddies. He was having an exciting time. He did not want to come with me, but when my friends told him the club was about to close, he reluctantly came along.

We left the club, talking, walking, and laughing. We'd had a wonderful evening. There was a round of goodbyes. They drove away and I returned to my barracks and *Tattoo* and *Taps*.

They came to camp Sunday morning and we went to church together — a very emotional service. Over the entry was this saying spelled out in wooden letters nailed in place: "Live Each Day So You Can Die Any Day."

At 0800 hours Monday, I was at company headquarters to pick up my orders and travel voucher. As I left, I grabbed my suitcase, which I had left outside, and ran to the station.

They were there waiting for me. As we drove through the gate, I looked back at Camp Hood and said goodbye to eighteen weeks of Herculean effort to become a combat infantryman — and to many an exotic night dancing under the big, bright stars deep in the heart of Texas.

I was much more mature — both physically and mentally — than when I had arrived — much, much more.

Chapter Three

Of Fort Meade-Camp Campbell, Bill Bailey, and Mrs. Day

Virginia had reserved two large adjoining rooms at one of Austin's finest motels — swimming pool, wading pool. She even thought to bring my swim trunks. We let Rebecca and Thomas Bruce choose their room and we took the other one.

It was just a little after 1000 hours. We decided to unpack and order sandwiches to our room for an early lunch. Afterward, we toured the State Capitol. We thought Thomas Bruce should begin to learn about the state government, so we spent the afternoon touring various important state government buildings. I asked Thomas Bruce what he thought of all of this. He shrugged off all of my questions — he was more interested in becoming a soldier.

When we returned to the motel, Ginny began to make arrangements for dinner. The operator told her they served Mexican food — and on gorgeous evenings like this one they served on their patio — and they had a band that played popular American and Mexican music. She put her hand over the phone and said to me:

"Bingo! This motel has everything."

Then she asked if they could serve a birthday cake with two candles. She turned to me and said:

"They are going to do more than I asked. In addition to two candles, they are adding two sparklers. Their waiters will light the candles and sparklers and serve the cake as they sing the *Happy Birthday Song.*"

This was his first party. It was a magnificent setting — under the stars, romantic music, good food. It was one to remember.

We did not dance. We ordered dinner and ate so we could get on with the party. It was an exciting moment when the cake was served. Three waiters came out of the kitchen with the one in the center carrying the cake with its candles and sparklers brightly burning. Thomas Bruce watched them but did not realize they were

41

bringing it to him. As they neared our table they began to sing the *Happy Birthday Song.*

They set the cake in front of him. His expression revealed this was entirely unexpected. One of the waiters pulled the hot wires out when the sparklers burned out, and Rebecca told him to blow out the candles — he nearly blew the top off of the cake. We applauded and he looked happy.

Virginia reached under the table and got his present. He quickly tore it open, and when he saw what it was, he cried out:

"Oh, Mommy! Oh, Dada! tank'ou. Gonna put on."

Virginia tried to talk him out of this, but he managed to get the toy .45 out of its holster. She let him keep this but wrapped the rest.

We ate the rest of the cake and went to our rooms. He immediately put on the uniform and began to march up and down the room as the fellows at Camp Hood had taught him. He was a very happy little boy and this made us all glow.

What a great feeling to be away from a military environment! Ginny and I were alone and together. We climbed into bed — snuggled very close — drifted off into sublime pleasures — covered very comfortably by the darkness of the night.

Thomas Bruce woke us up by wanting to go swimming. We put on our suits and went out to the pool. The water was clear, blue, and inviting. We jumped in and swam around for awhile. I noticed tables with brightly colored umbrellas around the deck. I climbed out to investigate, and a waiter from the dining room came over and asked if we would like to order breakfast and have it served poolside. Everyone was listening because they all yelled, "yes." He left menus and said he would be back and take our orders. We all ordered basically the same thing — the traditional breakfast. The exercise from the swim, and the clean, clear, invigorating early morning air made for large appetites. We took our time and ate and ate. It was nearly lunchtime when we finished.

The midsummer heat of Texas began to bear down so we headed for our air-conditioned rooms — a shower and a nap. When we woke up and began to move around it was dinnertime. Someone suggested ordering hamburgers, french fries, three beers, and a Coke to our rooms. This won a unanimous approval.

While we ate, Rebecca told us she needed to go home. This was fine with everyone. We planned to leave Austin at 0700 hours — a long way to Brownfield — ten hours of steady driving. I got anxious to visit some of my old friends.

We arrived about 1700 hours. Ginny and Thomas Bruce had moved in with her mother and father – Big Boy and Granny. Granny insisted we sit at the dining room table while she finished supper. The talking began – supper was served, then talking and eating; the clock struck 2400 hours – midnight was bedtime.

We gathered Thomas Bruce and went upstairs. Ginny put him to bed in one of the rooms at the front of the house – we stayed in the one across the hall. I remembered this room. . . . used to wave goodnight from it after I brought her home from a date. Many a time she did this – up to the time we were married. Now I was going to spend the night in it – I felt rather guilty – kinda like a dirty, yellow dog.

After breakfast, I left Ginny and Granny talking and headed downtown to visit some of my friends. It suddenly dawned on me that nearly all of my friends were in the military, serving their country. I ran across a few who were not – these disgusted me. They belonged to the DDD society – Despicable Draft Dodgers. They told me over and over why they were not in the service – their excuses did not impress me – I had known them for many years and knew they were lying. I could not stand to be around them so I moved on.

That night Virginia and I decided this furlough was for the two of us to be together. After lunch the next day, we headed west for Ruidoso, a popular resort high in the mountains of eastern New Mexico. We had been there many times, and we both enjoyed it. We left Thomas Bruce with Granny.

We were having a marvelous time when, bingo! we had used it all. I had to head for Fort George G. Meade, Maryland, for processing and shipment overseas. This really tore into heaven, but demands of war came first.

Here we were again saying goodbye. This time there were many unanswered questions. I was boarding the train at Lubbock, Texas, heading for Fort Meade. This was going to be a long ride – I didn't have a reserved seat, much less a pullman. Oh well, life was one big gamble, I bet I get a seat. . . .

This was the hardest goodbye yet. The date was Friday afternoon, 18 August 1944. The station was full of all kinds of people waiting to board.

"Bo . . . oard, Bo . . . oard," yelled the conductor.

I tenderly kissed Virginia – hugged and kissed Thomas Bruce – got sucked into the train and into the chair car. There were no vacant seats, so I stood. The train jerked to a start — I tried to find Ginny and Thomas Bruce but there were too many people. I prayed.

As the train pulled farther and farther away from my loved ones, all of my emotions exploded at once and sent rivers of tears cascading down my cheeks.

Ginny wrote me a letter when she got home. It was dated Saturday noon.

> I couldn't write you last night because I was so blue, and I didn't want to write you all of the things I was thinking and feeling. Anyway, I cried the whole night through and wished for you every minute with all my heart. Coming back here was horrible, and, when I think of the empty days and nights ahead of me, I can hardly stand it. Of course you know I have high hopes of our being together soon.
>
> I saw your train out of sight yesterday, and then we came straight home. I kept my chin up as you asked, but when I was by myself last night I just couldn't help crying for you. I'll be all right, only I can never get used to your leaving. I've been watching the time all day trying to think just where you are and what you are doing. I hope you are thinking of me. I suppose you will be in Chicago tonight — I forgot to ask you — and then you will get to Fort Meade tomorrow afternoon.
>
> We went to the show last night and saw *Ladies Courageous* and I enjoyed it. I hope you are writing me every day like you said you would because I am so lonely and blue for you, and your letters bring you a little closer.
>
> I hope you got a pullman and got some rest last night — got something to eat. I want you to be well and feel all right. Please write me the details of your trip when you have time.
>
> Thomas Bruce is already missing you, and he tells everyone: Rain took Dada way.
>
> You know, Bruce, I wanted to tell you "I love you" so many more times than I did. I am sure there are lots and lots of things I failed to tell you — I just didn't have enough time. You see, I need to see you soon. Good luck every day, my darling, combined with my love every minute.
>
> Ginny

> I wrote you this morning, but I didn't get to town to buy any stamps and besides, I just felt like writing you again. I forgot to tell you about two shirts, one pair of trousers and a cap you left. Do you want me to mail them to you?
>
> Darling, The Hit Parade is on and *I'll Be Seeing You* is in second place this week with *I'll Walk Alone* in seventh place. These are two of our favorite songs and it just makes me ache all over for you whenever I hear them.

V

After I got to Fort Meade, I wrote Ginny:

Monday night, 21 August, 1944
My darling:

It was a long, hard, dirty trip. I had to stand up all of the way to Kansas City, but when we left KC, I got a seat and hung on to it the rest of the way in. The trains were all crowded. People were coming from the north — coming from the south — from the east — from the west. I think they were moving around just to get out of each other's way.

Darling, leaving you last Friday was one of the hardest things I have ever done. Since then I have thought constantly of you and Thomas Bruce. Maybe it won't be too long before I can be with you two again and this time forever — just maybe.

I haven't been able to find out anything yet. Everything is confidential and classified. Before we say anything, we look around to see if there is anyone in hearing range. We talk in a whisper. There are signs all over the place telling us to be careful what we say, the enemy may be listening.

Tomorrow I'll write you a long letter and tell you about my trip here and anything else I find to tell you.

I did so enjoy those twelve heavenly days with you.

Bruce

The next day brought something new.

Tuesday night, 22 August, 1944

Another day of missing you and it's awfully hard to take. Now it looks like a long time before we can see each other again — a long, long time. Today we were issued all new equipment and clothing — new everything. This can mean only one thing — a trip across the Atlantic.

Now this bunch of cats is not as particular about how clothes fit as those at Fort Sill. If the clothes come close to fitting, that's good enough — move on down the line, soldier. I was glad to get new clothing and equipment. I hated to get a new rifle — had to remove protective cosmoline and this was a hard and nasty job — had to memorize its serial number — and had to take it to the rifle range and zero it in.

I'm sure you think I don't know what I'm talking about. First, I told you I would never be drafted. Then I told you I would never, never be placed in the infantry. Next, I told you I would never be assigned overseas under any condition — I'm thirty-one years old and father of a two-year-old son. Then I told you I would be assigned to duty in the States as a clerk or cadre at one of the training bases. Nothing I have told you has turned out to be right. Since I am going overseas, I want to go and get it over — get back home to you so we can pick up the pieces.

Before I board a ship, there is one thing I must ask of you even though it is morbid. I think it is necessary to bring it up.

While I am overseas, if I am reported "Missing-in-Action," please do not marry anyone else until there is a definite report I have been killed-in-action or have died of other causes. It haunts me to think of coming home and finding you married to someone else, thinking I was dead. Darling, please wait for me for I'll be seeing you.

This is a gloomy letter, but I had to get these things off my chest — the possibility of this happening is very real — it has happened in every war in recorded history.

Good night, sweetheart, I shall dream of your beauty and your love tonight.

Bruce

Wednesday night, 23 August, 1944
My darling:

I have read your letter of Saturday morning and Saturday night over and over. Every time I do, I cry like a baby. I am so blue and lonesome for you and Thomas Bruce I can hardly stand it. Your letter made me feel much better — kind of like talking to you during a five minute break on a busy day. It's raining tonight and that makes me want you all the more.

I finished processing today. I am mailing home my civilian shoes, some extra underwear and socks. I know for sure I'm being shipped overseas. We were ordered to the barber shop for an overseas haircut — this was a quickie — once over with the large clippers — you ought to see me now — look like a peeled onion — not hard to keep, not hard at all — had to pay for this cut — no say in how it was cut — that's not fair.

I'll hold you so very close to me in my dreams tonight.

Bruce

Thursday morning
31 August, 1944
My darling Ginny:

Well here I am at Camp Campbell, Kentucky. I bet you want to know, how come? At Fort Meade we were heavily censored. We were not allowed to call, wire or write when we were shipped out. All of us had our new uniforms and equipment packed — the army way — ready to board ship. Suddenly orders were changed — instead of boarding ship — we boarded train. It was a close call, very, very close. I get sea-sick just thinking about it.

There were 195 men on special orders transferring us here. We came on a special troop train — 13 pullmans — diners — club cars. This was all first class — we didn't pull any duty — just slept and ate. We were not allowed to get off for any reason. There was not any reason to get off. At every stop — small town — medium sized town — big town — the local people swarmed the train. They handed us all kinds of goodies through the windows — ice-cream — cake — sandwiches — milk — Cokes — hamburgers — hot dogs — magazines — newspapers — anything you could think of — they had it. We were treated like heroes at every stop. This was America supporting her troops. I was proud to be on that train.

Well, that's how come. We got here about 0600 hours—ate breakfast at 0830—at 0930 we are sitting around waiting for something to happen. We are to be assigned this afternoon.

Now let me tell you about Camp Campbell. It is about the same size and looks a lot like Camp Hood. It straddles the Kentucky-Tennessee border—about 15 miles from Clarksville, Tennessee—47 miles from Nashville—15 miles from Hopkinsville, Kentucky—260 miles south of Louisville.

Camp Campbell houses two armored infantry divisions—the 14th and the 20th. I have been transferred from the regular infantry to the 14th Armored Infantry Division. I have not, as yet, been transferred to any unit within the division.

The division has completed intensive training in preparation for overseas shipment. It needed the 195 men from Fort Meade to bring it to combat strength.

Service with this unit will be entirely different from basic at Camp Hood. I can get a pass to leave the base any night I'm not on detail.

Virginia, we will not ship out for another four weeks. This is a wonderful place and a beautiful time of the year. Why don't you and Thomas Bruce come spend three weeks with me? You will love the country—it's so beautiful. Gosh, I miss you. I'm just dying to see you. Now here's a suggestion:

Clarksville, Tennessee, is the place to stay. It is the home of C. W. (Bill) Bailey, Past-President of the American Bankers Association and, at present, President of First National Bank of Clarksville. He is the father of Corporal Bill Bailey who was orderly of my barracks at Camp Hood. I heard Mr. Bailey talk at University of Texas a couple of years ago on Soil and Water Conservation. He is taking the lead in this field. He knows how important this is. He has worked hard and is responsible for getting President Roosevelt to encourage Congress to place Soil and Water Conservation Service under the Department of Agriculture.

On the next pass, I will go into Clarksville and talk to Mr. Bailey and get his opinion on the plausibility of your coming here and what he thinks about the chances of your finding a place to stay.

I guess you think I had forgotten you from the very few letters I wrote from Fort Meade. We were censored on every move we made and were kept busy doing something day and night. I'm glad I'm out of that place!

I did get a weekend pass. A friend of mine—you met him at Camp Hood—Private Tinder and I went into Washington. Quite by chance we had a wonderful time. Saturday night we managed to get a cot at the United Nations Service Club. Hotel rooms were impossible to get—felt very fortunate with what we got.

Sunday, we walked to a restaurant for brunch. Afterwards we began walking down a street discussing what we were going to see

and how we were going to do it — two GIs out to see the nation's
capitol and wondering how to do it. The answer came quickly. An
elderly couple stopped their car along side us and asked if they could
show us the Capitol. Unbelievable! But it happened and renewed our
faith in our fellow man. We climbed in, and they did indeed show
us the city.

They showed us the beautiful memorials to Jefferson and Lincoln,
and just east of the Lincoln Memorial Reflecting Pool was the
Washington Monument — a tapering shaft of Maryland marble
piercing the heavens like a straight sword of triumph. They drove
us by the Capitol Building — the White House — Supreme Court —
many other beautiful buildings housing various departments of our
National Government — passed the sprawling Pentagon — many of
the Embassies — Dumbarton Oaks where the peace conference was
being held — the Episcopal Cathedral where President Wilson and
Admiral Dewey were entombed.

Then they drove us across the Potomac to their apartment in Alex-
andria, Virginia and served us coffee and cake. We ate and talked
for a long time — until 2400 hours — midnight, in fact. His name was
Oscar W. Gearheart. He worked for the Government Printing Office
and his wife worked for some department of the government. He
served in World War I and was in six major engagements. He had
some interesting stories to tell. This was a very incredible day, and
it came to pass because we were two GIs walking down the street
minding our own business — just minding our own business.

At Fort Meade I got to see America's reaction to the phobia of The
Enemy Within. Within the shadow of the Nation's Capitol, I saw a
Japanese Internment Camp complete with watch tower and armed
sentinels — a concentration camp.

I'll call you in three or four days and see what you think of my
suggestion.

I love you so much,

Bruce

I confirmed I could get a pass any night I was not on detail.
However, I had to report back in time to stand reveille at 0545
hours.

On Saturday, 2 September, I got a pass and went into Clarksville and to First National Bank to see Mr. Bailey. He was busy at
the time, and his secretary had me wait. I didn't wait long. Mr.
Bailey came out of his office and held out his hand. I shook it and
introduced myself — told him I was in the banking business in
Brownfield, Texas — had heard him talk at University of Texas — was
in his son Corporal Bill Bailey's platoon during my basic training at
Camp Hood. He very graciously invited me into his office.

He was indeed the picture of a Southern country gentleman —

beautiful white hair, polite, courteous, highly educated, deeply religious; and anxious to help. After we sat down, he asked me:

"How may I help you, Mr. Zorns?"

"Call me Bruce, please."

I told him about Virginia and Thomas Bruce and asked him what he thought about them coming and staying with me until I shipped out.

"I think you three should be together as much as possible. Finding a place for them is going to be difficult, but with a little time I feel sure I can find them a place. Have them come on. They can stay in the hotel for a few days. I'll make reservations. Bruce, I would like for you to come in tomorrow, Sunday, and go to church with me and my family and sit in our family pew and have lunch with us afterwards."

I quickly accepted.

What a day this had been! The first thing I did when I got back to camp was call Virginia. She was so excited — she began to talk so fast I couldn't understand what she was saying. When she calmed down, she told me she had been checking train schedules and she could get into Clarksville at 4:00 P.M. Saturday, 9 September. I promised to meet them and have a place for them to stay. When we hung up, I called Mr. Bailey and told him when they would arrive. He assured me he would have them a room.

"Remember, Bruce, we are expecting you for church and lunch tomorrow."

"I'll be there. Thank you," I responded.

What a memorable occasion! The Baileys belonged to the First Presbyterian Church. The building was beautiful, delicately aged, southern-functional gothic in design. The furniture was different from anything I had ever seen. Each family group had a pew which was semi-enclosed. Entry was from the center aisle through a door that served only that pew. Only family group members could sit in their pew except by invitation. I felt honored to have been invited to sit in the Bailey's pew.

After services we went to their lovely southern home — large, functional, and very comfortable. We ate in the very large dining room. What a meal it was! — fried chicken, cream gravy, mashed potatoes, fresh green beans — homemade hot rolls, tossed green salad. For dessert Mrs. Bailey served delicious chocolate pie she had made and the best coffee I had ever tasted. Compared to the Army chow I had been eating, this meal was "outta" this world.

After everyone had finished, Mr. Bailey suggested we sit on the back porch. It was shady and cool. The neighbors began their customary Sunday afternoon visits, and just by being quiet and listening I heard all of the town gossip in a short time. After visiting with these drop-in guests for about thirty minutes, Mr. Bailey looked at me and said:

"Bruce, would you like to see my farms? I would like to show you my application of *The Four Pillars of Agriculture,* or *How Agriculture Is Winning the War."*

"I would love to," I replied.

"I'll have Johnny saddle a couple of horses and bring them around — just keep your seat."

The Four Pillars of Agriculture was the title of the speech Mr. Bailey made at the University of Texas — which I heard. While he was President of the American Bankers Association, he made this speech all over the world. He told me in many countries the land had been so badly mismanaged it produced very little and what it did produce was low in nutrition. He said he saw many, many people of this world hungry and starving because of misuse of the soil. His plan called for crop rotation, to increase water holding capacity of the soil by adding organic matter — and planting legumes — to increase productivity by adding nitrogen. His plan revolved around the four pillars of sheep, cattle, wheat, and tobacco.

He was back in a very short time and said the horses would be around in a minute.

"Bruce, you take this one — he's extra gentle."

With Bill leading the way, we rode off across the red clay hills of Tennessee. He pointed to a lush, green slope and said:

"This is a patch of lespedeza, a legume. I have planted it for the first time to see how it holds the red clay soil on that slope — how much nutrition it adds and how much forage it provides."

We rode past a field of tobacco that had just been harvested.

"Here's how it all works," he said to me.

"We will plow this field — plant it in wheat. When it's large enough, we'll turn in cattle or sheep — let them graze until mid-April — take them to one of my permanent pastures of guar — let wheat mature — harvest it. We will immediately plow wheat stubble under for organic matter to increase water holding capacity of the soil — plant to a legume such as the lespedeza on the hill. When foliage gets big enough, bring in cattle or sheep — graze it until mid-October — move them to one of my perennial grass pastures like the fescue across the turn-row. We will plow under the legume in late winter — nodules of legume will release nitrogen throughout late winter and early spring. The soil is now conditioned to plant tobacco again. While adding organic matter and nitrogen to the soil, we have produced four cash crops: Wheat, cattle, sheep, and tobacco — *The Four Pillars of Agriculture.*"

What a beautiful lesson in soil stewardship! If only everyone around the world could see and hear what I had just witnessed — and practiced it — there would be no hunger in the world. In practicing this plan of soil stewardship we would be obeying Christ's command to us:

"Feed my sheep."

"Bill, will it ever come to be, that everyone will practice soil stewardship?"

"Under the Roosevelt administration, Soil Conservation Service is under the supervision of the Department of Agriculture. I feel sure the USDA will continue to bring this message to the people of the United States and maybe — just maybe — other nations will listen."

Under Bill's leadership, the American farmers were contributing as much — and maybe more — toward winning this war as any other industry. They produced enough food to feed the nation's military forces around the world, its civilian population, and its prisoners of war captured by the military, and enough fiber to manufacture clothing for them all.

Bill Bailey, along with the rest of America's farmers, deserved a medal — the Medal of Freedom.

When we got back from the farms, Bill drove me to the bus depot. What an insight into the importance of agriculture in winning a war! What an inspirational day this had been! On Thursday, I got a letter from Bill (see page 52).

The train was late — about one hour. Mr. Bailey was very calm and patient and did everything he could to keep me calm. When Virginia was getting off the train, I noticed she and Thomas Bruce were exhausted — Bill noticed it too. The introductions were kept very short, and he took us directly to the hotel. As he left, he turned to Virginia and said:

"I know a lady who has a beautiful plantation home between here and camp, and the bus runs right by it. She is out of town on a trip but will be back Wednesday. She lives alone and it just may be she would like for you to stay with her. If she does, it will be perfect for all of you. I will contact her when she gets home. In the

1603

THE FIRST NATIONAL BANK OF CLARKSVILLE

CAPITAL AND SURPLUS $250,000.00

CLARKSVILLE, TENN.

September 6, 1944.

Pvt. Bruce Zorns,
Company A, 62nd AIB.,
14th Armored Division,
Camp Campbell, Ky.

Dear Bruce,

        If you get off in time on Saturday, say
by 12:00 o'clock, and are in town at that hour, come on
to the bank and go home to lunch with me; then I will
take you by the railroad station to meet your wife and
baby. We will be delighted to have you.

        Sincerely yours,

CWB/mj

Letter from C. W. (Bill) Bailey. Note "Four Pillars of Agriculture" on bottom of stationery.

meantime, I think it will be smart for you to look around for something else—I'll look too. I have arranged with the hotel for you to stay there until you find a place to stay permanently.

"Mrs. Zorns—may I call you Virginia?"

"Please do," Virginia replied.

"Virginia, don't worry—I'll find you a nice place to stay. Mrs. Bailey and I want to have all of you for lunch soon. I am delighted to know you and your young son. If I can be of any service to you, please call me."

He bent down and kissed Virginia and then Thomas Bruce; we shook hands and he said:

"Good night, all of you." He pulled the door shut as he left.

"What a great person. It seems strange to run across anyone like him during wartime, and in an Army town at that," observed Ginny.

"In one of my letters I wrote you:

'There are still a lot of marvelous people in the world. Keep your eyes open for them — they are there, really lots of them.'"

We embraced and kissed and kissed. Thomas Bruce thought enough was enough and jerked on my pants leg. I picked him up and hugged and kissed him. He seemed so happy to see me. Heaven surrounded us — we three were together.

I went to bed early. I had to get up early enough to get to the base, change to the uniform of the day, and fall into reveille at 0545 hours.

I met the commander of Company A, Captain Daniel R. Ianella — my platoon leader, Second Lieutenant Richard J. Good — the company's first sergeant, Melvin T. Parker — my squad leader and platoon sergeant, Staff Sergeant Ernest Herrera. All of these were very capable men — they made me proud of my company.

The 14th Armored Division was filled to combat strength with the 195 men from Fort Meade. During the next few weeks, all units would undergo strenuous polishing-up training in preparation for combat somewhere overseas.

After lunch Lieutenant Good took our platoon, with full field equipment, on a ten-mile hike at a very fast pace. I could tell he was going to be very demanding and hard, but at the same time, a prince of a fellow.

After one hell of a rough day I showered, dressed in Class A uniform, picked up my pass from Sergeant Parker, climbed on the bus, and headed for Virginia's hotel room. When she opened the door, I could tell she had been through one hell of a rough day too.

She told me about it. She had gone from house to house dragging, but most of the time carrying, Thomas Bruce. At every house she asked if they had an apartment — or just any place they would rent for three weeks. Most told her no, but a few noticed she was carrying Thomas Bruce and told her they would not rent to anyone with children. This infuriated her — Thomas Bruce was at the crying, whining stage — she came back to the hotel exhausted.

We decided there was nothing to be gained walking from house to house, hunting a place to stay. She could stay at the hotel until our money ran out or just maybe Bill's friend would let us stay with her — he would talk to her the day after tomorrow.

I poured Thomas Bruce a Coke and mixed us a drink — we sat, relaxed and talked. I told her about my day — meeting the officers of my company, the first sergeant and my squad leader Sergeant Herrera — how much I liked all of them — we would be in combat together.

I gave her my new address — something new had been added:

> Pvt. Bruce C. Zorns, 38693068
> 14th Armored Division
> APO #446
> Camp Campbell, Kentucky
> U.S. Army

I mixed us another drink before dinner. We all jumped into bed afterward — exhausted — I had to get back to base, change clothes, and stand reveille at 0545.

We did not hear from Bill until Wednesday. He called and wanted to take us to meet his friend — said he would be by in thirty minutes: we were excited. We met him in front of the hotel. He took the road toward camp through the beautifully wooded hills of Tennessee. It was a gorgeous, five-mile drive. He turned into the driveway of a graceful, two-story, plantation mansion with tall, fluted columns supporting the roof of a massive front porch.

He led the way to the front door and rang the bell. As the door opened, we saw standing in the entry, a very lovely, gracious, and beautiful woman about sixty years old.

Her hair was silver-blue — she looked like she had just come from the beauty shop. Mr. Bailey made the introductions:

"Mrs. Day, I want you to meet some very dear friends of mine — they are from Texas — don't hold this against them. This is Virginia and Bruce Zorns and their young son, Thomas Bruce. All of you Zorns, I want you to meet my dearest friend, Mrs. Day."

"We're happy to meet you," I responded.

She curtsied and very gracefully moved her left hand toward her magnificent living room:

"Do come in," she invited.

She made everyone feel at ease. This was southern hospitality extended by its most gracious hostess.

"These are my friends I have been talking to you about. Bruce has just been transferred to Camp Campbell and has been assigned to the 14th Armored Division. As you know, this division will ship out in three to four weeks. Virginia and Thomas Bruce are here to spend as much time as they can with him. They need a place to stay."

"Bill, you know I live a very lonely life. I would love to have some company. With your recommendation, I extend them an invitation to stay with me. I am impressed with your Texas friends. I have a room upstairs with a separate bath and private entrance. It is a large room, and I have a baby bed I can put in there. I think it is just the thing for your friends.

"Virginia, would you want to see it?"

Virginia's face lit up—it even glowed. She looked like a great weight had been removed from around her neck. We followed our hostess upstairs. She showed us an elegant room. It was large, with its own private bath—with a tub and shower, a king-size bed, a sofa, two occasional chairs, two large closets, wall-to-wall carpeting, and a door opening to a covered outside stairway.

Virginia was beside herself. She could not believe this was happening to her. Mrs. Day put the icing on the cake:

"I want you to have the run of the house and join me for all meals. I know we will have a great time together, Virginia, driving to Hopkinsville, Kentucky, to buy the necessary supplies for my parties. Well, what do you think? Is this what you need?"

"This will be an idyll for us. I never dreamed of anything like this. Do you mean you are going to let us move in here?"

"I will be very happy and honored to have you. I just love this young son of yours! If you like the room and like me, I will drive in to the hotel tomorrow and help you move."

"Mrs. Day, I have never been treated this way before. You must be the Florence Nightingale assigned especially to watch over and lend a helping hand to all of the tired, frightened, and frustrated wives of GI Joes trying to find a place to live in an Army town, hundreds of miles from home and friends, and carrying a tired, hungry, crying baby. I love you so much. Of course I want to live here with you! I'll see you in the morning at your convenience. Thank you!"

It was apparent that the perfect transaction had been completed—perfect because all parties were happy. Mrs. Day was glowing over the prospect of having companionship for the next three weeks; Bill Bailey wore the expression of a boy scout who had done his good deed for the day; my family was dazed and in a dream world in anticipation of a three-week romantic interlude at this lovely plantation.

Mr. Bailey took us back to the hotel. When we got to our room I commented to Virginia:

"C. W. Bailey and Mrs. Day are two beautiful Christian people and I know we will never forget them."

"Never," replied Ginny.

As I look back over these events, it seems very strange I never knew Mrs. Day's first name as much as I was around her and as much as I loved her. I hope from high in heaven — where I know she is — she will forgive me.

I got a pass nearly every night and always on the weekend. The highlight of our stay came on each of the three Sunday mornings when we walked through the wooded area exploring the plantation. The country was magnificent — particularly in the early fall when the trees put on their brilliant garments and added color to the passing scene. There were all kinds of trees. I could identify a few — locust, poplar, maple, oak, elm, beech, pine, spruce, walnut, hickory, sycamore. Thomas Bruce discovered the orange-colored, globular-shaped, multi-seeded berry of the persimmon. Most were less than ripe and very astringent. He went around several days with his lips puckered. He thought this was funny.

The intensive training was terminated. We were told that a week from this date we would be restricted to base — no more passes, no telephone calls, all mail censored.

That night when I told Ginny, Mrs. Day drove us to the depot and Ginny made reservations to leave 29 September 1944.

Our beautiful romantic interlude at Mrs. Day's plantation came quickly to an end. Here we were standing in the cold, early morning Tennessee rain at 0430 hours waiting for the bus to carry me back to camp to stand reveille. As we stood there, we were ill at ease — neither knew what to do or say. So we stood there — and the cold, September rain floated softly down our faces.

My division had been ordered to our port of embarkation. When I got back to camp I would be restricted. This was the last time I would get to see Virginia in a long, long time, if indeed ever again! The bus stopped. The door opened. We stood there. Again I realized war does not wait for anything. We embraced and kissed each other. I boarded the bus. She turned and walked toward the mansion. Neither said anything. As the bus moved forward, I turned around for one last look, but the cold rain and darkness had swallowed my Ginny. I had the feeling of the emptiness of a vacuum, and the uncertain feeling of ever seeing my love again enveloped me.

When I got to camp the rain had slacked off. I hit the gound running and reached my barracks area and fell into formation just as Sergeant Herrera called:

"Zorns."

"Here," I answered, as though I had been standing there all of the time.

Sergeant Herrera did an about face, saluted our platoon leader, Second Lieutenant Good and reported:

"All present, sir."

"Very good Sergeant, carry on." He returned the salute, did an about face and walked away.

"At ease, men," the sergeant said. He turned and looked at me:

"Private Zorns, you're out of uniform."

"I'm just returning from leave, Sergeant."

"I don't give a damn where you're returning from — you're out of uniform. Look around and you will see the uniform of the day is Class C — fatigues, in case you don't remember. Now get your ass in the barracks and change — on the double. This platoon has to join the others of Company A in twenty minutes."

I dropped out of formation and headed for the barracks.

"Damn it, Private, I said on the double. Get your ass in high gear, change, and get back in formation — on the double — on the double, private."

I quickened my pace slightly.

Captain Ianella briefed the entire company on details of getting ready to ship out.

That night I wrote Virginia:

My darling Ginny:

It's 2000 hours and you are about to board the Rocket for an all night ride. I know your trip here was hard, and I know your trip home will be even harder. With four pieces of luggage and a very active two-year old son to look after and riding the chair car, it will be a killer trip. But knowing you, I know you will make it OK. I am anxious to get a wire from you saying you got home without anything happening.

I'm on guard duty from 220 to 2400 hours and from 0400 to 0600 tomorrow. It is raining hard, and this makes walking guard very disagreeable. However, I'll be walking along thinking of you, and this will make me feel close to you — the rain and sticky red clay won't seem so bad.

This morning I hated to leave you so badly. My heart broke into a thousand little pieces — only being with you will put it together again.

The three weeks you spent with me were like being in heaven. I shall never forget them. Thomas Bruce and I grew closer together. We all discovered how to spend a lifetime of happiness together.

When this war is over, we will pick up where it butted in and live
out our happiness together.

Good night, my sweet, don't get too tired on your crowded
train — remember, I love you so very much, Bruce.

Our shipping out day was 4 October 1944. Our officers ordered
us to do everything by the numbers, by the book, one way only —
the army way. Then came the moment. Lieutenant Good gave the
order for us to fall out of the barracks.

"Platoon, Fall . . . *in!* Tenn . . . *shun!* Right shoulder . . . *arms!*
Forward . . . *harch!*" He marched us to a waiting train and we
boarded. My luck was still with me. I drew KP and I saw the country
from my kitchen-sink view, from where I did get to see some interesting sights. Among them was the Statue of Liberty. I wanted to
stay close to this beautiful lady, but the train sped past her and came
to a stop at Camp Shanks, New York. We disembarked at our Port
of Embarkation, Friday, 6 October 1944.

We spent a week of inspections and physical examinations. For
the millionth time, I was told I was in A-1 condition, but there was
one last critical test that would be given the morning we shipped
out.

At 0800 hours on Friday, 13 October, we were ordered to take
off all of our clothing, including our boots. We were to wear only
our dog tags. Then we put on our raincoats and got the spoon out
of our mess-kit and fell in formation outside the barracks. We were
marched to a rather large building that served as a medical center.
Here we were ordered to take off our raincoats. There were several
doctors that checked us from head to toes. They checked our feet —
checked all of our exterior body to see if there were any visible
physical defects. We got the final short-arm inspection. Now it was
time for the last test — the critical, all important test we must pass
before we shipped out — the much discussed and famous spoon test.
We were each given our raincoat and told to carry it in our right
hand, told to carry our spoon in the other hand, and told to go to
room 101.

There was a corporal at the door. He took our coat, opened the
door, and told us to go in.

There were two doctors inside, each wearing a headband with
a light reflector. One got in front of me, the other behind. The doctor behind me told me to bend at the waist, put my hands behind
me, one on each cheek, and spread them as far apart as I could. The

doctor in front asked for my spoon. He told me to raise my head and open my mouth while he depressed my tongue. They turned on their lights. The doctor behind was looking up my ass, the one in front down my throat. In just a little while the doctor in front said:

"You pass. You're in perfect physical conditon."

When the corporal handed me my coat, I asked him:

"What's that test all about?"

"That's the final certification test. One doctor looks up your ass, the other down your throat. If they see each other, you're sent to the hospital. If they cannot, you are given the final certification. By the way, I've just been told all of your company passed."

Chapter Four
"Over There"

On Friday, 13 October 1944, we were marched to a waiting train to take us to a ferry and onto a waiting ship. We waited and waited. Standing began to tire some of us, so we sat down on the railroad right-of-way. I felt very miserable and stunned knowing I was being shipped out. I sat there and stared at the ground. I noticed we were sitting in a lush bed of clover. I thought it was very pretty. I continued to sit and stare. Suddenly, I jumped up yelling:

"I've found one! I've found one!"

"What's the matter, Zorns?" Lieutenant Good asked.

"I've found one, and I've never seen one before," I told him.

"You've found what?"

"I've found one!"

"Yes, yes, we all know you've found one. We want to know what you've found!"

"I've never even seen one before, but there it is — a beautiful, four-leaf clover."

"That's supposed to bring you good luck," Sergeant Herrera said.

"And you found it on Friday the 13th. That's double magic! I want to keep you around close so I can rub your head and rub off some of your good luck," commented the lieutenant.

I ran my fingers down the stem to the ground and pinched it off.

I threw away some cards that were in one of the plastic card holders in my billfold. I very gently placed my trophy inside and carefully spread the leaves with the stem behind the petals. I closed my billfold and put it back in my pocket. The superstition syndrome that had been hanging over my head all day because we were shipping out on Friday the 13th vaporized and I felt wonderful.

Finally we were ordered to board the train. After a rather brief ride, we disembarked onto a ferry that took us to a waiting ship in New York Harbor. We were lined up in alphabetical order. When my time to board came, the officer checking the list called out:

"Zorns."

"38-69-30-68," I responded with my army serial number.

"Board, soldier," he commanded.

I will never forget the struggle I had making it up the gangway and down the steep, narrow, steel steps that led to the hold and our compartment. I was carrying every piece of equipment, every piece of clothing that I wasn't wearing, and every piece of my personal belongings. I thought to myself:

"This is my net worth. This is everything I own." I had a new perspective of the true value of material things. The next day the convoy pulled away from shore, and through the dense fog I got a glimpse of the Statue of Liberty. She was the symbol of freedom, and freedom was what this war was about.

As the convoy moved farther and farther from the shore, the Lady gradually faded from sight. As she did, the full impact of leaving the United States for a destiny with war somewhere overseas stunned my mind. I could not comprehend the full effect it would have on my life. I prayed silently that I would survive and return to the United States and be welcomed by this beautiful Lady of New York Harbor. I prayed further that the Torch of Freedom she held so high would be burning brighter than now.

Our battalion had boarded the USS *LeJeune*, a luxury liner captured earlier from the Germans. She had been converted into a troop transport and assigned to the United States Navy. The *LeJeune* was part of an enormous convoy carrying the entire 14th Armored Division and all its equipment of war to somewhere overseas. The formation was made up of aircraft carriers, their planes, balloons, battleships, destroyers, minesweepers, and practically every piece of weaponry the Navy owned. It was an awesome sight.

When she was converted to a troop carrier, the liner's luxury was lost — she was anything but luxurious now. Our compartment was in the hold and much too small for the large number of troops packed into it. Bunks were stacked four high in rows two feet apart. The odor was horrendous. Most of the troops began puking as soon as the ship started moving. All of the four P's of troop-transport odors were prevalent — piss, puke, poop, perspiration. Most of the troops were doing all four at the same time — all the time.

A common sight any time of the day or night was a long line of naked men, each carrying a towel and a bar of brown soap. None was too eager to climb into the shower and turn on the cold, salty sea water. The brown soap was supposed to lather in this water. I could never get my bar to. After every shower with the brown soap in cold, salty sea water, I really felt as if I needed a bath.

Meals were a novelty aboard ship, especially for the enlisted men. The menu was the same for breakfast or dinner — only two meals a day. Every meal, every day, consisted of navy beans, cornbread, and hot, black coffee — that's all. I ate thirty-two of these meals and survived.

Every compartment of the ship was assigned a certain time to eat. Serving was continuous twenty-four hours a day. When my compartment's time came, we fell into the serpentine line at least one hour before serving time — it took this long to inch our way to the hatch of the standing/dining area. Here a sailor punched a number off our green meal tickets which had been issued when we boarded. Printed in large type on the front was:

Keep this tag tied on person and in sight at all times.

I ran a string through a hole in the top and hung the ticket around my neck. This satisfied the Navy.

I got prepared for any pitch the server might throw my way before I started through the chow line. I put the knife, fork, and spoon from my mess kit in the upper left pocket of my jacket, carried my canteen cup in my left hand and the plate and lid to my mess kit in my right hand. The coffee was thrown at me first. Quickly I thrust my canteen cup as far to the left as I could reach, caught the leading edge of the liquid mass, and all the coffee settled snugly to the bottom. Next, I noticed the server dipping a large ladle of soupy beans. He threw them in a different direction than I'd anticipated. Hard as I tried to catch them, some fell to the deck. He looked at me disdainfully. He took a large spatula and scooped up a man-sized piece of cornbread. He teased me with this, trying to confuse me. As he threw it, I reached as far to the right as I could and the cornbread landed in the center of the lid to my mess kit. This brought an approving look from the server. I moved out of the chow line and into the standing/dining area, where I hoped to find a shelf to hold my cup and plates while I ate. For sixteen days I went through this routine — twice a day.

Discrimination between officers and enlisted men was more noticeable aboard ship than in any other environment. We had to stand in line for an hour, have our beans, cornbread, and coffee thrown at us, then eat standing up. The officers were served three gourmet meals a day at a table covered with beautiful, crisp linen set with sparkling crystal, sterling silver, and elegant china. The *Le-Jeune's* mess boys, wearing immaculate white jackets, served them with politeness and zest.

Quite by accident one day, I walked into the galley—what a beautiful sight for a hungry infantry private who had been eating beans, cornbread, and coffee for seven days! There were fifteen or twenty large baked hams, an equal number of baked turkeys, several large pots of candied yams, pan after pan of cornbread dressing, vat after vat of giblet gravy, huge containers of creamy mashed potatoes, large pots of green beans and mountains of freshly baked rolls. There were about fifteen multi-layered chocolate cakes with chocolate pecan icing. Beside these were the same number of cream pies topped with mounds of whipped cream, and matching these were beautiful pumpkin pies also with mounds of whipped cream. I was just standing there fixing to scoop up a mouthful of whipped cream with my finger when a naval officer walked in and screamed:

"Soldier, what in the hell are you doing in the galley?"

"Just passing through, sir, trying to find a latrine."

"You mean head. There's not one around here. Now get your ass out of here before I call your commanding officer!"

I got my ass out of there, but I took a picture, etched deep in my mind, of the discrimination between enlisted men and officers. The gap was too wide. It needed to be narrowed.

Our company was lucky. We were not assigned any duties on this ride. Captain Ianella was responsible for this. He had won a lottery that determined units of 62nd that would work. All we had to do was sleep, eat, read, and write. I wrote Ginny fourteen letters. Instead of dating these, I numbered them and showed the address as "On-board ship" on the first and "Somewhere at sea" on the rest.

Letter no. #1:

Today is the day the superstitious would like to mark off the calendar, but I'm going to believe it is my lucky day. I have been unlucky in having to leave the States, but I'm going to look on the bright side and think I'm off to a lucky start. Friday the 13th is dreaded by the superstitious; they believe it is unlucky. I think it is my lucky day. As we were boarding our train this morning, I found a four-leaf clover—the first one I have ever found.

I have been thinking back over our lives together, from our very first meeting to that early Thursday morning when I left you stand-

ing in the cold Tennessee rain. Our days and years together have
been very happy, and to leave them behind is tearing my heart out.
I find consolation in the fact that I can count on you for everything — to take care of my heart, to take care of Thomas Bruce, to
take care of our love. I love you so very much, Bruce.

Letter no. #2:

The rocking, rolling movement of this ship gives me a queer feeling but as yet I have not gotten seasick. A lot of the men have. They
say it's an awful feeling.

It was hard to stand on deck and watch the shores of the United
States slip below the horizon, not knowing where I was going, how
long it would take to get there, what I was going to do when I got
there or how long it would be before I could come home to you. Yes,
it was hard to watach the horizon disappear. I was leaving you farther and farther behind.

Letter no. #3:

I went to church this morning and enjoyed the services. Somehow
I felt very close to you and Thomas Bruce. Maybe you were at
church at the same time and we were praying the same prayer.

This war is not going to last forever and before we know it I will
be home and we will be together. I believe this very strongly. There
is an old saying I heard somewhere, I don't know where — 'If you
think and believe a thing strong enough and long enough it is bound
to happen.'

It's crazy, in a way, to write you like this every day because the
letters won't be mailed until we land and there is so little I am allowed
to write you but I have to talk to you and this is the only way.

Letter no. #4:

The most unexpected thing happened today. We had a mail call
here in the middle of the Atlantic. I got a letter from you dated Tuesday, October 10, 1944. I feel so much better now. This is the last mail
we will get until we land. It is possible air-mail letters will be waiting
for us when we get there. I hope so.

You asked me if there was anything you could send me. There sure
is. I would like you to send me a real good picture of you. I want
to show it to the fellows. They don't believe you are as beautiful as
I tell them. Now get busy and have one made — no excuses and no
delays. I miss you terribly.

Letter no. #5:

I have not been seasick yet. I'm feeling fine. I can't say I'm enjoying this trip. One thing I can't understand is the big difference in the treatment of enlisted men and officers. Oh well, it's just the military's way of doing things — a way I hate.

I have at last gotten a book to read — *Aaron's Rod* by D. H. Lawrence. I have just started it. I think it's going to be very interesting.

I am missing you so very much, and I know you are lonely too. Your loneliness is what worries me. I don't want you to get so lonely that in desperation you find relief in someone else. My worries about such things don't last long. I finally realize I can always depend on you. I am sure you would not love me as much as you do if I were not just a little jealous. We both have too much happiness ahead to take any chances.

Letter no. #6:

I think, my darling, we have been misinformed about the work of the American Red Cross. Just before we came aboard ship they served us coffee, doughnuts, and candy — all we wanted. Then this morning when I came from top deck to my bunk I found a little bag from the Red Cross filled with a book — *Charlie Chan*, a deck of cards, sewing kit, razor and blades, shoe strings, mints, a pencil, writing paper, envelopes, and two packs of cigarettes.

Every man aboard got one and every man appreciated it for two reasons: First, because the items were useful, and second, because it made us all feel good that someone cared enough to remember us with a gift. This really gave all of our spirits a boost. The Red Cross is doing its job — but good. Help them whenever you can.

Today we had some entertainment aboard ship. The concert band and the orchestra played on main deck all afternoon. Both organizations are composed of Army men. I enjoyed the music. I wanted them to play our song, *I'll Walk Alone*, but they never got around to it.

I'm getting further along with my book, *Aaron's Rod*. I like it a lot. I think you would enjoy it.

It might be interesting to you to know what we pay for cigarettes — fifty cents a carton. That's five cents a package and that's $1.15 a carton cheaper than you pay. The difference is taxes — federal and state.

We are still moving and getting farther and farther from you and yet across all those miles of land and sea I can still feel the warmth of your love. It's a comforting feeling. You are really something to be able to reach this far.

Letter no. #7:

There is an old saying, "It's a small world after all." But ever since I boarded this ship this world has gotten larger and larger. Here we have been sailing day after day and all we have seen is water. Water, water everywhere — it all looks the same to me. Some days the water is smooth, others it's rough. Whatever its state, it's still water. Now I'm an ole West Texas boy from the South Plains, and I would like to see some land — even a little sand.

Early this morning while I was on top deck I heard someone sing *I'm Dreaming of a White Christmas*. This made my heart more lonely. It will be our first Christmas apart since we married.

I know the worry you are going through — waiting for a letter from me day after day and not getting one — expecting to get one tomorrow, and all you get tomorrow is another disappointment. I write you every day but I know you will not get any letter until 10 or 12 days after we land, and then you'll get a bunch.

I wonder so often just what you are doing. I try to picture every move you make. You know, darling, we are so much in love with each other. I wonder if any other couple ever loved as we do. The thing that pleases me is that our love grows stronger day by day and year by year. We are on our fifth year of married life and yet you are more exciting to me now than the day we married. In you, my dear, I found everything. I do not have to go elsewhere to satisfy my desires — I doubt if I could anyway, because nowhere could I find your equal.... I am looking forward to many more happy years together.

Letter no. #8:

Tonight, exactly one month ago we were celebrating your birthday. It was not an elaborate celebration, but I enjoyed it because I was with you. Time passes so slowly when we are apart and so fast when we are together. It seems ages and ages since your party, and yet it has only been a month. The three weeks you spent visiting me at Camp Campbell seemed to pass overnight.

Today has been just another day — typical day aboard a troop transport ship. Up at 0630 hours. Breakfast about 0715. Out on deck for a while. Back down to read for a while. Back up on deck at 1300 hours to listen to the band. Back into the hold about 1500. I read until 1630 and then into the chow line, ate, and then out on deck again. Back into this stinking hold for my cold sea water shower and a shave. Now I am writing to you at 1930. We have lights out at 2100 and try to make it through the night to 0630, so we can start all over again. I'm getting used to this two-meals-a-day business. It was hard at first but OK now.

I got out all the letters I received from you since you left Clarksville and read them again just a little while ago. It was kind of like a conversation with you. I treasure your letters very much.

Thomas Bruce, I would like to be with you so much, but you must understand that your Daddy didn't leave because he wanted to, but because he had to. It seems there's a job to be done before I can come home to stay. I will come home soon, and we will have a lot of fun together. Be a good boy and be sweet to Mommy.

Letter no. #9:

Today has been beautiful. The sea has been still and blue, and the clouds have piled up on the horizon — looking more like mountains rising out of the water of some lake. I have seen an occasional bird, small like a sparrow, skimming across the top of the water. We must be getting close to land — but what land?

What a perfect paradise this would be if we could bask in this beauty together, and this war was just a dream. Someday, my dear, I plan for us to view together the beauty of the sea. I have been so many places I want us to go after the war. There is so much for us to see and so much to do. We are going to enjoy every minute of life together. We have the capacity for such enjoyment, and to fail to take advantage of it would be wasting two lives — oops — three, I mean. Of course Thomas Bruce will be with us — and will he get a kick out of it all!

We have gotten the good news of the invasion of the Philippines by General MacArthur. The war on both sides of the world looks good for the Allies.

General Motors Corporation came to the front yesterday and gave each man in this convoy six packages of cigarettes via the American Red Cross. It looks like we will be well supplied with cigarettes, either given to us, or sold to us cheap.

I am going to church tomorrow, and I hope you and Thomas Bruce go too. We can at least be together spiritually.

Contrary to any of the philosophy set forth in *Aaron's Rod*, I think it is right and proper for two people to love as we do.

Letter no. #10:

I went to church services this morning. In fact I went to two. The one from 1000 to 1030 hours was conducted by the Navy chaplain, and the one from 1030 to 1100 hours was conducted by the Army chaplain. During the later service we had communion. I thought of you and Thomas Bruce throughout this service. In this part of the world there is a 4 ½-hour time differential between here and Brownfield. It was only 0600 in Texas when I went to church at 1030. I knew you were still in bed. At 1500 I could picture you in church.

I had a bad cold all last night and all of today. I made sick call this morning and the doctor swabbed my throat, sprayed my nose and gave me some pills. I feel much better tonight and will be OK tomorrow. I have not been seasick as yet and doubt that I will at this stage of the game.

So far we have seen only water. I never realized there was so much water in the world. I would welcome a sandstorm now. In fact if I were home, I'd sit out in the worst one all day long. Of all the places I have seen since I have been in the Army, I will still take the South Plains area of Texas to make our home.

My darling, it is so hard for me to tell you just how much I love you. I cannot find the right words. It's like sitting down at a piano to play. The music is there, but I can't bring it out. So it is with my love for you. The love is there, but I cannot tell you in words the depth and sincerity of that love. It is an all encompassing love that has engulfed me completely.

Letter no. #11:

This ship is really rocking around tonight. The sailors say it's not a rough sea, but it's the roughest we have seen. I saw a land-based aircraft this afternoon. We are not too far from land.

I haven't done much today but sleep. I went out on deck for a little while this morning but came back down about 1130, bathed and shaved and then slept until 1600 hours. The pills the doctor gave me for my cold made me sleepy. I'm feeling much better now and know I will be OK.

By the way, I have just seen what Prudential Insurance Company uses for its logo. Find one of their ads in any newspaper or magazine, and you will see it too.

Yesterday I had a very uneasy feeling from a dream that set me thinking along the wrong track. I am over it now, thank goodness. In this dream I saw you somewhere with someone else. That is all I can remember of the dream. You have no idea the hurt I was feeling when I woke up. I felt uneasy all day. Please forgive me, my darling; you know I have never doubted you and I never will, but the dream taught me something. Under these conditions, where we are apart like this, we must think straight and have the utmost confidence in one another.

Letter no. #12:

I have just come down from the top deck. The convoy was a very impressive sight in the sunset. The ships were bunched together like a flock of little chickens hovered over by a Navy blimp and other aircraft. We cannot be far from land, but as yet no sight of any. The only land I can see is Texas. In my imagination, as I look out over the stern into the setting sun, I see Texas. I know it is somewhere out there in the West.

The other day the censors were telling us what we could and could not write in a letter. Later that afternoon a Mexican soldier was trying to compose a letter to his family. Everything he thought of to write was in violation of the censors' regulations. Finally, in desperation, he wrote about the beautiful flowers, the brightly colored birds, the swarms of bees, and the varied-colored trees he had seen on board ship. He said he had to write something about something so his family would hear from him. It's not that bad with me. I can always find something to write you, but I cannot write you about everything I see, hear or do.

I can really feel the nip in the air. I like the Fall of the year. On the South Plains of Texas there are the cool days, crisp nights — the smell of the cotton gins and fresh-cut feed — the activity of people who go about their increased duties with extra and restored energy because of lower temperatures and the turn of a season — the change from baggy summer clothes to neatly fitting fall ones, bright and colorful — the gusty wind tossing the gaudy-colored autumn leaves around and around. Yes, Fall is that interval of time the Master Plumber requires to change the thermostat from heating to cooling.

Letter no. #13:

The number 13 is really popping up a lot during this trip. It's just got to be a lucky number!

We saw land for the first time, and it was really a welcome sight. We saw some beautiful and historical sights this morning — something I thought I would never see in my lifetime. It gave us all renewed strength. Now the land is gone, and we are again at sea. What a beautiful blue sea! It's the deepest blue I have ever seen.

Letter no. #14:

This ship is really bouncing around tonight. We are in some of the roughest waters we have been in so far. I thought the sea would be smooth since we are getting close to our destination. This is the last letter I can write from aboard ship. I'll be glad to get off. It seems like we have been aboard for years and years. We have come a long, long way. There is just one thing I am looking forward to — to win this damn war and come back to you and Thomas Bruce. I am hoping and praying it won't be long. When we blast the Germans into surrendering this time, it will be for keeps. I don't want Thomas Bruce to go through this 20 or 30 years from now.

I hope you receive all the letters I have written you from aboard ship. You should get a good impression from them of life aboard an Army transport. We have been on board longer than most troops — but we have come further.

We passed a convoy going west this morning. Oh, how I wished I were on it!

We had a good band concert on deck this afternoon. Two numbers reminded me of you — *Anniversary Waltz* and *Embraceable You.*

The censors just told us we had seen the Rock of Gibraltar some way back and could write about it. It was a very interesting sight. Just by turning our heads we could see two continents — Africa and Europe. We saw the coasts of North Africa and Spain. We are not allowed to tell you the date we saw these things.

I love you so much, Bruce.

There were loud cheers from everyone aboard when Captain Lawrence E. Kelley, skipper of the *LeJeune,* announced the ship would dock at the French port of Marseille. We were already in the Gulf of Lions, southwest of there. Here for the first time we began to see the devastation of war. In every direction we could see the stacks and masts of ships the French and American military sank when they liberated this port city. A channel had to be cleared through the wreckage so Captain Kelley could navigate his ship to the docks. During the night, 28 October 1944, the USS *LeJeune* docked. It had been a long, long trip.

Major Ernest Gifford, the battalion S-4 officer, came aboard the next morning. He was in the advance party and had helped select our forward staging area. He issued instructions to commanding officers on what to do and where to go.

We left the ship carrying everything we had brought aboard. I had the same struggle disembarking as I had embarking. It was a struggle up those steep, steel steps to the main deck and then down the gangwalk. I made it but it took all the strength I could muster.

It was Sunday afternoon when we began our march through the city of Marseille. We were startled at the bombed areas. The liberating forces had left scars that would last forever. Some of our men began to fall out because of the very heavy load they were carrying; they were out of shape from sixteen days of inactivity aboard ship.

Finally, some of the battalion's trucks were unloaded, and Lieutenant Colonel Myers passed the order down the column for us to set our duffelbags alongside the road, and the trucks would pick them up and haul them to the staging area. What a relief!

It seemed as though the entire population turned out and lined the streets to welcome us. They came bearing gifts — apples, wine, and flowers. They were joyously emotional — so much so they caused us to be as emotional as they. As we marched through this French city, we encountered the ragged, snot-nosed boys begging for themselves and trying to sell us their sisters:

"Cigarette pour mon père? Chocolat pour mon soeur?"

It was a long march — eight miles — through and far beyond the city, and terminated at the Delta Base Section, a wide expanse of open field where we pitched our tents in orderly rows — row after row of them — and prepared to spend two weeks preparing our minds, our bodies, and our weapons for war.

Chapter Five

My Forest Cathedral

It was Saturday, Armistice Day 1944, that the 62nd Armored Infantry Battalion broke camp and pulled out of the staging area north of Marseille and said goodbye to the bright lights. We were taken to the rail yards near the docks. Here we began preparation for our move north. We loaded our gear onto boxcars called 40-and-8s. These were the very same boxcars that had been used thirty years before to transport troops to the front in World War I. They were called 40-and-8s because they had been built for the French army to transport forty men or eight horses! Then, as now, we were on our way to the front lines in the same old boxcars to help our old allies, France and England, contain an old enemy, Germany.

The 40-and-8s did indeed show their age. They leaked like sieves and they were noisy, cold, and rough. Being crowded into this small boxcar with thirty-nine other men was an experience that still makes me shudder. I was as miserable as I have ever been. But we survived and four days later arrived at Portieux-la-Verrerie. It was actually a sleepy little village, but it looked mighty good to us even with cold fog and dense forests. This was to be our last bivouac area for a while. The front lines were only a few miles ahead—so close that artillery flashes, from both sides, were as vivid as lightning.

Our officers gave us ample sack time to rest up for the ordeal ahead. During this time we began to talk about the thing that, up to now, had been silent meditation—fear. Whether we admitted it or not, we were all afraid. Which of us would "get it" before this thing was over? We talked—even kidded about it in a light vein—but none of us took it lightly. The moment of truth had come. I don't believe any of us had any thoughts about being heroes of any kind. The fear of cowardice was always there. I don't remember the context in which President Roosevelt spoke about fear but what we feared was fear itself—a state of uncertainty and of apprehension. The fear of the unknown was, and would continue to be, the most grueling ordeal we were to undergo.

It wasn't all sack time and talk. We spent an inordinate amount of time cleaning our weapons and checking our equipment. Live ammunition was issued for the first time. Each man received enough .30-caliber shells, in clips, to fill his ammo belt plus one clip for his rifle; two bandoliers — one for each shoulder, crossing at the center chest; six hand grenades which were worn on our field jackets with the handles sticking through the buttonholes. Then came the platoon supplies: mortar shells, bazooka rockets, .30-caliber ammo for the BARs (Browning Automatic Rifles), and .30- and .50-caliber ammo for the machine guns. We were armed to the teeth and ready for the Krauts!

Sunday, 19 November, we were idle. That morning, division headquarters sent over a clergy team to conduct a church service. A big truck rolled up followed by two Jeeps. This was my first experience with the portable church. The vehicles contained a chaplain, a choir leader, an organist, an organ, an altar, hymn books, hundreds of folding chairs and Sunday bulletins with the Order of Worship. The chaplain directed the setup, selecting a clearing in the forest. He could not have picked a more beautiful place.

The clearing was large enough to accommodate 500 troops. Tall, stately trees were along two opposite sides. I don't know what kind of trees they were, but they were slender and must have been over 100 feet tall. Near the tops they bent inward toward the center forming an almost perfect Gothic arch. At each end of the clearing there were more trees — a different species — not as tall as the others and much fuller from the ground up. They completed the four walls of our sanctuary. The floor was carpeted with a thick layer of varicolored leaves — yellow, brown, red, and orange — that had fallen that autumn. It was a beautiful and inspiring setting in which to worship God! When I entered, I unslung my rifle and sat down in one of the chairs, placed my rifle between my knees, and let the barrel lean back against my body. I took off my helmet, helmet liner, and wool cap and held them in my hand. As I sat in silence and gazed around this beautiful place, I said to myself:

"This is my Forest Cathedral."

It was as beautiful as anything I had ever seen in my life. A warm, gentle rain began to fall. The peace and serenity of nature's Gothic-like cathedral was certainly conducive to the worship of God. Every chair was filled but the place was silent. Worship began with the prelude by the organist. The beauty of the organ music was in keeping with our surroundings. The chaplain stood and began the service with the invocation. We sang the doxology. One of the men read a passage from the scripture and we all said the Lord's Prayer. The chaplain's sermon was short. I was impressed with what he said. I wrote Ginny:

> . . . I went to church this morning and liked it very much. The setting was spectacular, to say the least — out in the open and under the trees. The sermon was short but very good. The chaplain made it plain that he could not offer us any supernatural protection against the dangers ahead. He asked us to bear the cross, as our Lord did, without bitterness for what the outcome might be. He asked us to not let the war change us, for us not to be bitter but to retain our tenderness and understanding.
>
> I think the thought he put across was very good. I feel sure I can do my duty and not become bitter and hard.
>
> I thought so much about you and Thomas Bruce while I was at this church service under the trees this morning. I could see you both as you went to church. You looked lovely. I wish I could have been with you in the flesh — but I was with you in thought and spirit. . . .

Following the sermon, we sang the closing hymn, and the chaplain gave the benediction. The last hymn was an old one — one I had sung all my life — *God Will Take Care of You.* I have always been touched by the words of this hymn, and this service was certainly no exception. The organist played the introduction, and the choir director led us into the first verse. Everyone sang solemnly but with gusto.

I joined in singing the first stanza and held up well. Then we began to sing the second, but when we began the chorus, my voice quivered a little and my eyes began to fill with tears. I stopped and listened until the chorus came to an end and then joined in with the third stanza.

Emotion welled up within me. My eyes filled with tears that spilled down my face. I didn't think combat soldiers were supposed to cry, and I sure didn't want my buddies to see me this way. I lifted my head and looked up through an opening in the trees of the cathedral. In the distance, toward the village of Epinal, the sky was a beautiful blue. As I gazed, the clouds overhead began to break up and the rain stopped. With a start, I realized I wasn't just looking into the sky, but something had caused my sight to be transfixed beyond and into the nothingness of space! As I looked, I could see deeper and deeper into infinity. I didn't know it was possible to see so far. Perhaps the atmospheric conditions were just right, and the refraction from the tears in my eyes formed a telescope-like lens that made it all possible.

As I stood there looking through space, I saw something that appeared to be a door. It was the doorway to heaven! The door opened, and I had a brief glimpse inside. Beautiful is not the word. No adjective could describe the brilliance, the color, the radiance, and the emerald-like sparkle. And just as suddenly as the door opened, the view changed, and I was aware of a presence. I couldn't identify what was there—but I knew.

Then I was with God.

And God saw me.

And God spoke to me. He said:

"Be Not Afraid, I Will Be with You."

Then the clouds came together over the cathedral, and I could not see beyond them—the rain began to fall again.

I was barely aware of the chaplain's benediction, and I wondered how 500 soldiers could leave without knowing it. The clergy team began folding chairs and loading all their gear back on the truck, so I moved out of the way and went over to lean against one of those stately old trees. I was not ready to leave what had been given me this morning, so I stood there. The rain became heavier, and it began to trickle down my neck and cheeks, washing away the tears.

The chaplain team had gone, and I was alone. I sensed, rather than heard, motion behind me at the end of my Forest Cathedral. I looked but saw nothing. I knew something was there in the trees just beyond where the altar had been. I asked myself:

"Is it He?"

And before I could answer, I remembered what He had said:

"Be Not Afraid, I Will Be with You."

I reasoned that if He is with me, He has to be where I am. Yes, what I sensed or heard had to be Him. There I stood with the rain coming down. I stood and cherished this very special moment in my life. Suddenly an ear-splitting yell shattered my reverie:

"Private Zorns, *where in the hell are you?*"

Staff Sergeant Ernest Herrera was calling me from just beyond the line of trees!

"Here, Sergeant."

"Captain Ianella wants all the men of Company A to fall in at the vehicles. Get your ass in high gear and get over there on the double and I said *on the double.* Do not mount your vehicle."

"Coming, Sergeant."

The whole company had gathered around the half-tracks by the time I got there. Captain Ianella had us stand at ease. Then he began to talk:

"Men, this is it. I have just received orders from Lieutenant Colonel Myers that as of 0100 hours tomorrow, 20 November 1944, all units of the 62nd Armored Infantry Battalion are committed to combat. As of now, we are under battle conditions. I want all men of this company to be here at these vehicles ready to mount up at 2145 hours today. We will roll out and move to the front lines at 2200 hours.

"Men, this is the moment your officers and non-coms have been training you for all these months. I hope and pray we have done a good job, and I hope further each of you has absorbed most of what we have been trying to instill in you. Our orders are as follows:

"Attack and drive the enemy out of the Vosges Mountains. Never in the history of Europe has this been done. Up to this point, the Vosges have always been considered a fortress that could not be conquered. We are not only to conquer them, but we are to cross them with all our armor.

"Attack and secure the Alsatian Plain on the other side of these mountains.

"Attack and conquer the Siegfried Line.

"Attack, cross, and secure a beachhead on the east bank of the Rhine River.

"Further orders will be waiting for us on the east side of the Rhine.

"Remember, you will be fighting the best trained, best equipped, and toughest army in the history of the world. I am confident that each of you, with superior training, superior equipment and with God's strength, will beat the hell out of the Germans.

"May God be with each of you — and with me, too.

"That is all. Dismissed."

Chapter Six

Crossing the Vosges Mountains and Beyond

Every soldier in A Company was at the loading area by 2100 hours. We milled around, smoked, and some of the guys talked a little. Sharply at 2145 hours Captain Ianella nodded to Sergeant Herrera.

"Mount . . . *up!*"

A wall of soldiers moved toward the vehicles. They carried backpacks, bedrolls, and a variety of weaponry in addition to rifles. It was only misting a little rain when we began loading but was raining pretty hard before we were finished, so we tied a tarpaulin across the top of our half-track. The driver buttoned up the cab by pulling down a windshield of heavy-gauge steel with oblong peepholes about 12" x 3" on the driver and passenger sides. Similar plates were affixed to the side windows.

Promptly at 2200 hours Captain Ianella and Sergeant Herrera appeared at the lead vehicle. Sergeant Herrera gave the order:

"Forward . . . *haarch!*"

Without lights on, the column of vehicles moved slowly into the cold, wet darkness toward a baptism by fire. We hadn't gone a mile when the column was halted. We sat there in the darkness with cold rain pouring down, not knowing what was going on. Our rifles were protected from the rain under our raincoats. And it really was a baptism by fire. A screaming barrage of heavy artillery shells from both armies criss-crossed over our vehicles. Their high-pitched shriek was bone chilling, and we ducked every time we heard one. Some wise ol' soldier in our 'track said we didn't have to be afraid of the ones we could hear—it was the ones we couldn't hear that would kill us. It was a noisy, miserable night and I felt like it would last forever. Our initiation into combat was hurry-up-and-wait.

We finally saw Sergeant Herrera coming down the line going from vehicle to vehicle. Our orders had been changed. Initially we had been committed to St. Die, but we were now to be moved to the outskirts of St. Quirin as the jumping-off place for an attack on the Germans entrenched on the outskirts of the village of Shirmeck. It was Tuesday, 22 November 1944, when the 62nd Armored Infantry Battalion began an assault that was a first. A first because it was successful in doing what had never happened before in the history of the Vosges Mountains. We pushed an occupying enemy force out and took command of this impenetrable natural fortress. It wasn't easy, nor did the victory come cheap.

A company of the 62nd became attached to the 45th Tank Battalion as supporting infantry. Our support role was unique. Each time the tank column halted, the infantry would dismount from their half-tracks and defend the perimeter while the lead tank opened fire at point-blank range on the well-made German roadblocks. When that tank started firing, everything became instant toothpicks — and we saw a lot of toothpicks that day. The Germans had thrown up roadblocks all over the place. We found them as close as every four or five miles. They were monstrous things. The Germans made them by felling hundreds of pine trees, most of which were in excess of twelve inches in diameter. When finished, each blockade was about six feet thick and six feet high. The Germans dug deep postholes across the road in parallel lines about three feet apart. They then set logs in these holes so they protruded about six feet above the ground — not unlike the way we still set posts to build a fence. The German engineers then filled the space between these parallel rows of protruding logs with tiers of big logs laid horizontally. These reached from the side of the mountain across the entire roadway to the cliff on the other side. To slow down the American Army's advance, land mines and booby traps had been planted at strategic places in front of the barricade itself. It took an awful lot of time to find and destroy the traps and mines, in addition to demolishing the barricades themselves. And it took a lot of artillery shells.

The infantry's job in this operation was to nursemaid the tanks. A stationary tank, blazing away at a barricade, was vulnerable to attack from ground forces using grenades, bazookas, or almost any kind of explosive device. Properly used, a cup of gasoline could destroy a tank — a tank that was built to withstand the impact of a mortar shell.

Our first casualty was at the first roadblock we hit. Second Lieutenant Richard L. Good was our platoon leader — and he was a good soldier. Our point-man went as far forward as was prudent and reported:

"No enemy action."

That wasn't good enough for Lieutenant Good. He went a few feet further, trying to see what was around a hairpin curve. We heard the sharp crack of a rifle, and we saw Lieutenant Good's body pitch forward into a big puddle of muddy water.

Sergeant Backman was watching from the line of trees.

"That German son-of-a-bitch got Lieutenant Good. We've got to get him out of that water before he drowns. Herrera, rake that area with hot lead. I don't want that bastard shootin' at me."

Sergeant Backman waited a few minutes while Sergeant Herrera sprayed the trees in the sniper's direction with .50-caliber machine gun bullets. Sergeant Backman didn't give anyone time to join him; he just took off down the road zigzagging all the way. Just as he reached down to pull the lieutenant out of the water, the sniper fired one more shot. Sergeant Backman spun sideways and fell across Lieutenant Good's almost submerged body.

Sergeant Herrera succeeded those two good soldiers as our platoon commander. His first order was to radio the tank commander to shell the area the sniper's fire had come from. The tanks to our right opened up with a barrage of heavy fire from the 75mm and the 105mm guns. Under this cover of fire we got the two downed soldiers back to a makeshift aid station.

In addition to being a qualified combat infantryman, I was also a qualified battalion aid man. As such, I carried a bigger first-aid kit than the other men — one that also contained morphine syrettes. Lieutenant Good was alive but bleeding profusely. He had been shot through the testicles. I applied a compress dressing and gave him a shot of morphine. That's all I could do. I attached to his field jacket a treatment slip that described his wound, what I had done for him, and the time and amount of morphine administered.

Sergeant Backman was dead.

While I worked on Lieutenant Good someone radioed for a Jeep from the aid station. We put the lieutenant on a stretcher and secured it to the brackets on the right side of the Jeep. We put Sergeant Backman's body on a stretcher on the other side. I didn't know it at the time, but these two men were only the first of many such mangled and dead, the picture of whom would sear to the very depth of my being before this war would end — and I was to be one of them.

The next day was Thanksgiving, 24 November 1944, but we didn't have time to think about Pilgrims, turkey, or the annual football game between Texas and Texas A & M. Instead, we had snipers — again. As the Germans retreated deeper into the mountains they left snipers behind to slow us down — and they did a damn good job of it. After a while they seemed to have run out of snipers, so it was relatively quiet for a few miles. We did nursemaid the tanks while they made toothpicks out of the roadblocks but there was no German activity.

Funny thing about tanks — you'd think Uncle Sam would be more thorough in the planning process. Like driving an automobile, you can drive a tank only as long as someone doesn't have to stop to pee. Airplanes have relief tubes so why don't tanks? The tankers rose to the occasion: spent shell casings. A 75mm shell case is about 18 inches long and 3 ½ inches in diameter and has the capacity to hold about one gallon. Those empty cases made perfect over-sized, handleless urinals — and they also had a built-in safety feature — they could be emptied from the turret of a tank, under fire, without undue exposure. When more solid relief was necessary the tanker was like any other GI in combat. He had to find a parking place for his tank somewhere near an unoccupied shell crater. Prudence, not modesty, dictated elimination of this kind be confined to the night hours, but there are times when nature can't wait.

This must have been the case late this afternoon. There were German tanks on the far side of a hill lobbing random shells to harass us and slow our progress. Pretty light action. Nothing even close. Up ahead of us I watched a tank pull out of the column and stop by the side of the road. The turret opened and out came a tanker. He removed a spade from its clips on the side of the tank and headed for the trees — not to garden, I'm sure, but to commune with nature in the privacy of these beautiful mountains.

Believing in privacy, I occupied myself with other things. I didn't hear the shot, but I did hear the scream of pain — and the profanity. Two of the tankers, waiting on the outside of the tank for their buddy, took off into the trees to the rescue. I found out what had happened when they brought the tanker to me for medical aid. The poor guy had found his spot to commune — dropped his drawers and assumed the position. The problem was he had stopped near a clearing and squatted sideways to a sniper in a tree on the other side. The sniper was either a poor shot or had a warped sense of humor. I had heard stories about someone getting shot in the ass, but this was the first and only time in my life I had ever seen it happen. The sniper's bullet entered the fleshy part of the right lower buttock and exited from the left lower buttock's fleshy part. Incredibly, no bone, gristle, or vital organ was hit — it was nothing more than a deep, painful, flesh wound. More incredible still was how the family jewels, as prominent and as close as they were, escaped unscathed. The tanker didn't bleed very much. I applied a light compress, gave him a shot of morphine and sent him back to the aid station — and out of the war. I've always wondered about the guy: What did he tell his kids about "how daddy got wounded in the war"?

Soon after this episode, we began to move. There were no friendly forces up ahead, only retreating Germans and a few snipers. By nightfall the column had advanced several miles into the mountains — and we continued to move, much to our chagrin and discomfort. A steady rain began falling about dusk and despite our rain gear everyone got soaked to the skin and chilled to the bone. I don't think I've ever been that cold. The temperature only reached the upper 30s during the day and was now close to freezing. The men in our half-track were shivering so badly we didn't even think about the enemy or where they were. We were very cold and very hungry. All I wanted was some dry, warm clothes and a cup of hot coffee.

It was late that night when we came to what proved to be our last roadblock for awhile. We rolled out of our 'tracks, outposted the column, and the tanker began demolishing the roadblock with its high-powered impact shells. By the time the barricade was about gone, so was the tank's supply of ammo, and there was no way to replenish it until supply could catch up with us tomorrow.

It was one of those very dark, moonless nights, so the going was slow. The commander of the tank battalion decided to rest the column where it was but sent an advance party on ahead. The advance party consisted of one tank company and one platoon of infantry. Lucky me, I was with the platoon sent to nursemaid the tanks. We had to leave our half-tracks behind because too much of the barricade remained for them to roll over. The tanks had no problem. With infantrymen riding on the top of the tanks, the mini-task force moved out and up the grade to the ridge ahead about eight miles from the main body. Once there, we pulled off the road into the trees and tried to settle in for the night. Two of our three tanks passed through a blockade that the Germans had just started — there was hardly any obstruction. The third tank stopped short of the blockade. We had a good seven hours to wait before dawn.

The tankers were warm and dry inside those iron monsters, while we infantrymen stood or squatted or knelt wherever we could get a little protection from the elements. After only two hours of it I was convinced that all of us outside would freeze to death before dawn. We knew the main column below wouldn't move out before dawn. That is a lot of hours to wait for dry clothing and hot food. I was standing there on the lee side of a tree trying to get as little rain on me as possible, but it continued to drip off the back of my helmet and down my back. I was so hungry I couldn't remember my last hot meal. Two soldiers from my platoon came to talk. We huddled ourselves together, hoping to reflect each other's body heat. What made matters worse were the sounds coming from the two tanks on either side of us. The sounds were long, rhythmic, and deep. Those bastards were snoring!

While we were fighting just to stay alive in this miserable weather those tankers were very warm and dry. The longer we stood there and shivered, the longer and louder the snoring came from the tanks, and the deeper our resentment grew for those inside. By dawn that resentment had grown into full-blown hatred! As I stood there by that tree, I fantasized about how much fun it would be to climb up to the top of that tank, lift the turret, and piss down on the whole damn tank crew! As I stood there savoring the thought, we heard a noise on the road directly below us—the road that joined the road we were on. The noise—footsteps and guttural conversation—was barely 200 yards beyond our lead tank. Behind the marching men we heard the low rumble of their vehicles. It was just before daylight. We couldn't see too well, but the sound itself made a good target.

Up to this point, A Company of the 62nd Armored Infantry Battalion was classified as combat-experienced. Up until now we had never fired a shot at an enemy we knew was there. We had been shelled, bombed, strafed, and sniped at by the Germans. This was our first time to see the enemy through the peep-sights of our rifles—and we were hungry for action!

On the signal from our platoon leader all hell broke loose on those Germans down below—.50-caliber machine guns, Browning automatic rifles, M-1 rifles, .30-caliber machine guns, bazookas, and artillery shells, both 75mm and 105mm, were fired at the sounds. The total action took maybe five minutes, but it just about annihilated the German force. A few of the Germans jumped on motorcycles and sped down the road to escape the carnage. Those who didn't crack up on the dark, winding road were picked off by the .50-calibers mounted on the tanks.

Thus ended my initiation into aggressive combat. Our assault began at dawn and was all over by sun-up. It was Friday, 25 November 1944. I was beginning to think the sun would never shine, and I knew that I would die from exhaustion, cold, and hunger while standing there under that tree. We heard noises coming from down the road, but this time they were coming from the direction of our lines! The familiar clatter of our half-tracks was a beautiful sound. It meant not only safety, but warm, dry clothes, and something hot to eat.

When the first vehicle pulled up, the new platoon leader dismounted and ordered us to fall in. He told us he was Second Lieutenant Richard W. Hawes — Lieutenant Good's replacement. He then nodded to the sergeant, who went from man to man handing each a small red box. Each box had the drawing of a wooden horse on the flat surface with the word *Trojan* printed on it and under that "one dozen." I had experienced some strange things in my brief Army career but nothing as bizarre as this — condoms, out in the middle of nowhere. The last thing I wanted right now was sex and besides that there wasn't anybody here to have it with! The platoon leader said:

"As per orders from battalion headquarters, you are to immediately utilize the contents of the box but not for the purpose they were initially manufactured and intended. You are to remove one rubber from your box, place it over the muzzle of your rifle and roll it down over the barrel. This will permit you to carry your rifle with the muzzle up instead of down. You can get into firing position much faster if your rifle is slung over your shoulder with the muzzle up. The rubber will not interfere with the firing of the rifle. It will blow right off. After each firing, reposition a new condom if the weather is inclement.

"This new ordnance device is not to be used for wenching. Its sole purpose is to protect your rifle.

"Further, it is my unpleasant duty to tell you no dry clothing will be issued at this time because: one, this rain will continue throughout the day and two, clothing will not be available from supply before 1300 hours.

"Hot chow is on the half-track. You have thirty minutes before we pull out.

"Fall ... out!"

One of the first lessons we learned as we moved into German territory was the Germans always left snipers, roadblocks, booby traps, and land mines when they retreated. Since our platoon had already suffered two casualties from snipers, we took extra precaution when we dismounted and out-flanked the tanks. We were all a little skittish when the column moved out that morning. Sergeant Herrera took over the .50-caliber machine gun when he mounted our half-track. We moved ahead at a fairly good clip for a couple of miles before the column was halted. We quickly dismounted and took our positions. It was quiet — too quiet. All we could hear was the distant sound of a tank blasting a roadblock.

Then it came — and we were expecting it. We knew the snipers were there; we just didn't know where.

Crack!

I was looking at Sergeant Herrera and saw him slump at the same time I heard the shot. Someone to my left yelled,

"Sergeant Herrera's hit!"

Under prearranged command succession, I immediately became squad leader. My first move was to take the squad to the far side of the vehicle — away from where the shot had come. It was protection and it was also the only way we could get the sergeant out of the 'track.

"You, and you. Get the sergeant out of there. Lay him on his back so I can look at his wound."

One man held the sergeant's head and shoulders while another gripped on his waist and legs as they eased him out of the vehicle. It took only a glance to know that he was dead. There was a hole in the center of his field jacket at pocket level. The bullet had gone through the center of his heart.

We buried Sergeant Herrera.

The aid station had sent word earlier for us not to send them any more bodies. They didn't have any way of disposing of them. Until further notice, we were to bury our dead in shallow graves and mark them according to Army regulations. Under combat conditions, we were to leave them where they fell. They would be picked up later.

I picked a spot for this burial near the road and under the cover of the half-track — away from the sniper. The grave was shallow.

"Get the mattress cover out of his pack," I instructed.

When our GI clothing was issued back at the induction center we received a canvas mattress cover about seventy-two inches long by thirty inches wide. The cover was to be slipped over the mattress of the bunk we were assigned wherever we were billeted. Actually, the mattress cover looked very much like the sack I'd used when I was a kid picking cotton in west Texas. Little did I know it might turn out to be my burial shroud.

Two soldiers slipped the cover over the sergeant's head, pulled it down his body, over ankles and boots, and pulled it tight. They then lifted him, very gently, by the knees and the shoulders and placed him in his shallow grave. The others covered the body with the loose earth. I took his rifle, affixed the bayonet, and stabbed it into the ground at his head. I hung the short-chain dog tag on one side of the rifle butt — and his helmet on the other.

We were about to fan out to look for the sniper when someone asked,

"Zorns, do you pray?"

"Then why don't you say a prayer over the sergeant?"

I already had, I suppose. Sometimes when I talk to God it's not exactly a conversation — even a one-way conversation, like my prayers always seem to be, but a prayer that's more like a thought process — something you know God understands without your having to verbalize it.

After admitting I prayed, I was morally committed. I began, not knowing what I would say:

"Gracious Heavenly Father, we have just buried our friend, Staff Sergeant Ernest Herrera. We pray, O Father, that You will take him into Your heavenly fold where he can live forever in peace. Father, he died as did Your Son, Jesus Christ our Savior, fighting for 'Peace on earth, goodwill to men.'

"Oh God, look down this morning on all of us, friend and foe alike. Let Thy Fatherly hand guide us; help the wounded, strengthen the dying, and keep our families safe.

"In the name of our Savior, Jesus Christ, we ask Thy blessing. Amen."

A primitive prayer, perhaps, but it did give me a measure of comfort and the men seemed to like it. Just as we turned away from the fresh-spaded earth, the order came to mount up. We climbed aboard. As we moved out, I noticed that every man in the squad kept his eyes on that fresh grave until it was out of sight. It was sort of a very personal goodbye to a friend and soldier.

Taking time out to bury someone became a routine operation as we slowly bullied our way through the Vosges Mountains. One of the war correspondents called us, "Seasoned Fighters" — and we were; we got that way by working like hell just to stay alive. For a while it seemed like the only thing we ever did besides fight the Germans was liberate an Alsatian village. I had the pleasure of being a member of the liberating Army almost a dozen times, and the memory of the American Army marching through the center of the village is sweet indeed. I had always heard the French people were sentimental and I found out they really were! As we rolled through a village, the people lined the streets hysterical with joy, waving at us, and crying. We waved back — and we cried a little, too. These people were so grateful to be out from under German domination they showered us with everything — flowers, wine, fruit — and when our arms were full, they threw whatever they were trying to give us into the open half-track.

And the ragged little boys with runny noses were there in every village begging and trying to sell us their big sisters.

"Cigarette pour mon père?"

"Chocolat pour mon soeur? Elle est bonne; elle est très bonne."

We gave them cigarettes for their daddies even though we knew they usually smoked themselves. I didn't find out about their sisters, but one time a kid had his sister with him; she looked good; in fact, she looked very good!

We not only brought those good people the joy of liberation, but we gave them the best belly laugh they'd had since before the German occupation. It usually took them a minute or two to recognize the condoms rolled neatly over the muzzles of our rifles, but when they did, it doubled them up and they roared with laughter pointing at our rifles! We were a little embarrassed the first couple of times it happened, but we eventually came to laugh with them.

The fighting thus far had been steady but not particularly fierce except for a couple of occasions, but by the time we reached the village of Barr on 29 November 1944, the Germans had begun making it tough for us. From all appearances the fighting had been going on there at least two or three days. Since we were the first of the Allied advance it must have been the French Resistance that had dealt so effectively with the Germans. All around the perimeter of the village we saw bloated bodies — both men and animals. The human bodies were awful to behold. Some were intact. Some were blown to bits. None looked comfortable in death; none were neatly laid out. Combat-dead bodies are almost always askew — a puffy jumble of arms, legs, and heads twisted and turned in unnatural positions — and their eyes and mouths were always open. The animals (mostly horses and mules) rolled over on their backs as they began to bloat. From a distance they resembled four fence posts sticking in the ground. To see it was bad enough; to smell it was nauseous beyond my wildest imagination. The odor seemed to coat the nasal passages and lingered for days — the memory of it has never disappeared.

Once inside the town our objective was a building-by-building mop-up operation. My partner and I were ordered to secure the buildings in one block at the edge of the village. We went from door to door down the street. We would toss a grenade in the ground-floor window and after it exploded kick in the door, rush through the building, room to room, then out the back door and in again in search of Germans. The buildings in the first block were empty so we went on to the next.

In the last store of the second block I saw the grisliest sight of my life. As we exited, our way was blocked by the burned-out shell of a Sherman tank. It had been hit by a German bazooka. The tank commander had apparently been standing with his head and shoulders above the top of the open turret, his arms resting on the rim, when the incendiary shell hit. He was immediately burned to a crisp. The cinders that were once his arms still rested on the rim. When the tank burned, the crew was incinerated. What had once been their warm, dry shelter was now their giant columbarium. Since that very moment I have never looked inside another tank nor have I ever had any desire to take shelter in one when I was wet, cold, or tired, and whatever resentment I once had for tankers is gone forever.

After the village was secure, guards were posted around the perimeter. My post turned out to be a small winery. I soon learned it produced some of the finest Rhine wines in the country — smooth, whole-bodied, and without even a hint of sweetness, yet also without tartness or acidity. I don't know how the Germans missed a place like this but they had! Or perhaps they were in so much of a hurry to get out of the way of our advance that they didn't have time to take much with them. Whatever the reason, the wine cellars were stacked with thousands of bottles of this delicious and precious stuff. I was able to get a half-track to bring up supplies and when it did, we filled that vehicle with bottles of wine. Fearing we might run out of wine before the war ended, we jettisoned such nonessential items as gas masks, extra gas cans, spare tires, etc. just to be sure we had enough to last. We did leave room for the driver and eight soldiers.

The day I caught guard duty at the winery, one of our patrols discovered one of the prettiest little hotels I have ever seen — something you would expect to find only in a storybook. It was two-storied with the lobby, bar, kitchen, and split-level dining room on the ground floor, and eighteen rooms upstairs. The kitchen was well stocked with staple foods; the bar was filled with exotic liquors. How I wished Ginny and I could spend a holiday in a place like this. She would have loved everything about it, especially the china, crystal, and silver. The chest of silver was elegant with its Alsatian coat of arms. If there was some way I could have gotten that chest in my pack, I would have tried to get it home.

The hotel was big enough to serve as headquarters for Company A. We could all sleep there, the enlisted men using the lobby as barracks and the officers and senior enlisted men using the private rooms. I was fortunate enough to get a room — and how I looked forward to sleeping between clean, white sheets! When my relief was finally posted, I headed for my room, shut the door, and shucked my clothing down to my long johns. I was asleep in that gorgeous bed almost immediately and dreaming blissful dreams when the most god-awful screaming roar I ever heard literally knocked me out of bed. I hit the floor running, yelling at my room-mate,

"What the hell is that?"

There it was again. We knew we were being shelled by something but not anything we had ever been shelled by before. It sounded like clusters of projectiles of some kind that gave off a screaming-swooshing sound. Eerie.

"I'm going down to the command post," I said as I bolted down the stairs.

The Duty NCO didn't know any more than the rest of us. He was already on the telephone trying to get battalion headquarters — and so was everyone else. When he finally made connection he didn't even have to ask the question. As he sat there and listened, he kept nodding his head. Finally he said:

"Thank you, Sir," and hung up.

"Those are German rockets being fired at us. They're something new and G-2 has been expecting them for a while. Headquarters says they're not very accurate, but the noise does make them effective as an anti-personnel weapon.

"Headquarters calls them, 'Screaming-Meemies.' Four rockets are fired at one time from a launcher. Our orders are to take the same precautions as we do with conventional artillery fire."

We didn't know until later — just before the fighting was over — how ambitious Hitler's plans really were. The rockets we got that night, and the buzz-bombs being fired on London were highly destructive, but they weren't accurate. Their being fired at us was a testing process. Their trajectory and accuracy were slowly but surely being perfected — and when they reached whatever goal the German scientists were looking for, they would then be refitted with atomic warheads and the war would be over — the Third Reich victorious. We learned from history that Adolf made one critical mistake in his research and development: he gave too high a priority to atomic energy and rocket research and development and neglected the production of conventional fighter and bomber aircraft. Allied action had taken its toll on the Luftwaffe, making German air ineffectiveness an invitation to the Eighth Air Force to bomb the German industrial complex!

But we in our pretty little hotel in Barr, France, were not privy to what was going on in Hitler's War Room in Berlin. I went back upstairs and repeated to the guys standing in the hall what the Duty NCO had told me. Not a single one of the hundreds of screaming-meemies launched at or over us fell in our general area. Nevertheless, what had promised to be a night of beautiful sleep in a semi-private room, in a warm bed with clean sheets and down comforter, turned out to be a sleepless nightmare.

On the last day of November 1944 battalion headquarters ordered A Company to move to a village to the southwest — we were to join another outfit in a mop-up operation. The Allies had taken the village but there were still pockets of German resistance scattered all over the place. When we arrived, we were sent immediately to the northeastern sector, a residential neighborhood, to make a house-to-house search similar to what we had done in Barr. We worked in pairs — first one and then the other sidling up to a window, knocking in the windowpane with a rifle butt, then tossing a grenade inside. Immediately following the explosion, the other soldier would kick in the door and rush inside. We took turns throwing the grenade and kicking in the door.

At the fifth house it was my turn to smash the window. I edged my way up, holding a grenade in one hand while I smashed my rifle butt through the window with the other. I slung my rifle over my shoulder, grabbed the pin of the grenade—and nothing happened! There was nothing wrong with the grenade; I was incapable of pulling the pin. My hand simply refused the mind's command to pull!

My buddy yelled,

"Zorns, pull the pin and throw that son-of-a-bitch."

"I can't pull it. I don't know what's wrong, but I can't pull the pin!"

"You dumb bastard, you're going to get us both killed."

"Okay, okay, but get the hell out of the way and shut up. I'm going in. I take full responsibility."

I positioned my rifle, jumped over, and kicked in the door, then moved quickly aside. Nothing happened. I swung into the empty room, then over to the basement door and kicked it in. I don't know what I expected, but I was stunned by what I saw. I slowly backed out of the room and called to my partner,

"Come give me a hand. I've got a room full of 'em, maybe thirty-five or forty. Everything's under control, but I need some help. Don't come in here shootin' or throwing grenades. I've got 'em. Move on in."

Half a dozen soldiers raced into the room and over to the basement door where I stood guard over the enemy. My buddy looked in and said:

"Goodgawdamighty. You'd of killed 'em all if you'd of pulled the pin on that grenade."

Huddled together in one end of the basement were thirty-five or forty German-speaking Alsatian kids! Some were not much more than toddlers—the oldest couldn't have been much more than ten years old. They were all dirty. Their clothing was ragged. They were thin—and they were all scared half to death.

"Let's go down and do what we can in the short time we have."

Once we were in the basement, nobody seemed to know what to do. Each man kept looking at the other waiting for someone to make a move. Finally I said:

"Somebody get that big bowl over there. Pour what water you can spare in it so they can have a drink. If you want to give all or part of your D Ration, break it up and put it on that plate so the little kids can eat that hard chocolate."

Every man there emptied his canteen into the bowl, and each gave his D Ration chocolate bar. A sight like that warms the heart and wets the eye. I had to smile though when I saw two of the guys hacking away with their bayonets to make the pieces of chocolate small enough to go around. It didn't take long at all for the kids to know how we felt. Their big, trusting, blue eyes and shy smiles made it all worthwhile.

We weren't there as long as we would have liked to be, but the war wouldn't wait. Funny how we talked to those kids in English and they talked to us in German, neither understanding the other's language, but at the same time we understood each other completely. Love and trust seem to transcend barriers of that kind.

"We have to move on; we've done all we can here. The water and the D Rations will hold them till the main body moves up. I'll have Sparks telephone headquarters to alert the MPs to take over the minute they get in.

"We'll join the rest of the battalion at Wickersheim. That'll be the first time we've been a complete unit since we started combat. Move out."

We left the kids behind munching pieces of chocolate and drinking water from the canteen cup someone left. As we walked out into the street, my buddy turned and said to me:

"Zorns, why didn't you throw that grenade?"

"I don't know; I really don't know. I tried, but it was like there was something there that kept me from it."

"Well, whatever the reason, the guys in the squad say, 'Thanks.' They liked being out of the war for a little while, and like one guy said: 'being clean again.' You know what I mean."

As we plodded down the road to Wickersheim, I kept thinking back about the events of the morning. First, I was threatened with a court-martial because I refused — or couldn't — carry out an order, and my buddy thought I was either a coward or a traitor. Then the squad treated me like a hero because I didn't kill thirty-five or forty kids.

And I heard Him say: "...I Will Be with You."

A Company got to Wickersheim a couple days before the rest of the battalion. With no duties of any kind we caught up on our sleep, did some laundry, and wrote some letters. I wrote to Ginny:

> ...just got back from a church service in a beautiful cathedral. You would have been impressed. Sitting and kneeling there in that old church I thought of you and Thomas Bruce and prayed for your safety.

There is something about this war we're going through makes me realize there is Someone great who guides my way. I'm conscious of it all the time, and I give thanks to Him constantly for the way I have been guided through so many dangers.

It's a wonderful feeling to stand here in the quiet and holy atmosphere of this church after all the noise and confusion of the fighting. I thank God again for the safety of another day. I'm not the only one around here that feels that way. There are a bunch of us. One of the guys said that we are "God-conquered men" — and I hope we are! Forgive me if it sounds like I'm preaching, but Someone does guide the way.

I can't tell you where I am, but we are allowed to say that we are attached to General Patch's Seventh Army. That should give you a pretty good idea about where we are and what we're doing.

We've been very comfortable the past two days and I'm about caught up on sleep. It's surprising how long you can go without sleep when you have to.

I love you very much...

Bruce

The 62nd Armored Infantry Battalion was billeted in Wickersheim for ten days reorganizing and refitting for the next offensive. When we left on 13 December we moved north to a village named Soultz-sous-Forêts. The Seventh Army, with the 14th Armored Division attached to it, was preparing for a cartwheel maneuver. A cartwheel is something that rolls — and that's what we did to the Germans. We rolled over the enemy on our sweep toward the German homeland. The casualties were heavy, in both men and machines, but the 62nd alone captured Schönerbourg, Ingolsheim, and Reidseltz, all on or near the French border of Alsace.

We continued to roll, and the 62nd captured its biggest prize to date: the city of Wissembourg on the French-German border. From there, the fighting raged back and forth. We did push into Germany itself and captured two villages — Schweigen and Rechtenbach — but had to withdraw when the Air Corps was called in to soften up the area with saturation bombing.

Back in Alsace, from our bivouac area south of Wissembourg, we watched the giant bombers fly into Germany and drop their loads. We saw the black puffs of smoke from the anti-aircraft fire and the Luftwaffe fighters tear into the bomber formation. We watched the ragged formation of survivors head back toward their base in England.

It was late afternoon on 17 December 1944, that we captured the German village of Schwischoffen. We didn't exactly capture it;

we just occupied it. There was hardly any opposition. The German troops had pulled back to the Siegfried Line to take a stand against the advancing Allied troops.

Company A was in the first contingent of the occupying force. We were sent to secure the eastern sector of the village. Lieutenant Hawes posted guards and sent out a patrol before he went back to reconnoiter a farmhouse he had seen earlier — one that looked like it could serve as our command post. There were nine of us in the half-track that pulled up in front of the barn. The farmer was shoveling hay but he stopped and glared at us when Lieutenant Hawes jumped out of the 'track.

"Do you speak English?"

"A leetle," he replied.

The old man looked pretty hostile so the lieutenant spoke to him in the most authoritative tone he could:

"The American Army needs your house for its headquarters."

He told him he and his family would be allowed to remain there.

"You may keep one room for yourselves and may use the kitchen when it is not in use by the American Army. Not under any circumstance will any of you be permitted to leave the immediate area without my permission."

The old man continued to glare but finally shook his head in silent resignation. In answer to the lieutenant's question about his identity, he said:

"Von Schmidt. Hermann von Schmidt."

He put down his pitchfork and walked toward the house. The lieutenant and three of us followed him.

The house was big and well constructed of rough-hewn timber. We entered through a big front door into a family area comprised of the kitchen, dining room, and living room — this area occupied more than half the downstairs. One of the doors from the family room was open to what appeared to be a big bedroom. The bed was a four-poster, piled high with a down comforter and big, fat pillows. Von Schmidt looked at Lieutenant Hawes and nodded toward his wife:

"Frau Schmidt."

She looked exactly like what I'd expected a German farmer's wife to look like — short and a little dumpy, her hair in braids coiled around the crown of her head; she wore an over-sized blue apron and clod-hopper shoes. She smiled, did a little curtsy, and said,

"Gute abend."

We hadn't eaten since breakfast. I was pretty interested in the aroma coming from a pot on the wood-burning stove. What I could see looked like vegetable soup, or a meatless stew. I motioned the lieutenant aside and asked him if we could requisition their supper as well as the house. He didn't think we could, but he did suggest to the Schmidts that we pool our food and share supper. She didn't understand English. Von Schmidt told her what we wanted to do. She smiled, curtsied again, and said:

"Ja, Ja."

Lieutenant Hawes sent two men to the 'track for two Ten-in-One rations. Our company cook began to show Frau Schmidt how to use them but she didn't need or want any help. She gestured him aside and began preparing what turned out to be a rather sumptuous meal of German-style stew made with their vegetables and our Spam. There was plenty for ten soldiers and the four Schmidts. We didn't know they had daughters until they were called to supper from upstairs. They were young — and pretty. One was about eighteen and the other about twenty-one.

I don't know what the old farmer had been told about American soldiers, but whatever it was, we apparently didn't fit the picture. And by the same token, this German family didn't fit the picture of what most of us had been told about the Germans. This family seemed to be pretty nice folks!

While the meal was being prepared and put on the table, we talked to the old man and to the girls. The elder girl spoke a little better English than her father. When we were motioned to the table, the old farmer sat there for a minute, looked at us, then excused himself and went to a cupboard just off the kitchen. He came back with four big bottles of Rhine wine. We still had some of the wine liberated from the wine cellar in Barr, but it didn't compare to the quality of what we had with supper that night.

While we were eating, the lieutenant gave us orders for this mission. About all they amounted to was that half the squad would pull guard duty for four hours while the other half slept, then vice versa. I was in the group that got the second shift. This meant I could hit the sack after we finished eating. During supper I kept looking through that bedroom door to the big four-poster bed with its beautiful down comforter. If I got there first it would be mine for the first shift. Except for those miserable few hours in the hotel in Barr, I hadn't slept in a bed for over a month.

The only other thing that distracted me during supper was the farmer's elder daughter. She kept looking at me and any time there was conversation, she directed her remarks to me. And those big, blue eyes had something else to say. They told me she had something more on her mind than the food on the table! I had a pretty good idea about what it was, but I just wasn't interested. Not only was I bone-tired and half dead from too much combat and not enough sleep, but Ginny and I had talked about the temptations we would probably be subjected to while the war separated us and how we would handle them. The answer was simply to just say "no." Neither of us would stray from the marital fold. It sounded easy enough, but I never expected the kind of pursuit that was about to come my way that night!

I was the first to finish eating. I excused myself and rushed into that bedroom claiming squatter's rights. I thought I had closed the door but apparently I hadn't. I laid my helmet on a table, removed my field jacket, turned toward the bed to sit down and take off my boots — but didn't get a chance! I didn't hear the door open, nor did I hear anyone come into the room — but there she was, the farmer's elder daughter, right there in front of me. I was startled to see her and then shocked when she threw her arms around my neck and kissed me hard on the mouth!

My response was negative but my reflexes were not very fast. It must have taken me ten minutes to untangle that girl's arms from around my neck!

In retrospect, I had a lot to learn! Having been raised in a small west Texas town in what I was later to discover was a rather sheltered life, there was a lot I didn't know about world trade. I sure didn't read anything about it in any high school or college textbook, but the kind of world trade I was being introduced to right then was as old as the first battle ever fought on this earth: sex for the necessities of life. The needs of war have always taken precedence over the needs of the civilian population — which means the occupying force usually finds the conquered civilians half starved and half naked and with nothing to trade, except sex. My being older than the other soldiers in the farmhouse that night caused that poor German Fräulein to assume I was their leader. She also assumed if she was nice to me then I would be nice to her and see that she and her family were well treated and well provided for. I will admit it was a blow to my ego when I discovered it wasn't my virility and male magnetism that turned the girl on.

At supper von Schmidt had not introduced his daughters; he had simply told us their names. The elder was Eva; her sister was Gertrand. I was to later fantasize if the original Eve had been anywhere near as persistent and persuasive as the Eva in the bedroom with me, ol' Adam would have eaten every apple on the tree! No sooner had I gotten that girl's arms from around my neck than she did it again.

"No, Fräulein, nein."

Smack. She kissed me again, hard on the mouth. What lips! Again we were a big bundle of arms and legs. I kept repeating:

"No, dammit, nein, nein!"

I don't know how it happened, but somehow we lost balance and fell — on the bed. I've heard of quick-change artists, but Eva had to be the best. As entangled as we were — and her hands were all over me — all of a sudden she was stripped to the waist! No slip, no bra. Nothing.

"Nein, dammit, no!"

Even though I had a firm grip on her right wrist, and she had a hammerlock on me with her other arm, somehow she got her skirt off. The drab peasant's skirt and blouse covered a multitude of surprises! 36", 22", 34", were my visual measurements. The long, hard days of combat and the sleepless nights in a foxhole had finally caught up with me. I was tired of fighting. I felt a little foolish at the thought of this 110-pound Fräulein outmaneuvering me.

When I relaxed, so did she. She buried her head in the fold of my shoulder and neck and then draped her right leg over my hip. . . .

I haven't the foggiest idea how long we laid there, but I did drift off to sleep — and was jarred back into the reality of war when someone started pounding on the door yelling:

"Air raid. Take cover. *Air raid!*"

Eva hit the floor pulling on her skirt and blouse while I tied the laces of my combat boots and got my field jacket on. Her arms were around my neck again but without persistence this time. She kissed me softly and whispered:

"auf Wiedersehen, liebling," and was gone in the darkness. I responded:

"auf Wiedersehen."

Some of the members of our platoon were going out the front door as I left the bedroom.

"What the hell's going on?"

The sergeant had just come up from the barn.

"German gun emplacements at the edge of town. They may or may not be manned but battalion headquarters is not taking any chances. Air Corps bombers will be over the area in ten minutes."

We made our way down the road to a gully we had crossed on our way in just a few hours before. No sooner had we settled in than we heard the sound of a lone aircraft. It was one of our fighters coming in low to drop a flare for the bombers not far behind. In another couple of minutes we heard the drone of the bombers and then the scream of the bombs they dropped on the town. There were two waves of bombers. The bomb run was over in little more than two minutes. We were close enough to the target to see the countryside light up with the explosion of the bombs. We could even smell the cordite. There was no anti-aircraft gunfire from the enemy; the Germans had abandoned their guns and retreated to the Siegfried Line several hours before.

When we could no longer hear the drone of engines, we went back to Schwischoffen. It had been completely destroyed. Fires were burning everywhere; we saw no sign of life, only the rubble and the shells of what had shortly before been homes and shops and schools and churches. The platoon reassembled and marched back the way we had come that afternoon. Our route was over the road by the von Schmidt farm but there were no buildings, only a burning, smoking pile of rubble. And there were no people. The Siegfried Line was not far down the road; perhaps they made it there before the bombs started falling.

At supper that night von Schmidt had told us this village was over three hundred years old, and the villagers, all of them, could trace their ancestry back to the founding fathers who had settled there after the Prussian wars. Three hundred years of living and we had destroyed it in less than three minutes!

The insanity of war!

And I heard Him say:

". . .I Will Be with You."

We pressed on until midnight and arrived at another small village named Steinfeld, on the Siegfried Line. We spent the rest of the night in an abandoned cowshed and blacksmith shop. Next morning we found ourselves in the middle of a sector called the "Dragons' Teeth." It was aptly named. The "Dragons' Teeth" consisted of row after row of pyramid-shaped, steel-reinforced concrete projections measuring about three feet in height and two feet at the base. These projections ran the entire length of the line, five deep.

The German military referred to them as the West Wall. Their sole purpose was to prevent the invasion of enemy vehicles—tanks, in particular. The Siegfried Line took several years to complete and it cost millions of Deutschmarks—yet it took the Allied forces only seconds to penetrate it. They did not do it with tanks. They flew over it in airplanes!

The Siegfried Line was not a thin line of heavy fortification; it was, instead, a band one to five miles deep of more than three thousand small, mutually supporting pillboxes. Each pillbox was capable of defending itself and assisting the pillboxes on either side of it. The entire line was covered with "Dragons' Teeth."

Along the length of the "Dragons' Teeth" and the pillboxes were heavy, reenforced concrete shelters for German troops. These were used as protection against the weather, small arms fire, artillery shells, and bombs.

Out of curiosity I went into one of them.

On the inside, running completely around all four walls, was a concrete ledge about three feet wide and about two feet above the floor. The soldiers could throw their bed rolls on this and lie down for sleep and rest.

It was very clean. The only thing I could find was a very thin book that was open. I walked across the room and picked it up. Never, never in all my wildest dreams would I dream of finding this book in a German troop shelter! What kind of enemy are we fighting?

I looked at the cover and the title was *Sonnets from the Portuguese*. It was opened to the next to the last sonnet, number forty-three, which was the most popular of Elizabeth Barrett Browning's forty-four sonnets,

> How do I love thee? Let me count the ways.

And the authoress concludes:

> . . .I love thee with the breath,
> Smiles, tears, of all my life!—and, if God choose,
> I shall but love thee better after death.

There was something written in German on the inside front cover. I could not interpret what it said. The composition suggested it was to be a present for someone—wife, sweetheart, mother. Whatever it said, it was signed "Hans."

Hans apparently was intrigued with love and death. In the publisher's note, before the beginning of the sonnets, the publisher quoted some of the writings of the authoress that were not in the sonnets. Some of these Hans had underlined:

> *I had done living I thought;*
> *Was ever life so like death before?*

> *My face was so close against the tombstones,*
> *that there seemed no room even for tears.*

He had underlined parts of some of the sonnets:

> *I yield the grave for thy sake, and exchange*
> *My near sweet view of Heaven, for earth with thee!*

> *And a voice said in mastery while I strove...*
> *"Guess now who holds thee?" – "Death," I said. But,*
>   *there,*
> *The silver answer rang ... "Not Death, but Love."*

I closed the little book and put it inside my jacket.

"This I will take home with me – my very first souvenir of the war – straight from the Siegfried Line in Germany."

When I came out of the troop shelter, I noticed a combat unit had moved into the line to relieve us. I found out we were going to Oberseebach, France, for rest and relaxation.

As I marched along toward our rest area, I could not help but think of Hans. I could picture him, young – about twenty-one – blonde, clean-cut, highly educated, reared in the Christian faith, fighting because he was forced to. He had nothing against any of the Allies. Apparently he was very fond of English literature. He was reading *Sonnets from the Portuguese*, the finest sonnets written in English, or any language, when he had to make a hasty retreat from the shelter – so hasty he left his gift behind.

The first phase of our combat was over; we had been under almost constant enemy fire for a month and in some of the most bitter fighting in the ETO. We had done exceptionally well; we had successfully carried out the orders given us at our bivouac at Portieux-la-Verrerie: We had crossed the Vosges Mountains. We had captured the Alsatian Plain (except for a few isolated pockets of resistance), and we had secured a portion of the Siegfried Line. In all this heavy fighting only twelve men from Company A had been killed; many had been wounded, however.

On the second day of our R and R, I wrote to Ginny:

> The big news today is I got to take a hot shower, only the second one I've had in thirty days. I feel almost like a human being again. Next news of importance is the Red Cross came through again. I got two chocolate bars, three packs of cigarettes, three boxes of matches, a package of pipe tobacco and a pack of chewing gum. Didn't know I could miss, or appreciate, things like that so much.
>
> We are allowed to send home some French money as souvenirs, as much as forty-nine francs. Enclosed is a ten franc note. The franc is worth about two cents — money over here doesn't mean very much. About all we can spend it for is wine. You can buy more with a chocolate bar or a pack of cigarettes than you can with a $20 bill. Some of the fellows have gotten as much as 120 francs for a pack of cigarettes — at one place I got two gallons of pretty good wine for a chocolate bar.
>
> It's beginning to sleet so guess I'll have to move inside the tent to finish this letter. The fire is warm and feels good. It gets pretty cold at night. We can only have a fire from 0800 to 1600. We go to bed early just to keep warm.
>
> I don't know how long it takes my letters to reach you, so I'll take this opportunity to wish you and Thomas Bruce a Merry Christmas and a Happy New Year. I wish I could be with you but I can't — I can't send you anything from here but you will get a gift from me just the same. I took care of that before I shipped out. From here I send you my love — all of it. Don't worry about me. I'm okay.
>
> Bruce

Chapter Seven
Defending the Alsatian Plain

When we left Oberseebach on Christmas Eve, we had no idea we were about to participate in some of the most bitter fighting in the European theatre, but there I was celebrating Christmas sitting in a foxhole, miserably cold. A few snow flurries were coming down and with nothing to do but sit there and let the Germans shoot at me, I couldn't help but think about happier Christmases of other years. I decided to write to Ginny and tell her everything that was going on. While we were still in Oberseebach, I had heard scuttlebutt that our letters home were no longer being censored and we could write anything we wanted to. I didn't believe it but the way the Germans had us pinned down it looked like none of us would get out of this battle alive anyway, so I really didn't give a damn what I wrote. I thought if the letter did, by chance, get through without being censored, Ginny would at least know what was going on and where I was killed — and if the military censors did get it and didn't like it, they could cut what they wanted! I wrote:

[The words or phrases in parentheses were cut by the censors.]
(Phillipsburg) France
24 December 1944
It is Christmas Eve — the night of the birth of our Savior Jesus Christ. The night when people around the world traditionally sing, "Peace on the earth, goodwill to men." There is no peace on the earth this Christmas Eve — only war. Nearly every nation on earth is fighting some other nation or nations. I do not and I cannot understand the insanity of it all.

We are encountering some of the most bitter fighting since we were committed to combat. The enemy is making a very strong offensive move to drive us back over the (Vosges Mountains). Our entire battalion is on a line of defense committed to halt and if possible annihilate the forces of (Field Marshall Gerd von Rundstedt) that threaten the entire (Alsatian Plain) sector.

The (Province of Alsace) is located in the north-eastern part of France. It is sandwiched between the (Vosges Mountains, the Siegfried Line, and the Rhine River). In the last century it has belonged to Germany as much as it has to France. Its people have developed their own dialect. It is a mixture of both with some other languages thrown in. Its people are very independent. They don't care who claims their country; they just want whoever it is to stay out of their way, and let them do things the way they have been doing them for centuries. The capital of (Alsace) is (Strasbourg), and that is where we are supposed to be Christmas Day. The way things are going, we are not going to be there for another ninety days. The going is tough!

We are pinned down by the heaviest enemy fire we have experienced. So far I have not been hit by anything they have thrown my way. I am in a foxhole some other soldier dug and for some reason abandoned. I am thankful to him. It has given me time to write you instead of dig. I am as well off in this hole as I would be in town. There is nothing for me to do but keep my head down and sit in this ice-encrusted hole and listen to the sounds of war, smell the odors of war, taste the bitterness of war and feel and see the madness of it all.

I may not survive this heavy artillery attack; I don't see how any of us can. It is indeed the fire of hell that engulfs us.

Since I began writing, the firing from the German lines has lightened and now has almost stopped completely. I cannot for the life of me understand why, because they definitely had the upper hand. The quietness and stillness are as hard on my nerves as the thunderous roar of constantly exploding shells.

As the noise of fighting fades, I can hear — coming from both sides through the cold air — the music of Christmas. Each Army seems to be serenading the other. Very faintly — sounding almost like the last reverberation of an echo — I can hear coming from the German lines:

"Still nacht, heiling nacht."

Our men a few holes down the line from me respond:

"Silent night, holy night," and "Hark, the herald angels sing...."

I hope I can finish this letter during the lull. I have already addressed the envelope. All I have to do is fold it and put it in the envelope. Maybe when the burial team comes to clean up this battlefield one of them will see it and mail it — along with my other personal belongings — to you.

I had just finished the letter to Ginny when a tracer bullet, fired from our battalion headquarters, arched across the frigid French skies. It was a signal that we were about to launch an intense counteroffensive. Moments later all hell broke loose! The sky seemed to be on fire from the barrage of heavy artillery. The thunderous explosions were almost constant from the firing on the American side to the explosions on the German side.

Our artillery had opened up with the big stuff and were lobbing the 155mm shells about midway into "No-Man's-Land," and with each firing of the guns the trajectory was raised a fraction, aiming the shells closer and closer to the German lines. Next we heard the roar of aircraft. It sounded like our B-17s, but we couldn't be sure because it was too dark. We saw the bombs as they exploded in about the same places the artillery shells were hitting; each succeeding wave dropped their load a little closer to the Germans. A few of the planes broke formation and flew low over German territory looking for heavy gun emplacements.

Then came our signal: a green flare fired by Captain Ianella. It was our signal to crawl out of our foxholes and follow the artillery and bombs into the German lines. We worked in teams of two. Our immediate objective was to finish off any of the Germans who had survived the onslaught. We used bayonets fixed on our rifles. We didn't want to shoot for fear the flash might draw enemy fire. We found Germans — lots of Germans. Those who had not been blown up were cowering in foxholes or craters. It must have been past midnight but we had light from our artillery as they continued to fire, dropping those big shells further and further into the German lines.

I never knew a soldier who liked the mopping-up operation — and to me it was particularly distasteful. Even now I wince when I think of the short thrust and the quick jerk to pull the bayonet out. The sound of the blade crushing the ribcage, and then the chilling, grating sound the blade made as it was being pulled free against the clasping edges of the shattered bones, is one I can never forget. And there was always that awful gush of blood that came with it.

It took less than an hour to clear the Germans out of our part of the Alsatian Plain. There were fewer live ones than we expected. Sergeant Barber later told us a good many had fled toward the safety of the Siegfried Line. That part of the line had been abandoned as a fortification some days before, but it was safer than the plain. We were ordered not to pursue them.

Our counterattack was an almost unbelievable maneuver. What made it believable was the fact that I had not only seen it but had also been a participant! What made it so successful was the deadly accuracy of our heavy artillery and the pinpoint bombing by the Air Corps. As the last plane dropped its load and banked to head back to the base and the last 155mm shell fell deep behind the German lines, I gave a tip of the ol' helmet to two great military units — the Air Corps and the Field Artillery — because their timely entry into the battle probably saved my life!

After the area had been declared secure we were ordered to take five. While we rested we asked Captain Ianella why the Germans had ceased firing when we were pinned down. He didn't have the answer but said he would find out at the battalion briefing later in the day. The fighting over for the time being, Company A went back on regular routine. I did not pull any duty and had a little free time. No guard duty. No patrols. Those of us with no assignments went to Phillipsburg to a warm, dry building. That it was an awfully small building made no difference. All we wanted was a warm, dry place to get a little sleep. We were wall-to-wall people, literally, with our bedrolls spread out.

As I lay there on that floor, drifting into sleep, the thought came to me that this was Christmas Day! As in the foxhole the night before, my thoughts drifted back to my last Christmas with Ginny and Thomas Bruce — the tree and all the presents, the turkey and dressing, and all the trimmings — and then I drifted off into that merciful deep sleep of the totally exhausted.

It wasn't the bugler that got us up; it was the Germans, firing 88mm mortars. We took cover — in our underwear — but came back and dressed when we saw they were firing wild. None were coming close to us.

After a breakfast of cold C rations, the battalion commander, Colonel Myers, called Captain Ianella into headquarters and told him to send a patrol into the Neuhafen area to get intelligence on troop strength, gun emplacements, etc. Sergeant John Barber was chosen to lead the patrol and I was called to be his point-man. It was one of those patrols where everything seemed to go wrong. We drew enemy fire from the beginning. Germans were everywhere and we were finally forced to retreat. One of our soldiers was wounded by a bazooka shell and was unable to come back with us. Strangely enough, the patrol was by no means a bust. We got lots of first-hand intelligence about German positions and strength. After Sergeant Barber made his report, most of the patrol went back to get our wounded comrade and bring him back. Again we drew enemy fire and this time Sergeant Barber was wounded. We were able to get the sergeant back but we never did find the other soldier.

When we reported back from the rescue mission, we were told Colonel Myers had told Captain Ianella the German shelling had stopped the night before because our Air Corps had so completely demolished von Rundstedt's supply lines that his artillery had run out of ammo! We were also told the Air Corps did not encounter a single Luftwaffe aircraft — which meant our saturation bombing of German military installations had dealt crippling blows.

The week following Christmas was uneventful. A few replacements did come in to fill slots open by the wounded and missing. Actually, our casualties from combat were unbelievably low, considering what we had been subjected to. Other than the loss of the man on patrol and Sergeant Barber's wound, there was an occasional wound from fragments but no casualties. The weather was a different kind of enemy. We had men taken from the line every day with frost-bitten hands and feet.

We didn't have an Auld Lang Syne kind of New Year's Eve celebration. German patrols had been nipping at both flanks of the battalion, and G-2 told us to expect a frontal attack on the battalion itself. I pulled guard duty — in a foxhole — at midnight. It was a double watch. Our rifles were clean, oiled, loaded, and ready, but we kept them inside our field jackets for fear they would freeze up and not fire properly. The rest of Company A was on hold in the village, ready to go on a moment's notice. It was cold sitting there in that hole but not unpleasant. Moonlight flooded the snow-covered countryside — a factor much in our favor because we had a pretty good view from our well-camouflaged foxholes — we thought. At about 0300 hours a flare was fired in our company's sector of the barbed-wire barricade. In the brilliant light we saw the German combat patrol, camouflaged in white uniforms, crawling toward us not fifty feet away! We began point-blank firing and called on the artillery for help. Some of the shells fell on our lines, but we had anticipated this and had covered our holes with multiple layers of logs. We were so well dug in we didn't have a single casualty.

The Germans breached a part of our left flank. It was pretty bad and looked for a little while like the company was going to be in deep trouble. Before the Germans began their maneuver to encircle, battalion headquarters ordered the first and third platoons of our company to pull back and set up a second line of defense.

It was 1 January 1945, New Year's Day!

My platoon was one of the two on the way to set up the new line of defense. A Luftwaffe fighter spotted us and came in low to strafe and drop anti-personnel bombs. The bombs missed and so did the bullets. We had seen the plane in plenty of time to scatter like a covey of quail. I took cover by a little stream that was frozen over. From where I lay, I saw trees and rocks on the other side — a good place to be if the German pilot decided to make another pass. I was half-way across, inching my way on elbows and knees when I heard the ice crack. Before I knew what was happening, I was in that freezing stream up to my armpits. Everything was wet — except my rifle. Instinct forced my arm up as my body sank in the water. Only my rifle and my helmet were dry!

It is amazing how the mind sometimes reacts in crisis situations. My first thought as I was being plunged into that icy water was one of elation!

"Maybe I'll get a cold or pneumonia or maybe get frost-bitten hands and feet. They'll have to send me back to the hospital, and the war will be over by the time I get out, and I'll go home."

Wishful thinking. I crawled out of the stream on the opposite side, and my clothing instantly froze board-stiff. I began to jump up and down and wave my arms so there would be some flexibility in the clothing at the knees, hips, shoulders, and elbows.

The camouflage-striped Luftwaffe fighter plane kept making passes over the area — not firing, just looking. Headquarters figured this was the area the Germans would use to attempt a breakthrough and relayed this information to us. The site of our secondary defense was near the top of a hill at a point where three roads ran together. It was not an ideal spot because the ground was rocky, frozen, and impossible to dig, but the location was good. As we looked for protective cover, we found an old trench about half-way up the hill. Only half of it was usable but we had to make do. Our platoon's radio was on the blink, and there was no contact with battalion headquarters. We ran a telephone line from our new position to Company B. They had contact with battalion and could relay orders back to us.

Lieutenant Bailey was in command of the two platoons in that snow-filled trench on the side of the hill. It was bitter cold, and we had no protective cover from either the weather or low-flying reconnaissance aircraft. There wasn't much sleep. It was impossible because of a combination of anxiety, cold, and discomfort and the continuous firing going on from about a mile down the road. Both sides were really shooting at each other.

Dawn finally came. As we were trying to uncramp our arms and legs, one of our scouts motioned us to keep down and keep quiet; there was activity in the direction of Company B. I crawled out of the trench and made my way to the top of the hill. I could hardly believe what I saw: hundreds of German soldiers, perhaps a thousand, walking in our direction! They were in loose formation, talking and singing as they approached. They were totally unaware that we were dug in there in front of them. I made my way back to the trench and reported what I had seen to Lieutenant Bailey. The lieutenant had been on the telephone. He told us the Germans had infiltrated Company B's defenses and were unaware Allied troops were beyond. Company B immediately alerted us to the hard fact that we were faced with superior German troops both ahead of and behind us!

We were facing about 4-to-1 odds. We had about 240 men from our two platoons, plus all of Company B. At a given signal, we opened fire. Initially, the rifle fire was not satisfactory. The intense cold made the firing mechanisms sluggish and caused some misfires. The soldiers having the most trouble put their rifles down and began throwing hand grenades. The only progress we made was to keep the Germans from advancing. They finally withdrew to an outcropping of rock some 1,000 yards away and settled in. After about three hours of each force holding its own ground, the men from the two platoons of Company A began to run out of steam. Morale reached an all-time low and our determination and dedication began to wane. We were all bone-tired from too many days in combat.

And I heard Him say,

". . .I Will Be with You."

We continued to fight. I think the will to survive — and win — had been instilled in us the day before when we'd heard the stories about the atrocity committed to the north of us by the German SS troops. They had taken more than one hundred prisoners and rather than send them back to a POW camp, they had marched them to an open field. While they were halted for what they thought was a rest stop, the tailgate of the last truck was dropped and a machine gun began firing. They slaughtered every last prisoner of war. I guess we remembered that when they called on us to surrender; whatever the reason, we fought with a determination we had not had before, giving no ground and ignoring other demands to surrender.

The fighting was so intense we soon began to run out of ammunition, and at the time it appeared the battle was over — and lost — there was a shell-burst on the hill occupied by the Germans! And then another, and another, and then the bursts came in pairs. Whoever was firing was doing so with such uncanny accuracy the Germans began surrendering — and they surrendered in droves. We sat up in our trench in awe and wonder, and watched two Sherman tanks rumble into view. Colonel Myers from battalion headquarters had called on the 25th Tank Division and asked them to divert some of their armor to help us. As the tanks were attacking, Captain Ianella had readied the remainder of Company A for a counterattack. Every single man in the company was armed and on the line — the walking wounded, cooks, and orderlies — everybody. The main part of the company, along with the ragtags and those of us who were almost too tired to hold a rifle, were not exactly what you would call a superior force but the Germans didn't know that. They, too, had been on the line a long time and were not psychologically prepared to do combat with new enemy strength. To our amazement, the enemy troops crawled out of their holes, came from behind rocks and from wherever else they were entrenched, laying down their rifles and placing their hands behind their heads in defeat — and surrender!

For such a hard-fought battle our casualties were nominal but it was a costly one for the Germans. The casualty rate was 23 to 1 — 23 Germans killed for every American casualty! The 2 platoons of Company A were credited with capturing 942 elite German soldiers. We thought it was quite an accomplishment for 80 cold, hungry, exhausted American Army combat infantrymen.

While we were still inflated a relief regiment came down the road. Fresh out of the replacement center, they had not seen combat. As they neared the battlefield they were repulsed by the sight and smell of the mangled, the dead, the wounded, and the captured Germans. It was horrible. But to those of us who had survived and won, it was a grimly satisfying picture we would not soon forget.

Just before the relief regiment came I was wondering if our two platoons would have to babysit those 942 prisoners.

Colonel Myers was with the commander of the relief regiment. They spoke briefly about the prisoners and he then turned them over to the replacements. He had ordered the mobile kitchen to our position, well stocked with hot coffee and sandwiches. I filled my canteen cup with the hot coffee and gulped it down, and ate the first two sandwiches along with another cup of coffee without bothering to taste them. I got the third cup of coffee and a sandwich for the road and joined the platoon. We headed toward the village of Ingweller and some much needed rest. We did pull guard duty there but little else. We slept for most of two days. After that, what was left of our battalion was moved to Kindweller for reorganization. Eight days later the combat veterans were rested and the battalion was back to full strength.

On 11 January the 62nd Armored Infantry Battalion was once again committed to combat. Our objective was to recapture the ground lost to the German army's counterattack.

We assembled at Woerth and moved up to Hohwillern the next day. Things moved so fast we had time only for a quick hot lunch before we were again in battle. In armored style — tanks and infantry — the attack began north of Kuhlendorf in an open field. Captain Ianella was leading three of Company A's platoons; the fourth had been assigned elsewhere before we left Kindweller. Our objective was the ground west of a village named Hatten. The temperature was below zero and there were about ten inches of snow on the ground. Dressed in combat, forest-green fatigue uniforms, we made beautiful silhouettes against the white snow.

The Germans were ready for us, and they had an ideal fortification: trenches that commanded a 180-degree range of vision, perfect camouflage, and ten inches of snow on the ground, and it seemed they'd been careful not to disturb a single flake. Their position was so well concealed we walked right into it without any suspicion they were anywhere around! The minute the last of our men came into sight, they opened up with every weapon they had. They had MG-34 machine guns (the very best machine gun ever made), 88mm mortars, bazookas, and hundreds of infantry troops.

In the opening burst of gunfire, I saw Captain Ianella fall forward in the snow. Then my buddy on the right fell. I was on our right flank and immediately dropped to the ground, rolling over into the safety of a snow-covered furrow where I lay flat as a pancake. The Germans couldn't hit me with small-arms fire while I was flat on the ground in the furrow, so they began lobbing 88mm mortar shells. At first they fired impact shells — which require a direct hit to be effective because the trajectory of its fragment was upward — in the outline of an inverted cone. If one hit just a few feet away, there was a good smack from the concussion, but the flying metal fragments would go upward and outward. When they saw the impact shells were not effective, they began using time shells. A time shell is just that. It is set at the time it is fired to explode at an elapsed interval of time. It exploded above ground level. The pattern of the trajectory of its fragments was downward and outward. The downside area the fragments covered depended on the height of the shell at the time of explosion.

The first time shells fired my way went too far over for me to get any fragments. The second was short and missed again. The third exploded directly over me. I felt small, hot metal dig into my body from the waist down. Then there was another explosion, closer, and I felt large, red-hot fragments hit me on the right side of my right ankle and others tear across the inside of my left shin. I knew immediately I was badly wounded and needed medical assistance. I called,

"Medic."

When he did not show up by the time I thought he should, I called again, this time as loud as I could.

I was getting ready to call again when I heard him coming across the icy snow. I didn't dare raise my head and look. The enemy would shoot me. When it sounded like he was alongside me, I looked without raising my head. It was the medic, wearing all the insignia necessary to identify him. He was unarmed. He was carrying his black medical bag. He had the red cross painted on the front, back, and each side of his helmet. He wore a large red cross patch on each arm. Even from a long distance, he could not be mistaken for a combat soldier. I felt relieved he was so conspicuously identified. I didn't want him to get hurt helping me.

He was less than three feet from me when I saw and heard it happen. He was standing straight up looking down at me, and I saw the top of his head disappear, and instantaneously I heard the sound of the rattle of a machine gun. The first shot hit him in the center of his forehead and seemed to blow his helmet and scalp off. The Germans filled his chest and abdomen full of holes. His lifeblood gushed from every hole and arched downward into the snow. He slumped slowly forward on his face and settled into the blood-soaked snow not two feet from me. I cried out:

"Oh, no God! Not the medic! He hasn't hurt anyone. He saves lives. Why take him, God? Why? Medical Aid men are not supposed to be harmed! They help the wounded—friend and foe alike. Every Army in the world respects the medic. Every one except these god-damn German sons-of-bitches—if only I could get my hands on them—I would kill every last one of them—if only. . . ."

I had become hysterical—I was ranting and raving—out of my mind, and then from high above I heard Him say:

"Be Not Afraid, I Will Be with You."

I began to drift back into the realm of cold reality and came face to face with a deep feeling of guilt.

"If only I had not called him—he would be alive. I killed him! I killed him!"

A dark black feeling of remorse, and a deep, deep feeling of guilt engulfed me, and these feelings would never let me go — never.

As I lay there — wounded and in great pain, I began to wonder what I should do. I was lying in an open, snow-covered field somewhere in France. I was cold. I could not hear any sound of any kind coming from anywhere. Had all the men in three platoons of my company been killed? Was I a lone survivor? How could I get out of here? Was there no help? Would I freeze to death? Did anyone know where I was? Could anyone help me? These questions dazzled me. I felt alone, so alone. I felt utterly helpless. And again I heard those words float down to me, as they had from the ceiling of my Forest Cathedral in the forest of Epinal:

"Be Not Afraid, I Will Be with You."

I was not alone! God was with me! I wanted to rise up and look around. Then I heard steps approaching across the frozen snow. More questions began running through my mind. Who was this coming? They had to be some of the enemy troops; they were coming from their direction. Were they coming to capture me? Were they coming to kill me? I became motionless. I dared not breathe. They walked past me. By opening one eye just a little, I could tell they were SS troops. They walked to the opposite flank of the downed platoons.

I could not tell at first what they were doing, but suddenly the grating sound of the bayonet as it was being pulled from the body against jagged bones painted me a clear picture — they were making sure all were dead — no prisoners today. I became so afraid — scared stiff!

They worked their way slowly toward me and my fear became intense. I stopped breathing. I lay motionless. I was on the verge of passing out. They were next to me — alongside the medic. I opened one eye just a little and watched with horror as they went to work on him. One of the men worked his booted right foot under the body and quickly flipped the medic over on his back. The other one jabbed his bayonet into the lifeless body three or four times. Then they turned to me . . . .

The SS trooper had a hard time getting his foot under my body — I was lying in a furrow. He finally made it, and I began to feel the tension as he prepared to flip me over, and fear enveloped me. I was afraid to pray — afraid they would hear me. Finally my mind addressed Him:

"Dear God, help me! I need your help, God! You are the only one, God, who can help me now! Help me, God, help me!"

And then I felt the tension ease. The two began to talk to each other. Their conversation became punctuated with excitement and more excitement and more excitement. I felt him remove the booted foot, and the two of them took off across the icy snow in a run. I did not breathe; I did not move. There was some kind of trick to this. I lay there in the snow for a long, long time . . . breathing just enough air to survive. Time passed, and I could feel the cold of the approaching night. Finally I got enough courage to rise up and look around. There was no one anywhere around. The rays of the sun were getting long. I needed to find some protection from the cold wind before night settled in. I raised up on my hands and knees and began to crawl in search of shelter. Suddenly there was this whizzing, hissing, screeching, whining whistle, followed by a thunderous explosion and I was knocked flat on my face again.

This shell came from behind me. This was from the 62nd Battalion. Now I was going to be killed by shells from my own outfit! I didn't know what to do. I had been fired on by both armies. I guess my battalion thought everyone had been killed. They were going to lambaste the area and get all the Germans. They didn't know I was alive. They would get me with their shelling. I would stay close to the ground and observe the pattern of their fire. Maybe I could figure a way to get out of here. I lay there as close to the gound as I could, but nothing else happened.

The lone shell had gone about fifty feet over me before impact and explosion. The concussion knocked me to the ground. The explosion threw snow, rocks, and dirt all over me. I couldn't tell from where I was lying just how deep the hole was, but from the amount of debris it had to be plenty deep to protect me from the cold wind.

I lay there for a long time to determine if my Army was going to do any more firing. It was getting dark fast and getting cold, cold, cold. I had to try to make it to this crater. I could not survive this cold without some kind of protection — this crater was the only thing around. I raised up on my hands and knees and began to torturously pull myself through the deep, icy snow. The going was painful and slow. Tenaciously I kept inching my way toward the crater and made it to the rim just as darkness took over. I peeked into it and discovered it was about six feet deep, twenty feet in diameter, and the sides sloped at about 45 degrees. This was too steep to crawl into, so I curved my body around the rim and rolled to the bottom. I knew this would be a painful maneuver but didn't realize it would hurt so badly. When I recovered a little from the excruciating pain, I began to move around and make myself as comfortable as possible. It was going to be a long, cold night. I made a pad out of the fresh, loose earth and positioned myself on it with my back against the leeward side of the crater. The fresh earth was warm. The wind zipped right over me. This was not too bad if I didn't have to stay long.

When I got settled, I decided I would look over my wounds. I unlaced my right boot. It wouldn't budge, even though I pulled and pulled. I looked closely to see why the boot wouldn't come off and then saw that my wound had bled profusely, filled my boot with blood, and this had frozen. The same thing had happened to my left boot. I thought:

"This will control the bleeding — I won't lose much more blood; this will lessen the pain, and this will reduce the risk of infection. I'm in good shape now, but I can't last too long in this bitter cold. There's hope as long as I'm alive. Maybe battalion headquarters will send patrols in search of all of these frozen soldiers lying scattered across the bloody snow of this massacre field — and for me. I will listen very carefully. I know they will come. They have always sent out patrols. I have been on them. I will keep quiet and listen very carefully. They will come before too long."

The night dragged on and on. I was getting miserably cold. My pain was acting up — becoming unbearable.

"Why don't they come for us? Why do they let us lie in this cold and freeze to death?"

It was still night and it dragged on and on. The cold got colder and *colder* and *c o l d e r.*

"Why doesn't day come?" The night hung on. The dark of the night and the light of day fought to see which stayed. Finally darkness gave way to light, but that was the only difference — the day was bitterly cold.

"And there was evening and there was morning, a second day."

I felt like the marrow in my bones was frozen. Every time I moved, I could hear and feel something crack.

The day was quite dreary. There was a thick, overcast sky with a ceiling of about 4,000 feet. I wondered how I could wile away the endless hours. I could look at the snow and count the flakes. I could look at the dark, gray clouds and try to find the outline of something hidden there. I could spend the time looking at the dark, dreary, dull, and gloomy atmosphere that wrapped me with its copper coils of refrigerant; freezing me colder and colder with each passing second. Silence punctuated my misery and emphasized the delicate balance existing between life and death.

Abruptly the silence was broken by the roar of an aircraft engine. I looked in the direction of the sound and saw plunging through the bottom of the clouds one of our sleek, twin engine, twin fuselage, Lockheed P-38 Lightning fighter planes heading toward home base. Again I got the feeling of jealousy. In just a short time the pilot and the plane would be home. He would spend the night in a clean, warm, soft bed with clean, crisp, white sheets. He would eat all the delicious hot food he wanted. He would shower with hot water and soap. He would put on a clean uniform and indulge in many other niceties of life. All this he would do while I lay wounded in the bitter cold, in great pain, filthy, hungry, thirsty, lonesome, weak, and doubting I would ever head for home base again.

While I jealously fantasized about all the good things the pilot could do when he got to home base, I heard a strange, earsplitting whine — a sound I had not heard before. I looked for the source and saw a German fighter plane moving in on our P-38. It was not the Luftwaffe. I had been strafed by them and knew exactly what they looked like. As it got closer, I noticed it did not have propellers. There were two motor pods mounted under the wing, one on either side of the fuselage, but at the front of each engine, where propellers are generally located, there were large, gaping holes. The sound was not that of a piston engine but was an earsplitting whine. It was moving much faster than our P-38. This had to be their German plane we had heard so much about in our lectures on Enemy Aircraft Identification — the Messerschmitt ME 262 jet fighter. Only a few of these planes were in operation at this time. It was the world's first jet fighter plane, and it had a lot going for it. It used low-octane diesel fuel. It had the unprecedented air speed of 540 miles per hour — much faster than any other fighter plane in the war.

It was zooming in on the tail of the P-38. When it opened fire, the Lightning made a sharp dive, and the ME 262 streaked by like a meteorite. Its pilot pulled the nose of the jet up and the plane climbed vertically and disappeared into the dark, gray clouds.

The pilot of the P-38 pulled his plane out of its dive and did a 360-degree turn and headed straight into German territory, hoping to put enough miles between the two planes so the pilot of the jet would have a hard time finding him.

The ME 262 came out of the clouds and began to circle as the pilot tried to spot the P-38, which had managed to get completely out of sight, but it had left behind two brilliant, white vapor trails called contrails, which pinpointed the location of the Lockheed. The jet pilot spotted these and took off at top speed. When he got close enough to identify the P-38, he climbed above it and then dove down on the Lightning with all his guns firing.

Immediately I saw smoke trailing the P-38. Then it began to roll while in horizontal flight and then went into a spinning, vertical dive.

I saw the pilot eject from the burning plane and clear it. His chute opened, and he descended slowly into German territory. I began to feel remorseful over the jealous feeling I had of the pilot. I began to wonder about him as he floated down:

"Will the enemy on the ground strafe him as he descends? Will he be captured and taken prisoner of war? Was he badly wounded? Will he have to lie in an open field without any protection from the cold and wind? This man is in a worse situation than I am. I have my shell crater to protect me. He will freeze quicker than I. I don't guess I will ever know the answers to these questions. I know this: I will never again feel jealous of anyone serving in other units of the military. They face dangers the same as we in the infantry."

Now what do I do? Why doesn't the battalion send out search parties? Were they going to abandon us? My wounds were beginning to hurt—the pain had become excruciating. The cold lessened my pain at first, but now the pain was overriding the anesthetic effect of the cold. The pain was becoming unbearable. Then I remembered—I was a battalion aid man. In this capacity I carried a packet of twelve morphine syrettes. These were for pain. I would shoot myself with one of them and this would ease my pain. This was going to be the easy way. Then I remembered the instructions I'd received in the use of morphine. I remembered one of the big "don'ts"—don't give to anyone in extremely cold weather. They would go to sleep and not wake up. No, I don't want to do this now. I'll put up with the pain for a while longer.

I kept listening for a scouting party from battalion headquarters to come in search of all of us. I listened and listened but no one came.

Finally the second night took over and time dragged ever so

slowly. I began to wonder what time it was and looked for my watch. I remembered it had been broken by the first shell burst. Then I reasoned I could not see the face of my watch in this darkness, much less the hour and minute hands, so I forgot about time. I knew it would be a long, long time before morning would overtake the night.

I put my right ear to the ground, hoping this would amplify the sound of anyone approaching. I listened and listened. All I could hear was the rustling sound of some kind of animal. Then I heard the bone-chilling sound of chalk being scraped across a blackboard. There was no chalk; there was no blackboard. The sound came from the teeth of the animals I'd just heard scraping across the frozen bodies of my buddies lying scattered across this snow-covered battlefield.

I kept listening and listening, waiting and waiting, but nothing happened—no one came. I got colder and colder, and the night dragged slower and slower. I was in intense pain from the cold. For a while the cold had killed the pain of my wounds. Now I was in great pain all over my body. I was one big mass of pulsating pain. I did not think I could stand it another minute. My condition was unbearable. I began to think of alternatives open to me. Again I remembered the morphine syrettes. If I gave myself two of them, I would drift painlessly off to sleep and never wake up. There would be no more cold, no more pain. At first this seemed to be the most sensible and the easiest thing to do.

Then I reasoned:

"It would be easy but there would be no rescue possible, no recapture, no return to control of the American Army, no return to God's promised help, no return to Ginny and Thomas Bruce and their love. Such action would be final—that was all. No, I didn't like this way out. I would continue to suffer this intense pain for a while longer."

Chapter Eight
A Time to Surrender

The darkness of night was once again swallowed by the light of day.

"And there was evening and there was morning, a third day."

I realized I had to make some serious decisions and make them fast. I could possibly make it through this third day but there was no way I could make it through another night. I needed help! To whom could I turn?

As the day got brighter, my mind got clearer and I realized there was only One to turn to. Again I called on my God.

"Oh God, I'm in trouble and I need your help. In my Forest Cathedral outside of Epinal you said to me, 'Be Not Afraid, I Will Be with You.' I cannot see you or hear you but I know you are here. I need you to help me decide: Should I stay in this shell hole and wait some more for the American Army to come and take me back under their control, or should I crawl out of this hole toward the German line and hope they take me prisoner of war?"

I waited a long time for an answer but God did not acknowledge in the manner I expected — but then He works in mysterious ways. As I lay there in the cold morning, I felt something strange. I did not know what it was but it felt as if my mind was being cleared of its cobwebs. I felt I could make the right decisions, so I began to think:

"If I stay in this hole another night I *will* freeze to death before morning. The verb 'will' expressed inevitability; there is no other possibility. If I climb out of this hole and crawl toward the German lines they *may* take me prisoner. The verbal auxiliary 'may' expresses a contingency, a chance. The answer is clear. I will do whatever gives me a chance."

It was mid-afternoon. I knew I had better get started. Torturously I began to pull myself out of the crater. The going was slow. Every wiggle, every twist, every turn was severely painful. With tenacity I kept twisting, turning, and pulling myself up inch by inch. I finally made it to the top and pulled myself out of the hole and onto the flat surface. I lay there and rested for a few minutes before I began the crawl toward the enemy. As I lay there I thought to myself:

"This is crazy, deliberately surrendering to the enemy. We have been taught throughout all our training to avoid being captured. Our instructors had led us to believe surrendering to the enemy was something less than honorable. But here I am: if I want to survive, I have no choice but surrender. To evade capture another night will mean certain death. I do not want to die. I want to live and go home to my wife and son. I want to live more than anything. The only thing to do is to start crawling. This way I have a chance."

I got up on my hands and knees and started to pull myself through the deep snow. This was as torturous as climbing out of the crater. I kept trying and edged along inch by inch. Any moment I expected to hear the staccato rhythm — tata-ta-ta — tata-ta-ta — tata-ta-ta of enemy machine guns but heard nothing. Either they didn't see me or they were ignoring me.

Maybe I needed a white flag? I had noticed in the movies when someone wanted to surrender, they waved a white flag. I began to wonder where I could get a white flag. I didn't think I had anything on me that was white. My handkerchief, my underwear, and everything else I was wearing that was not khaki or forest green was a sickening dirty green color. And I said to myself:

"Oh well, I'll just have to surrender without a white flag."

I continued to crawl toward enemy lines. They must be looking me over pretty close — trying to figure out whether to shoot me or capture me. I hoped they decided soon — I was running out of strength. I was so thirsty! I was so cold! I was so tired! I had committed myself — I had to carry through. I kept crawling and crawling inch by inch. Every once in a while I laid down and rested a little, but every time I did, I got colder. I had to keep going even though it was draining my strength. I had to carry through — there was no turning back now.

I thought I saw some movement in the enemy lines. I must have had a whiteout. Their lines were so well camouflaged I did not know where they were. I kept crawling, kept pulling myself through the deep snow, kept my fingers crossed and kept praying. This effort had to work! There was nothing else!

After what seemed to me to be an eternity, I looked up and saw an enemy soldier coming toward me. I became frightened. I hoped he was not one of the SS troops that had mowed us down day before yesterday. When he got close to me, he said something in German, but I could not understand what he was saying. I could tell he was not from the SS. Everything about him was shoddy. He acted uncertain about what he was supposed to do. He stood there looking down at me. He stood and stood. Finally he said something else to me, but I did not understand this either. He bent down and took hold of my right arm and tried to pull me to my feet. I was not able to help him any, and he was not very strong. He let go of my arm and I settled back into the deep snow. He backed off a few feet and looked at me — it was a very puzzled look. He was trying to figure out what he should do.

He tried again to lift me. I could not help him and he dropped me back into the snow. Our problem was we could not communicate verbally. At last I wondered if we could visually. I pulled my pants leg up as far as I could, and that was enough for him to see the bloody ice and snow that wrapped my ankle. He looked at my wounded ankle, nodded his head, said:

"Ja," and turned and walked away. I thought to myself:

"Well I'll be damned! That goddamn German son-of-a-bitch is not going to take me in — he's going to leave me out here in the snow to freeze to death. I am worse off than I was in the crater — there, I had protection from the bitter cold wind. I will freeze to death much faster without this protection."

It was getting dark and I began to panic. I didn't like the idea of freezing to death. I would suffer a lot if I froze. A lethal dose of morphine would cause death instantly. The freezing process had started. I was getting numb in my legs and arms. This made up my mind.

I reached into the pocket of my jacket and pulled out the package of syrettes. I took two out of the package, and then thought:

"I've got to cut a hole through all this clothing to find a place to give the shot. My thigh would be the best place. What would I use to cut the clothing? My bayonet, of course! And it's easy to get to."

I reached back to my backpack to pull it out, but nothing was there. Oh, no! I'd taken my backpack off when I'd started crawling toward my crater. I relaxed a minute to think. About the only part of my body I could get to was my hand. This was not a very good place. I took the glove off my left hand and took a look. The fleshy

part on the top of my hand between the thumb and index finger
would be all right. I was getting more numb with each passing second. I had to do this thing now and get it over. I took the protective
cover off the needle of one of the syrettes and held it in my right
hand. I placed my left hand on my left knee. This was just right. I
placed the needle of the syrette in the area I was to shoot myself. All
I had to do was shove the needle in. At this very instant and as fast
and as quick as a bolt of lightning could strike the ground from the
clouds above, a few lines from my favorite song, sung by the lonely
shepherd, David, flashed through my mind:

> Yea, though I walk through the valley of the shadow of death, I will
> fear no evil; for thou art with me....

Before this song was finished, I heard a noise and looked up.
Standing over me was that goddamn German son-of-a-bitch. He
had another German soldier with him, and between the two of them
was a homemade wooden wheelbarrow that even had a wooden
wheel. I had not realized that goddamn German son-of-a-bitch had
been gone long enough to grow a set of wings. There, in the presence
of my enemy, I cried, and through my tears I plainly saw the
beautiful white wings that had grown out of his shoulders. Never
had I dared to dream of being happy over seeing my enemy. There
he was and with him some help and a wooden wheelbarrow. A
beautiful halo glowed brightly around his helmet.

The wooden wheelbarrow was a work of art, and I prayed the
farmer from whom it was stolen would get it back after my captors
had delivered me to wherever they were taking me. It was larger
than most wheelbarrows I had seen. The bed had three vertical
sides. The front sloped out at about a 40-degree angle. This allowed
the operator to empty his load by simply tilting the wheelbarrow up
from the rear. The frame was A-shaped — very simple construction.
The bed sat on this frame with the front, sloping end, at the apex
of the frame. The wooden wheel had been cut from a single piece
of laminated wood. It was about 2 ½ inches thick. The apex of the
frame did not come to a point but was squared off and was about
12 inches wide. The two structural members of the frame angled
back past the crossbeam and the rear of the bed. At this point they
were 3 feet wide and were used for the handles. This was very sturdy
construction.

When the loading process began, I noticed they had a long rope coiled in the bottom. They took this out and began the loading process. One of the soldiers put his arms around my shoulders, the other put his around my thighs. Even as careful as they were, the pain was excruciating. I was placed in this contraption with my back and shoulders resting on the front end, the sloping end, and my legs hanging over the vertical rear end. That goddamn German son-of-a-bitch very carefully handled my right leg to reduce the pain as much as possible. He very carefully placed the bottom of my right foot on top of the left beam, cut a piece off the rope and tied my foot to this beam. They had me ready to go.

They tied the rope to the apex of the frame with one end tied on each side and the wooden wheel in between. The newcomer got inside the rope and let it fit snugly around his waist as he faced forward, very much like a dog harnessed to a sled. The goddamn German son-of-a-bitch took his position at the handles at the rear. He could watch my right foot better from this position. The first soldier gave the signal — the new soldier pulled, the first pushed. We didn't get very far. The snow was very deep and slick. As they tried to push and pull they'd slip and their rifles would slide off their shoulders. They kept trying but they did not get anywhere. Finally they called a conference and did some serious talking. When they finished they headed toward me. They took their rifles off their shoulders and handed them to me — butt first. This helped a little but the going was tough. They pushed and pulled and huffed and puffed.

Now here was the picture: I was the prisoner, I was carrying my captors' rifles, and in addition I had six hand grenades hanging on my jacket. I was lying in a wheelbarrow being pushed and pulled by my captors, and they were now unarmed. I could blow them to kingdom come if I wanted to, but I would be alone again in the snow, in the cold, in an open field somewhere in France. I wanted my captors to get me to wherever they were taking me. I stood a chance of getting out of this alive. I didn't want to mess up now.

They kept pushing and pulling. We moved forward at a very slow pace. Night settled in, got darker and darker. This didn't bother my captors. They seemed to know where we were going and how to get there. Finally they stopped, took their rifles from me, left me and the wheelbarrow parked and walked forward into the darkness. Now where in the hell was I?

In about twenty minutes they returned. When they got close enough I could see they were carrying a stretcher. They lifted me out of the wheelbarrow onto the stretcher and headed off into the darkness. Now the bombardment began — both sides — and we were in the middle. If I ever got out of this war, I would never come back — never. I had had enough of war. The shells were not landing very close to us, but they made a lot of noise and gave off a lot of light. Now I could see where we were. In front of me was a large hole. It hadn't been made by an exploding shell, but had been dug by the French.

From the bottom of this massive hole rose a monumental structure. It was one of the giant bunkers of the Maginot Line — France's offset to the Siegfried Line. That goddamn German son-of-a-bitch and his helper picked up the stretcher and began carrying me down a long flight of stairs. These, I later discovered, led to the back entry of this giant fortification which faced east into Germany. My captors got me down these stairs and through a door that led to the massive interior. This was great — nice and warm in here. They laid me in front of a German officer who said something to me in German, but I didn't understand. My captors were getting ready to leave. They had been mighty good to me. I looked up at them, held out my right hand, and each of them put out his right hand. I shook hands with my captors and said:

"Danke."

They smiled, nodded their heads, and walked out.

The officer said something else to me but I didn't understand this either. He came around, squatted down, and began to examine my leg. I was so thirsty I asked him:

"Trinkwasser?"

He replied:

"Ja," and headed off into the massive darkness. He was carrying a glass full of something when he returned and handed it to me.

I was so thirsty. I took one big swallow, but it did not go down. I gagged, coughed, and spit out about half of it. This was a big glass of wine. Nothing could quench my thirst but water.

"No! No! I wanted water. Water, not wine, trinkwasser."

He took my glass and returned with it full of something else. This time I sipped it and immediately spit it out. This was apple cider. I didn't want to cause all this trouble, but when I was this thirsty nothing would quench my thirst but water. I hadn't had any water in three days. I handed him the glass and asked again:

"Trinkwasser?"

The next drink he handed me was beer. I took a sip and handed the glass back to him.

"Water? Water? Trinkwasser? Trinkwasser?" I asked him over and over.

He turned to me and said:

"Nein trinkwasser, trinkwasser kaput."

So that was it — the drinking water was ruined.

As much as I would like to have a glass of water, I would make do with this beer. It was better than anything else he had brought.

He squatted down again and began to examine my legs. He tried to get the boot off my right foot but it would not budge — it was frozen to my foot and leg. He tried the left one, but it was frozen too. He walked over to the table where he had been sitting and got something that looked like a scalpel. When he got back he squatted down and began to cut my boots from the top to the sole in one-inch strips. Then he told me he would have to wait until the boots thawed before he could do anything else. He told me to relax.

The pain was getting severe again, or I was just beginning to notice it after the elation of being captured and brought into this warm, safe room. I thought of the morphine syrettes in my jacket pocket, pulled them out and handed them to him, thinking he would give me a shot. He looked at them disdainfully and casually threw them into a dark corner. He walked over to the table, got a syringe, filled it from a bottle of medication on the table, and injected me with this. I didn't have any idea what it was and just didn't give a damn. I immediately began to relax and to glow with the wonderful feeling of warmth. And I heard Him say:

"Be Not Afraid, I Will Be with You."

As the boots began to thaw a little, the officer pulled the strips down and soon had the boots off. This did not help him much in determining the extent of my wounds. Both of my legs were frozen. He didn't hasten the thawing process, but allowed my legs to thaw at room temperature.

The shot he gave me did not make me pass out but it took me to the very brink. As my legs thawed, I lay there in the comfort of the Maginot Line and passed in and out of consciousness.

It was very late by the time my legs had thawed enough for the doctor to make his examination and determine the extent of my injury. There was nothing he could do in the way of treating my leg. He put a make-shift splint on it to keep it from hurting so badly and to prevent any further damage to it. He had my stretcher moved closer to the entry so it could be loaded into the next ambulance and moved to an aid station further into Germany.

It must have been between 0200 and 0300 hours when I was loaded into the ambulance. As they opened the door to this fortification, I could tell the artillery fire was fierce, worse than anything I had experienced, and it was coming from both sides. As they carried my stretcher up the stairs to ground level, it looked like the whole world was on fire. I didn't like the idea of leaving the warmth and safety of the Maginot Line, but the ambulance attendants didn't seem concerned. When they finished loading, they headed east into Germany.

In about one and a half hours they stopped at a building and began unloading. From the outside it looked like a school. They took me into one of its rooms and placed me in front of a German officer who was going to question me. He was a tough-looking character. I bet he'd get mean before he got through with me. He spoke fairly good English and began the questioning quickly and gruffly:

"Is this your outfit?" he asked as he pointed to the patch of the 14th Armored Division on the right sleeve of my jacket.

I looked him in the eye and responded as we had been trained to do:

"My name is Bruce C. Zorns, my rank is Private First Class, my Army serial number is 38693068."

"Oh, you are going to act like one of those smart-aleck Americans. I have dealt with them before, many, many times. I'm going to deal with you as I did with them. It was very effective. Now, damn it, tell me what unit of the 14th Armored you are with."

"My name is Bruce C. Zorns, my rank is Private First Class, my Army serial number is 38693068."

"Damn it, you have already told me that; now answer my question."

"My name is Bruce C. Zorns, my rank is Private First Class, my Army serial number is 38693068."

"Where is your unit located?"

"My name is Bruce C. Zorns, my rank is Private First Class, my Army serial number is 38693068."

"How many men are in your unit?"

"My name is Bruce C. Zorns, my rank is Private First Class, my Army serial number is 38693068."

"Who is commander of your company?"

"My name is Bruce C. Zorns, my rank is Private First Class, my Army serial number is 38693068."

"Who is commander of your battalion?"

"My name is Bruce C. Zorns, my rank is Private First Class, my Army serial number is 38693068."

He was puffing on a cigar. By the way he was puffing I could tell he was getting mad. He began to puff hard and fast. He got up and stuck his face in mine and blew smoke in it. He continued blowing smoke in my face and said:

"I want some answers and I'm going to get some answers one way or the other. Make it easy on yourself and on me and answer my questions, OK?"

"My name is Bruce C. Zorns, my rank is Private First Class, my Army serial number is 38693068."

He bent down, grabbed my shoulders, and began to shake me while he yelled,

"Now, goddamn it, answer my questions..."

Before he could finish, two of the medical team came and picked up my stretcher and carried me into a room being used as an operating room. One of the men who spoke a little English told me they were going to put me to sleep and pick the shell fragments out of my legs and thighs. Before I could say anything, a mask was placed over my face and I could smell ether. The next thing I remembered was riding in the ambulance again.

When they stopped, they unloaded me and carried me into a room that was large and full of rows upon rows of cots and bunk beds. It took me a little while to figure out where they had brought me. I finally figured out I was in a German military hospital in a room full of wounded German soldiers. I thought to myself:

"How will this work out? I am the captured enemy in the midst of many of my captors, all of whom have been wounded by action against my Army – the U.S. Army. Will they be bitter toward me? It didn't take long to find out. When I was settled, the wounded German soldiers began to speak to me. I didn't know what they were saying, but they were saying it in a friendly way. They asked all kinds of questions. I talked back to them in a friendly tone. We talked and talked, not knowing what the other was saying, but we said it with a smile and smiles transcend all language barriers.

A high-ranking German officer entered the ward and everyone came to attention, raised their right arms to about 75 degrees and shouted:

"Heil Hitler!"

I lay there bewildered. Finally one of the hospital attendants came over and raised my right arm to about 75 degrees and told me to say:

"Heil Hitler!"

I protested:

"I am a prisoner of the Germans. I fight Hitler, not heil Hitler."

A German officer walked up about this time and noticed I was having trouble adjusting to the role of prisoner of war. He began to indoctrinate me in the protocol of being one. I must say he had read a lot of English literature because he began to tell me what Prime Minister Winston Churchill had written about his experiences as a prisoner of war during the Boer War in South Africa while he was serving as a war correspondent:

"You are in the power of your enemy. You owe your life to his humanity, and your daily bread to his compassion. You must obey his orders, go where he tells you, stay where you are bid, await his pleasure, possess your soul in patience."

I butted in on the officer's indoctrination:

"But what about the Geneva Convention?"

The officer smiled and quickly said:

"How a prisoner of war fares under the Geneva Convention depends not on the humanitarian provisions of the Geneva Convention but upon the attitude and customs of his captors — and during wartime conditions. A prisoner's welfare may hinge on the men who happen to be guarding him. Many a guard has tapped his rifle and said, 'Here is my Geneva Convention.'"

I kept looking at the officer and his jaunty uniform, complete with bright yellow scarf and an odd-looking medal I had never seen before. I asked him about the medal.

"Oh, this one? This medal is for being a pilot of our jet fighter plane, the Messerschmitt 262A."

"I saw one of those a few days ago — the day after I was wounded — near Hatten. It was in a fight with one of our P-38s. The jet shot our Lightning out of the sky."

"They are faster than anything in the sky. We could have beat the hell out of your Air Force if Hitler had taken Göring's advice and built more of them. We only built 1,300 of them and built them too late. I was flying the jet that shot your P-38 down."

"You were! I've been wondering about the American pilot — was he killed; did he bail out; was he strafed on his way down; was he taken POW?"

"I watched him bail out. He landed safely and was taken POW. He didn't get a scratch, but I hurt my thumb," and he held up a bandaged thumb on his right hand.

"Hurt badly?" I asked him.

"I mashed it opening the canopy of my cockpit after the fight. I can't fly with it in this condition."

"You poor German," I thought to myself as I looked around the ward full of seriously wounded Germans.

He then came out with this startling question:

"Why are you Americans fighting us Germans? We should be allies fighting the Russians."

"For one thing, my friend, you declared war on us, and you invaded Russia."

"The way things look now, we should have been allies."

"Maybe for you Germans. We are doing quite well and so is Russia. By the way, what are you going to do after the war?"

Without hesitation he replied,

"Go to the United States of America."

I was very startled by this answer, especially since it came from our enemy, and in a questioning voice I asked him:

"Go to the United States? You are fighting us. Why would you want to go there?"

"Everything here is kaput. There is no future, no opportunity. I want to go where there is an opportunity. The Americans will like me; I will like the United States, ja?"

Two hospital attendants loaded me onto their stretcher and carried me away, so I didn't have to answer the egotistical German flyboy's question.

I was admitted to this German military hospital on the morning of 16 January 1945. Throughout the rest of the day I was interviewed, and all kinds of tests and X-rays were begun. There were several conferences among physicians and surgeons. For the next four days they did everything in their power to try to save my right leg. Late in the afternoon of the 20th I was taken to the operating room — not quite to the operating room, but placed in line to be admitted into the room. I was placed at the end of this line. Men were taken into the room in the order they were placed in the line. It didn't make any difference what nationality you were — there was not any discrimination. Enemy soldiers were taken ahead of Germans, if they were ahead of them in the line.

As I moved slowly forward, hospital attendants came by and

took my temperature, brought me water, or whatever I wanted, if it was not against doctors' orders. I was treated just like a German soldier.

Finally I was admitted. A very distinguished-looking man came over to the table and began to talk to me in perfect English:

"I'm your doctor. I'm afraid I have bad news for you. We are going to have to amputate your right leg. Gangrene has set in and is spreading fast. Your temperature is 105 degrees and rising. If we wait any longer, we risk having to amputate above the knee. It is very important we save the knee if we can. Then you will be able to walk again without any discernible limp. You will be able to participate in sports other than the more strenuous ones. I am familiar with the prosthetic appliance you will be wearing. You see, I graduated from one of America's more famous medical universities — Johns Hopkins, Baltimore."

His perfect English made me ashamed to say anything. Finally I asked him:

"Do I have an option, Doctor?"

"Yes, you do."

"What is it?"

"Death within a short period of time."

"Well then, let's get busy and cut it off. Doctor, you will give me something for the pain?"

"I will give you something to 'rest your blood,'" and with this the doctor left the room.

This reference to "rest your blood" upset me. Only this morning I was in a ward of wounded Germans when the door opened, and the ambulance crew brought in another wounded German, laid him on one of the bunks, and called a doctor. The doctor raised the sheet, took one quick look, and called a nurse. She brought him a syringe. The doctor injected the patient and pulled the sheet over his head. The ambulance crew carried him out.

This picture flashed through my mind when the doctor told me he would give me something to "rest your blood." I wished the doctor would get back in here. I needed to talk to him. I thought I heard him coming.

"Doctor?"

"Yes," he responded.

"What do you mean, 'I will give you something to rest your blood'?"

"Oh, I see what is bothering you. 'Rest your blood' is a phrase we German doctors use in referring to the effects of a new anesthetic we have developed. We have been using it now for several years. I don't believe you Americans have developed it yet. It is called 'Sodium Pentothal.' We find it to be very good. It acts quickly, is dependable, and leaves very little aftereffect.

"OK, Doctor, I'm ready when you are."

"This anesthetic is injected into a vein. Now I want you to count backward from ten to zero."

"Ten, nine, eight, seven, si . . ."

I was in the corner of an upstairs room when I started coming to. When I opened my eyes, I saw a nurse, and recognized her as the doctor's nurse and secretary. Before the sodium pentothal knocked me out, I had noticed her taking notes prior to the operation, and presumed they were about the amputation. She spoke English about as well as he—I guess she had to if she worked for him.

"The doctor wanted me to stay with you until you came to and were completely out from under the anesthetic. He wanted me to tell you we amputated your right leg below the knee. For some people the shock of hearing this causes them to jump out of bed and try to run. He didn't want you to do this and hurt your stump. You are aware your right leg has been amputated?"

"Yes, it's beginning to hurt. It feels like I have stubbed my big toe and it hurts."

"You will feel all kinds of pain and in every part of the missing limb. Some of them will be very painful. This will get better in time, but it will never go away completely."

"I need to scratch my ankle. It sure does itch."

"This is something you will have to live with the rest of your life. We hated to cut it off. You gave us your permission. It was necessary to save your life.

"The doctor also wanted me to tell you he only did a 'guillotine' type operation. He did not have time to make the closure—just too many wounded lined up in the hallway. You will have to have a re-amputation when you get home. Your stump will heal alright; you just can't wear a prosthesis with it in this condition.

"You will notice the bandages are all paper. Not the best, but better than nothing. Germany does not produce nor, with all the blockades of our shipping, can we import any cotton. Paper is nearly as good, and it's made out of wood and wood out of trees, and we have plenty of trees. We use our trees for nearly every-thing.

"It is now 0300 hours, 20 January. You will be shipped to a prisoner of war camp in just a little while. The medical attention you will receive there is not very good. We are sorry, but there is nothing we can do about this. We can take care of anything you need before you leave here, but after you leave there is nothing we can do.

"If you don't need anything else, I must go," and she got up and headed toward the door of this dark room. When she got there, she turned and smiled sympathetically and said tenderly:

"auf Wiedersehen."

And once again, I was alone and in the dark, waiting to be taken to a prisoner of war camp deeper inside Germany.

Chapter Nine

Of Lice and Fleas and Stalag XIIA

Wham!

I nearly jumped out of my skin. The sound was so loud — and it sounded like an artillery shell exploding. I cautiously looked around to see what was going on. There were two German corpsmen — they had very boisterously kicked the swinging, double doors open and these had hit the wall, sounding like an artillery shell exploding. They laid their stretcher on a nearby table, loaded me onto it, and carried it to a conventional-looking ambulance. When they shoved me in, I noticed three stretchers had already been loaded. I was loaded on the bottom with another — there were two on the row above. I didn't know where we were going and from the inside of this contraption I couldn't tell either. I thought we would be going over the Autobahn but as slow as we were moving, I didn't know for sure. We were moving mighty slowly to be traveling over a super highway.

We had been traveling less than an hour when we stopped. I heard both corpsmen get out and immediately something very heavy was hitting the ambulance. I called out to my traveling companions:

"What the hell's going on?"

"They are loading logs."

"Is this ambulance powered by a steam engine?" I asked my companion on the left.

"No, it's internal combustion."

"Don't give me that shit. I know you can't run logs through a carburetor into a cylinder and have a spark explode them."

"Any shit-ass knows that, smarty. These are green pine logs and they are thrown into a little furnace-like contraption that trails behind the ambulance. The gases that are given off are run through coils and this gas comes out — methane gas, a very high quality gas, and this is what is injected into the carburetor. It works. This ambulance won't run very fast. But fast enough, I guess.

"And so the Krauts run their ambulances on pine trees. Very, very interesting. What do they call these things?" I asked my companion next to me.

"I don't know. I haven't heard them called anything."

"Then let's call them our 'woodchippers.'"

"That suits me. We are now riding in a 'woodchipper.'"

"I'm Private Bruce Zorns, Seventh Army, General Alexander Patch," I introduced myself.

"I'm First Sergeant Charles M. Holmes, Third Army, General George S. Patton—Old Blood and Guts, he's called."

"The Third and Seventh Armies have been crossing paths all the way across France. We landed on the shores of the Mediterranean and came north across France. The Third Army joined the invasion forces and helped them break out of the Normandy hedgerow. Patton drove his army hard—gaining up to forty miles a day. I ran into your General one day not long ago—a few days before Christmas."

"Where was this?"

"It was during the Third Army's attack on Strasbourg. I was on a hill about five miles south of the city. I could see the fighting and hear the loud noises of this vicious battle. I was pulling guard duty on a two-rut dirt road that ran into Strasbourg. My orders were not to let anyone pass who could not give the password, 'Yellow Bird.' This order was passed down from General Patton himself. The city was under siege and he didn't wany anyone going down this road and running into the fierce fighting taking place."

"I remember that battle. It was hell. We lost a lot of men."

"There was not anything going on in this area of the hill so I walked back and forth across the road. There must have been a very deadly battle there not many hours earlier; there were a lot of dead Germans lying around and they had not begun to bloat as yet. I came across a young soldier who was wearing something I'd wanted for a long time. Some of the fellows in my company had picked some up from dead enemy in the field. Everyone wanted one as a souvenir."

"Bet it was one of their P-38 pistols—a beautiful little gun. They fire 9mm shells. I think we named them P-38. I don't know why. They are not .38-caliber."

"This was the prettiest one I had run across. The blue steel of the gun did shine as bright as a mirror. The holster, belt, and shoulder strap were out of the very best leather. I could tell he had worked very hard to keep it shined. He had finally polished it to a satin-sheen finish. He wasn't going to use it anymore, so I took it off him and put it on. It fit me to a T. I didn't have to change a single buckle. Oh, I was proud of it! This was something I would take home as a souvenir."

"Those are mighty attractive little guns. I never did get one. Do you still have yours?" Sergeant Holmes asked.

"No, thanks to your General."

"How's that?"

"I was telling you about my being on guard duty and watching the battle of Strasbourg. Well, after I found my little gun I saw a cloud of dust down the two-rutted road. Whatever was raising the dust was a long way off. Just the same, I kept my eye on it, and as it got nearer I could tell it was moving very fast. Finally I could make out the outline of a Jeep. I thought to myself: "That's some drunk GI. He won't know the password and I'll have to shoot him, and I'm not in the killing mood today."

"Did you have to kill him?"

"No, Sergeant, I was worrying about nothing. When it got close I could see flags waving from all fenders. I thought: 'My God, I've got me some top brass; I had better get on the ball and shape up — top brass indeed! I could make out four stars on the flags and four stars on the license plates.'"

Charles asked me: "Didn't the thought of having to stop a Four Star General and ask him for the password frighten you?"

"It scared the shit out of me. I felt as out of place as a whore in church. I wanted to find a place to hide where he couldn't see me."

"Well what did you do?"

"Charles, I got out in the middle of the road and stood at attention — present arms. I thought that damn driver of his was going to run over me before he got that four star Jeep stopped. He missed me by about six inches. I did a right shoulder arms, walked back to the General, saluted with present arms, and said: 'Sorry to stop you, sir, but these are your orders. Give me the password.'"

"What did he do?" the sergeant asked.

"He leaned forward in his seat and replied: *'Yellow bird.'*

"I said to him: 'You may pass, sir,' and I saluted him with present arms, did a right shoulder arms, did a smart about-face, and walked away. I didn't get very far before I heard the rather high-pitched voice of the General yelling: *'Hey, you son-of-a-bitch!'*

"I turned and asked him: 'Sir, to whom are you talking?'

"Very savagely he replied: *'I'm talking to you, Private. Get your ass over here on the double.'*

"On the double I got my ass over to the four star Jeep and again saluted him with present arms. He waved his finger at me and asked: *'Private, don't you know my orders?'*

"Sergeant, I answered him: 'No, sir. I'm not in your Army. I'm in the Seventh Army under the command of General Patch. I was ordered to pull this duty by my company commander, Captain Ianella, who told me what the duty was and that was all. I did my best to carry out these orders. I'm sorry, sir, if I have goofed.'

"He proceeded to set me straight. *'You are in territory assigned to the Third Army by General Omar Bradley, Commander of the Twelfth Army Group. I'm Commanding General of the Third Army and I outrank General Patch. You are under my command! The order I am referring to forbids Allied troops from carrying enemy weapons. When these are fired, the sounds they make are different from the sounds of our weapons and this causes confusion among our troops. Private, hand me that enemy weapon you are wearing.'*

"I unbuckled my beautiful trophy and handed it to him. When he stood up to take it, I noticed a pearl-handled .45-caliber revolver hanging from each hip. I wondered just how much confusion would be created if he fired these weapons. I kept these thoughts to myself and didn't bother the General with them. I saluted him with present arms and turned and walked away.

"His driver gunned the Jeep, but stopped just as quickly. Again, I heard the high-pitched voice of the General and wondered: 'Now what in the hell does this old son-of-a-bitch want.' I turned, stood at attention, saluted with present arms. The General said: *'Soldier, you carried out your orders in a precise military manner. I commend you. Carry on.'*"

"Zorns, you should have had a motion picture — with sound — made of this incident. Nobody is going to believe you when you tell this story. Very few men in this war have ever been given any complimentary remarks by old B and G."

"I was so stunned I just stood there with my mouth wide open. I didn't even finish my salute. This then, is the story of why I don't have a P-38 gun. Charles, who are those Joes above us?"

"I don't know. They were loaded before I was. They haven't said a word since I've been aboard. They are either under the influence of an anesthetic or they are dead and being hauled away from some hospital. If they come to I guess we will hear them."

"What's your injury, Sergeant?"

"I was leading my platoon in retreat out of a little town the Germans wanted more than we. When we captured it we cleaned out all the land mines, we thought—except one. That was the one we left for me. I didn't have any trouble finding it; in fact, I stepped right in the middle of it the first try. It blew off my left leg."

"Above or below the knee?"

"Above; it's an AK."

"Well, between the two of us we left a pair of legs in France. I wonder what they do with them—bury, burn, or just throw them in the trash. I would like to know where that missing part of me is. I might want to come back and pay my respects."

The ambulance stopped and we could hear them throwing logs into the trailer. I made this observation:

"Logs for the engine of woodchipper."

"Private, what are your injuries?"

"A German 88mm shell broke above me and crushed my right ankle. A German doctor amputated the leg yesterday."

I told Charles about my lying in the open field after I was wounded and watching and hearing the SS troops flip over the frozen dead and either run their bayonets through their chests or bash in their heads with the butts of their rifles. I told him about me being next, about my feeling the booted foot under my stomach, feeling the lessening of the tension, listening to their excited conversation, and listening to the crunch of the frozen snow as they took off in the direction of their lines. I told him all the story up to my surrender.

"Charles, when I decided to surrender, my main concern was that the Wehrmacht and SS troops would kill me and not bother to take me prisoner. I was never so surprised, and happily so, as when that shoddy, poorly trained German came and tried to pick me up, dropped me back in the snow, left, and returned with a buddy and a wooden wheelbarrow."

"Bruce, you were lucky or someone was watching over you."

"Yes, He was really watching over me."

Charles told this story:

"Hitler conceived of this massive German counterattack himself and had it executed against the advice of most of his top generals. It was to be a surprise thrust that sent Panzer divisions through

Belgium's Ardennes Forest. This onslaught began on 16 December 1944. After the German's initial success, British armies under the command of General Montgomery attacked from the north and American armies under command of General Bradley attacked from the south. This put a hard squeeze on the Germans.

"General Patton and many of his men were pulled out of our southern lines and so were many officers and enlisted men of the Seventh Army. Bruce, this left our southern line as thin as tissue paper and the Nazis let us have it. I don't know at this time how the Battle of the Bulge came out.

"I do know our high command was shaken out of its complacency by the viciousness with which the enemy could strike in its death struggle.

"Just a few days ago, about the time you were in the field wounded, all the Wehrmacht and SS troops were ordered to join German forces fighting in the Battle of the Bulge. That's where the two SS men who were about to execute you went. Their places were filled with men from the bottom of the barrel — green, very young, untrained soldiers. Your 'goddamn German son-of-a-bitch' and his buddy who hauled you to the aid station in the Maginot Line were some of these greenhorns. They had not been in training long enough to lose their compassion.

"I got all this information a few days ago when I was in Third Army headquarters. Someday we will find out how the Battle of the Bulge came out."

They stopped again for logs for the engine of woodchipper.

"These Joes above us must be dead ones being hauled off," I said. I wondered if the Nazis would notify American headquarters of their deaths or if some mother would forever wonder about her son — reported MIA — and day after day return from the post office in bitter anguish because there was no expected letter from the War Department telling that her son had been returned to control of the American Army. The Germans paid little attention to such details.

"Sergeant, what will they do with these bodies?"

"Take them somewhere and burn them. They are very good at this. You know they are not going to the trouble of burying them," he replied.

"Sergeant, they are turning this thing to the right off the highway. Feel how rough it is? Now they are stopping. I wonder where we are. Going by the time we have been traveling, we are deep into Germany."

We heard the corpsmen as they opened their door and climbed out of the cab. They opened the doors to the ambulance and the brilliant, mid-morning, winter sunlight of Germany poured in. we saw the two corpsmen standing off to the side in the snow looking bored with it all but making no move to unload us.

Soon two GIs came out of the building where we had stopped. They were thin and pale and looked dejected. They walked to the door of the ambulance; they didn't say anything but looked in, and the expressions on their faces painted a clear picture of what they were thinking:

"We are cold, hungry, and weak from starvation. We doubt we can carry you fat cats in. You look stronger than we are." They greeted us with an uncivilized expression and a single word:

"Hi."

We got the feeling they were resentful of our coming to this camp — it had caused them to have to exert themselves.

Sergeant Holmes asked them:

"Where are we?"

"This is a prisoner of war camp. It's a stinking, filthy, lice-and-flea infested hellhole where you will be warehoused until you starve to death, freeze to death, or the lice and fleas suck all the blood out of you. It was an insane asylum before it was turned into a prisoner-of-war death trap. The bunks have mattresses of burlap stuffed with straw that house myriad lice and fleas that are happy to have a new body with a fresh supply of blood. There are no sheets. You are issued one thin blanket. The food? There is very little of it. For breakfast there is one thin slice of dark bread, made mostly from sawdust with one cup of ersatz coffee, made mostly of roasted sawdust and barley. There is another slice of the dark sawdust bread with a small bowl of thin potato-peel soup, rotten spots and all, for dinner. You are served this same diet, day after day, eternity after eternity. Medical facilities are nonexistent.

"Enough of the doom and gloom. What is the name of this prison?" asked Sergeant Holmes.

"Stalag XIIA."

"Where is it located?"

"In Heppenheim, in the Black Forest of Germany. It is on the Autobahn between Mannheim and Frankfurt.

The prison commandant came out of the building and walked over to the ambulance. The two starving GIs introduced him.

"This is Major Zeigler."

Major Zeigler looked us over, turned to the two GIs, and told them:

"These two will have to be bathed before I admit them. They look filthy. American troops never pay much attention to making a sharp, clean, military appearance. They never shine their boots or wear fresh uniforms. Take this one first," and he pointed to me.

"Why in the hell does he want us to give you a bath and then put you on a filthy, lice-and-flea laden mattress? That's Ziggy for you. Ziggy is what we call Major Zeigler. Kinda fits him, doesn't it? Well, we have our orders; let's get moving," and the two GIs began unloading me from the ambulance.

With all the strength they could muster, they pulled my stretcher out of the ambulance and carried me up the stairs, moaning and groaning every step of the way. I began to believe these men were not putting on, but they were sick and weak from malnutrition. They took me into a room that had a bathtub—nothing else. With some help from them, I managed to get out of my dirty clothes. They turned on the faucets and began to draw water for my bath.

"Make it warm. I'm cold," I requested.

"Funny, funny man. There is not a bit of heat in this building anywhere and hasn't been for years. The water is near the freezing point. That's the best we can do. OK, in you go. I'll hold your leg so it won't get in the water."

"*Damn!* Damn! This water's cold. Goddamn it! Get me out of here."

"Let's wash you off a little. OK, now we will take you out and dry you," and one of them went to a corner of the room and brought back the most filthy, dirty towel I have ever seen.

"Don't use that nasty towel on me," I yelled to them.

"Be quiet; you're no better than the rest of us, and we all used it. This is the only towel in this camp."

"This bathing farce must be part of the torture they have programmed for us. I can't think of any other reason for going through this ritual. Am I going to put on the same dirty, filthy, stinking clothes I took off? I've been wearing them since we left Oberseebach on Christmas Eve. They've been through all my fighting—my dip in the ice-covered river on New Year's Eve, my lying in the cold after I was wounded, my capture, my amputation, my trip here. By the way, I don't have any boots. The doctor in the aid station in the Maginot Line cut mine off. I've gone barefooted since then. Come to think of it, until I can walk again and am fitted with a prosthesis, I don't need but one – the left one."

"Surely you don't think they are going to issue you pajamas, robe, and house shoes. We are putting back on you the dirty, torn uniform we took off you. You will not be going to any social functions while you are registered here. You will wear these until you get out of here. Here we go. We have got to find the ward and bunk you are assigned," and they picked up my stretcher and carried me out into the hallway.

They put the stretcher down and one of them took off down the hallway to the office to find out where to take me.

"You're on the second floor."

They carried my stretcher up the stairs and at the top did a sharp left turn into my new home. This ward had twelve home-made, wooden bunks. All but three were occupied. These were all together, down the wall from the door we entered at the opposite end. I was placed on the center bunk – just laid out on the burlap mattress.

"Well, here you are. Your new hotel room. Someone from the staff will bring you your thin blanket. Spread it over you; cover up, and get acquainted with your myriad of new friends. Don't get in any hurry; you will have plenty of time to get acquainted with each and every one of them. I imagine they are moving in to explore this new body and get a taste of some new blood. Well, this is all we can do for you. Gotta go get the other occupant of the ambulance. He's assigned to the bunk on your right. Have a good day!"

And they left me to go get Sergeant Holmes. I bet he'd raise holy hell when they took him through the routine I had just finished. He would be next to me – I'd get to find out before long. Some of my friends dropped in; they began to sample my blood. When they punctured my skin getting to my blood, it stung like hell and then began to itch. And so began my itching, bitching, endless days of scratching at Stalag XIIA.

I was so cold; the temperature in my ward was about freezing. I hadn't been warm since before Christmas. That stupid cold bath made me colder. Here I was lying on my bunk in a room that was not heated, the temperature was near freezing. I was in my old dirty uniform on a burlap mattress stuffed with straw inhabited by lice and fleas that had come out and were eating on me. I had never been so miserable. When I thought of the endless days of torture ahead of me, I asked myself:

"Can this be what you deserve? Is this the glory of fighting for your country? Maybe I should have been a draft dodger and stayed out of this war."

Then I thought:

"Yet, if I had to do it over, I'd do the same thing all over again."

"These goddamn Germans!" raved Sergeant Holmes as the two starving GIs brought him to his bunk.

"They are not complying with the terms of the Geneva Convention. They should be treating us the same way they treat their own troops."

Then I told the sergeant what the fly-boy officer had told me about what Winston Churchill had written of his experience as a POW in the Boer War.

"Maybe we do owe our lives to their humanity. I still don't like the way the damn sons-of-bitches are treating their prisoners."

"What are you going to do about it, Sergeant?"

"Possess my soul with patience," he responded in a disgruntled voice.

A short time later, the two GIs carried in someone else and put him in the third bunk—the one in the corner.

"Who's that?" asked Holmes.

"The name we were given is Moore—Marvin Moore. He was out cold when they brought him here, and he hasn't come to yet. We couldn't give him a bath. His entire torso is in a cast—just his head and feet sticking out. His right arm is in a cast. There is a brace from the torso cast to the arm cast that holds his arm away from his body at about a 45-degree angle. His right hand is not in the cast. He can have some use of it. He's in one hell of a shape—doubt he will make it. The lice and fleas will run him crazy. He doesn't look to be over eighteen years old. You guys watch him, and when he begins to come to, call a nurse."

"Oh, we have nurses?" I asked.

"Only for the very worst cases. You call them by yelling: 'Fräulein.' Their station is not very far down the hall. They know when they have a patient in a certain ward. So long—we are going to leave it with you," and they took their stretcher and left.

We both looked at Marvin and shook our heads. He looked so uncomfortable. He could only lie in one position—on his left side with his right arm sticking up. I asked:

"Sergeant, won't the fleas and lice get in that cast and give him fits? He can't scratch or do anything except lie there and bear it along with the pains of his wounds. Poor guy, I feel so sorry for him I don't know what to do."

"He's got a hard row to hoe, and he's so young. I think it's a crime for our government, or any government, to draft men this young. They haven't had a chance to do any living. Why don't they go on up and draft men a few years older than they are drafting now? Private, I think it's a hell of a note to tell a young man like Marvin he's old enough to carry a gun, fight, kill, and be killed, but he's not old enough to vote or buy a bottle of beer. I want to tell you, and anyone else listening, these young kids are getting screwed. I don't like it, and I don't care who knows it. Older men start wars and want the young to fight them. Maybe there wouldn't be as many wars if those that started them fought them," said the Sergeant as he did his editorializing for the day.

Marvin began to stir a little and uttered continuous moans.

"I think we should call the nurse," I said.

"I think it's time. Call one," the sergeant answered.

"Fräulein," I called.

Nothing happened so I called again, this time louder.

"*Fräulein!*"

In just a short time a nurse popped in. She went straight to Marvin's bunk and began checking him. As she turned to leave she shook her head in doubt, looked at me and said:

"If his pain seems to be getting worse, call me and I'll come give him a shot."

The blanket man finally came around with his cartload of blankets. He very carefully dealt one to Charles, and with the same care dealt me one. We had been told they would be thin and thin they were — but better than nothing. He pulled his cart over to Marvin's bunk, selected a blanket, threw it over Marvin and stepped back and looked. It didn't fit. With Marvin's right arm sticking up in the air, the blanket covered less than half of him — there was an awful lot of fresh air circulating over much of Marvin's torso. He turned the blanket first one way, then the other, but it wouldn't cover. I called and asked him to bring the blanket to me. I showed him how to cut it so it would lie flat over Marvin. He then took his cart and rolled it out.

By this time it was getting close to dinner and sure enough, in just a little while, the man with the dinner cart came around with the evening meal. To those he was serving the first time, he gave a beat-up tin cup with a matching tin plate. He served the slice of bread on the plate and ladled out enough soup to fill the bowl half full. The bread should have had a label "Tree-Top" bread. It seemed to have been made mostly of pine tree sawdust as a filler mixed with milled, roasted barley for nutrition and flavor. In time we became so hungry we developed a craving for this dark sawdust bread and looked forward to mealtime.

The coffee was ersatz also. It was made mostly from ground roasted barley. It too, in time, became tasty. Little imagination was used in the preparation of the potato-peeling soup. The peelings from potatoes served to German troops were put in a very large vat — water was added — the amount depended on the number of POWs to be fed. Nothing else was added. It was served after cooking to POWs — dirt, rotten spots, and all. We even got to liking this concoction, which came close to being garbage.

After dinner, preparation for "lights out" began. This consisted mainly of the medical aid man coming around and giving everyone some pain-relief medicine. At each bunk he stopped, filled the tin cup he was using with water, and with a dropper very carefully put two drops of medication into the cup of water. This caused the water to turn cloudy. Someone asked the aid man what the medication was.

"Opium in saturated solution," the aid man replied.

I didn't know what it was, but it didn't seem the two drops of opium in saturated solution improved the pain-relieving ability of my cup of water any.

And so endless number of cold, restless, miserable, itching, scratching nights began. The silence was broken almost continually by the moaning of the badly wounded men. Marvin did his part of the loud moaning, but no one could blame him. We could all take comfort in the fact that Marvin was the most seriously wounded in the ward. Poor little fellow. It was a struggle for him to stay alive, and being alive had almost unbearable miseries. He would have been uncomfortable if his cast was his only problem, but the cast created other problems — it became a haven for hundreds of blood-sucking lice and fleas. He could not scratch them. He could just lie there and bare his misery and issue out cries of moaning. He had heard us calling his nurse, so he tried it.

"Fur-line," he called in a very low, weak voice. We thought his effort was great considering it was the first time he had said anything since he came to this camp. I said to him:

"Marvin, a German nurse is called 'Fräulein,' not 'Fur-line.'"

"I can't say what you call them; besides I like 'Fur-line' better. Oh Fur-line, I need some help."

His voice was so weak the nurse could not hear him, so I called for him:

"Fräulein."

She popped into the room in just a short time. After examining him, she gave him a shot that knocked him out. She kept him knocked out for the next three days.

On the third day of my internment the medical aid man — the same one who'd served the opium drops two nights before — came around with his cart and told me he had orders to change the bandage on my leg. He uncovered me and began to unwind the paper bandages.

"Ouch!" I yelled when he got down to where the blood had dried on the bandage.

"Don't you have any hydrogen peroxide you can use to soften the dried blood so the bandages can be removed without hurting?"

"No, we don't have any. I'll be extra careful and not hurt you."

When we continued to unwind the bandages, I felt the sharpest pain I had ever felt. I let out a scream that could be heard all over camp.

"Don't touch that bandage again you goddamn French son-of-a-bitch. Get away from here."

The French son-of-a-bitch backed off, but quickly came at me again saying:

"I have orders to change your bandage."

"Stay away from me, you phony. You are not a qualified aid man. You are just a French POW pretending to be one. Now, get the hell out of here before I call the commandant."

I didn't have to call him — in he popped. He shoved the French aid man away and took a good look at what the Frenchman was trying to do. Then he called Marvin's nurse and had her take over. She spoke English and talked constantly. She told us Ziggy had heard my screams from way down in his office and had come running to see what was going on. She said he had not heard a scream that loud or that agonizing in his life, and he had not trusted the Frenchman since he first applied for the job — but he was all that was available. POWs wanted these jobs. They got more freedom — a trip to town now and then. Ziggy stayed around until the nurse got started. Then he got the Frenchman by the arm and led him out.

Marvin woke up during all this commotion and heard his nurse. He called her, and she went to his bunk and asked him what he needed.

"Fur-line, I'm hungry. I want some of my mother's cheesecake. She makes the best cheesecake you ever tasted."

"I'm sorry, Marvin, but I don't have any way to get you a piece at this time."

"My mother is the best cook anywhere in the world. She can cook anything, and it turns out delicious. She cooks the best beef pot roast—the brown gravy is delicious. She can really do fried chicken good. She excels in her pork chops and cream gravy. Even now I can smell her pork chops cooking. She always has hot biscuits with them. I love to put cream gravy over the hot biscuits."

Charles looked at me. His tongue was hanging out with saliva dripping off. He leaned over to me and whispered,

"That kid is making me so hungry I can hardly stand it. Everything he describes that his mother cooks sounds delicious to me. Can we get him to shut up before I die of starvation?"

"Charles, I don't think we should say anything to him to make him not want to talk about his mother's cooking. The poor little fellow doesn't have much else to talk about. I think we should talk with him about all the good things his mother cooks. It will make us more hungry, but I think we can take it."

"OK. You're right. We won't say anything to him to discourage him from talking. When his nurse leaves we'll talk with him about all the goodies his mother cooks."

When the nurse left, her tongue was hanging out with saliva dripping off. Charles remarked:

"I bet she has never tasted anything like the food his mother cooks."

The endless days of misery, monotony, hunger, cold to a point of numbness, itching, scratching, bitching, wondering what the next day would bring, thinking constantly of Ginny and Thomas Bruce and whether the War Department had notified them I was missing in action, speculating on how Ginny would react to this news, afraid she would think I was dead and marry someone else and wishing I could write her, continued to roll over, one day after the other, with the following day bringing only what the previous day had produced and leaving each of us more and more depressed and feeling like we had reached a place of no return.

The balance of January finally slipped away and the calendar

CLASS OF SERVICE		SYMBOLS
This is a full-rate Telegram or Cablegram unless its deferred character is indicated by a suitable symbol above or preceding the address.	WESTERN UNION 1201 A. N. WILLIAMS PRESIDENT	DL = Day Letter NL = Night Letter LC = Deferred Cable NLT = Cable Night Letter Ship Radiogram

The filing time shown in the date line on telegrams and day letters is STANDARD TIME at point of origin. Time of receipt is STANDARD TIME at point of destination

UC36 44 GOVT=WUX WASHINGTON DC JAN 29 63 1P

MRS VIRGINIA M ZORNS=

521 EAST TATE ST BROWNFIELD TEX=

THE SECRETARY OF WAR DESIRES ME TO EXPRESS HIS DEEP REGRET
THAT YOUR HUSBAND PRIVATE FIRST CLASS ERUCE C ZORNS HAS
BEEN REPORTED MISSING IN ACTION SINCE TWELVE JANUARY IN
FRANCE IF FURTHER DETAILS OR OTHER INFORMATION ARE RECEIVED
YOU WILL BE PROMPTLY NOTIFIED=

ULIO THE ADJUTANT GENERAL.

(613P).

THE COMPANY WILL APPRECIATE SUGGESTIONS FROM ITS PATRONS CONCERNING ITS SERVICE

Telegram to Virginia advising her I was missing in action.

carried us forward into February. The second day of February brought something different — something none of us had dared dream would happen. Ziggy came into the ward with one of his aides, who was carrying an armful of paper and a fistful of pencils. Ziggy didn't speak English, so his aide acted as interpreter. He began:

"Major Zeigler is pleased to inform you he has been instructed to allow each of you to write a letter home. He received some special stationery you will use. You will print plainly. Do not write. You will say you have been captured by the Germans, you are in a German hospital, slightly wounded, and you are getting good care and treatment. Ask that they not write you until you send your permanent address. I will pass to each of you one sheet of this stationery and a pencil. Your letters will be censored."

Major Zeigler stood off to one side looking very benevolent. His round, fat little face was wearing a smile because he thought he was every bit as good as God.

When I received my sheet of stationery, I looked it over to familiarize myself with it before I began to print. It had been carefully prepared for Stalag XIIA. It was approximately 5 3/8 inches wide by 10 3/4 inches long, and had a 2 ½-inch wide tab for sealing. The form was designed to be folded as follows: The tab was to be folded down so the rest of the sheet was a rectangle. The bottom edge was to be folded up one third of the length of the sheet, and then the remaining portion was folded double. When this was done, there was a slot on the bottom of the first fold for the tab to slip into to form a seal. On the back of this stationery, when it was folded, was a place for the name and address of the addressee. I printed in this space the following:

> An "Mrs. Virginia M. Zorns
> 202 East Cardwell
> Empfangsort: Brownfield
> Strafie: Texas
> Kreis: United States
> Land: America
> Landesteil (Provinz usw.)
> Gebührenfrei!

On the back was:

> Absender:
> Vor-und Zuname: "PFC Bruce C. Zorns 38693068
> Gefangenenummer: _____
> Lager-Bezeichnung: M.-Stallager: XII A
> Deutschland (Allemagne)

After reviewing the form carefully I began to print a letter to Ginny.

> February 2, 1945
>
> My darling Ginny:
> I know you have spent many anxious moments, but this is the first chance I have had to write you. I am a prisoner of war in a German hospital. I am slightly wounded, but am getting along alright. I am getting good care and treatment.
> I will write you as often as I can, but that won't be too often. Do not try to write me until I send you a permanent address. Do not worry about me. I am getting along fine. Keep your chin up and be brave. I love you, my darling, with all my heart, soul, and body. I hope and pray that you and Thomas Bruce are well. God bless you both and keep you well and safe.
>
> [Signed] Bruce Zorns

Ziggy's man came around and collected the finished letter and pencil from each man. At first Marvin was upset because he couldn't write. I assured him I would print him a letter if he just dictated it to me. He dictated one of the most emotional epistles I had ever read. I am not going to violate my pledge not to reveal to anyone what he wrote. I will say his letter home revealed that Marvin and his family were of the stuff that made and kept this great nation free and strong. I developed a very high regard for Marvin and his family. When I finished printing the letter and he read it, he wanted to know what all those German words meant. He particularly wanted to know what *Gebührenfrei* meant and why it had the exclamation point and was underlined. I could answer him because I had just asked someone. I had found out it was an adjective and meant "free of charge." It was underlined and with the exclamation point because the Germans liked to brag about the fact that they let their POWs mail letters without any charge.

The next two days were just as monotonous, if not more so, as any of the preceding days. The third day brought something different again, and something none of us expected because we had written home only two days ago. Major Zeigler and his aide came into the ward. The aide was carrying some more paper and pencils, and he began explaining:

"Major Zeigler is again pleased for me to tell you he has received instructions from his headquarters in Frankfurt to let you write another letter home. This form is different from the one you used a couple of days ago. I am going to pass these and pencils out to you. These forms contain complete instructions."

When I got mine I discovered it was a postcard. I looked this over carefully. It had the message you could send already printed on it in multiple choice fashion.

Kriegsgefang
  Postkarte
An
Mrs. Virginia M. Zorns
202 East Cardwell St.
    Empfangsort: <u>Brownfield, Tex.</u>
    town
    Land: <u>United States of America</u>
    country
    Landesteil: <u>Terry County</u>
    (Provinz usw.)

county
Gebührenfrei!

The other side looked like this.

Prisoner of War Camp

Date Feb. 7, 1945

No. of Camp only; as may be directed by the Commandant
of the Camp
I have been taken prisoner of war in Germany. I am — Slightly
wounded (cancel accordingly).
We will be transported from here to another Camp within the next
few days. Please don't write until I give new address.

Kindest regards

Christian Name and Surname: Bruce Zorns

Rank: Private First Class

Detachment: 38693068

(No further details — Clear legible writing)

The cold, endless days and nights of February 1945 slipped off
the calendar forever, and I know they will never be missed. The first
of March turned up with just a hint of spring. The men were more
hungry and they were thinner. Those who came in about the time
Charles and I did had lost more than thirty-five pounds. They were
so hungry they became cannibalistic. Soon after the first, the guy
who had the bunk straight across the room from me died. They had
just served him breakfast. The men close to him were sitting tensely
on the edges of their beds. When the blanket was pulled over his
head and he was carried out on a stretcher, these men dove for the
cup of coffee and the slice of dark bread. There was a good battle
over this meager amount of food. The best man won, and he quickly
drank the ersatz coffee and gulped down the dark bread. He looked
around the room to see if anyone was watching him and saw a
roomful of disapproving eyes, and he fell down on his bed and
pulled the blanket over his head. We all felt as guilty as he because
there was not a one of us who would not have done the same thing.
It was such a dirty, filthy feeling we all got sick at our souls.

The GI in the bunk on Charles's right was a "Wheeler-Dealer."
He was able to walk around, so he explored the whole camp. He told
Charles the Russian POWs had some kind of arrangement that permitted them to go into town and buy whatever they could find
available. He further told Charles they had lots of bread and cigarettes in their ward.

"Bruce, he told me they wanted to trade bread and cigarettes for almost anything such as rings, watches, pocket knives, etc. Would you want to do any trading with them?"

"I don't have anything to trade. My watch was broken when I was wounded. Are you going to do any trading with them?"

"I don't have anything either. All my stuff disappeared after I was captured. Say, isn't that a ring on your left hand?"

"That's my 32nd degree Masonic ring Ginny bought me just before I was drafted. It has a little diamond in it. It's not very expensive – I think she paid $250 for it, but I wouldn't take anything for it. She really had to save to buy this for me."

"I don't blame you; I wouldn't trade it either."

As I lay there in my bunk thinking of the cannibalistic scene I had witnessed just a few moments ago, I turned to Charles and said:

"We are all getting mighty hungry. Maybe I should let your wheeler-dealer friend take my ring and show it to the Russians and see if it is something they would want to trade for and how much they would pay."

"Not a bad idea. Let me have it, and I will get him to show it to his Russian friends. I will get with you when he returns with an offer."

And I saw the wheeler-dealer take off to do business with the Russians. He was gone a long time – about two hours. He must have had a rough time with our allies, the Russian POWs. I saw him return and get with Charles. When he left, Charles turned to me and said:

"He can make a trade, but it seems to me your ring is going mighty cheap, and bread and cigarettes are very expensive. He can trade your ring for two loaves of the dark bread like we have been getting and a package of Camel cigarettes."

"The price of anything is only what it is worth to you at the time it is traded. The diamond ring is not worth anything to me – I cannot eat it, and food is the most important thing to me at this time. It will nourish my body and prevent me from starving to death for at least ten days. That is very dear to me. If I can live ten days longer, my chances of going home to Ginny and Thomas Bruce are greater. This is the only thing worth anything to me at this time. All right, I'll trade. How much does the wheeler-dealer get in commissions?"

"Not anything from us. The Russians pay him. I bet, though,

that whatever he makes comes from you by his juggling the price he quoted us."

"Charles, I'll still trade. Let's close the deal now."

And for two loaves of dark bread and a package of Camel cigarettes I traded a $250 ring. I could get ten slices from each loaf. That was twenty slices in all. There were twenty cigarettes to a package. That made forty units, each with a cost of $6.25. Very, very expensive for a slice of bread or a Camel cigarette. When you are hungry to the point of starvation, you cannot put a price on food.

It could be worth your life.

Charles came back from closing the deal and handed me two loaves of dark bread and a package of Camels. I told him:

"I want to share the bread with you and Marvin as far as it will go. Maybe I can trade the cigarettes for bread. Thanks, Amigo!"

As I sat on my bunk with my bread and cigarettes, I looked around the room and realized I really had problems. Every man in the ward had witnessed the transaction and every man was looking at me with hungry, hollow, pleading eyes. No, I couldn't feed everybody, but how was I going to explain to a room full of starving men? I said to them:

"Men, you all witnessed the transaction when I acquired the bread and cigarettes. In case you don't know what I paid for them I will tell you. I traded a $250 diamond ring for them. You see, they cost a lot. Now I am going to share the bread with Charles and Marvin. The cigarettes are for trade. Who wants to make me an offer?"

Some GI way across the room said he would trade me one slice of his daily bread ration for a cigarette.

"That's fine; you just bought a cigarette. Now the rest of you choose one from among you to represent each of you. Every cigarette that I trade for a slice of bread will be given to him to be distributed in keeping with your instructions. This is the best I can do. Does this sound okay?"

They all enthusiastically said,

"Yes, thank you. You're going the extra mile."

And the international trade of "Bread and Cigarettes for a Diamond Ring" was completed.

On 7 March 1945, Major Zeigler and his aide came into the ward with some more postcards and pencils. We got to write home again. I wrote Ginny:

Datum: March 7, 1945

My Darling Ginny & Thomas Bruce:

I am getting along fine. My wounds have healed. I am missing you both so much. Keep your chin up. I will see you soon. I hope and pray you are both well and safe. God bless you both and keep you well and safe.

Bruce

The wheeler-dealer continued to prowl around POW camp and snoop into every nook and crevice. One day he came to my bunk with one very primitive crutch and one very worn boot for my left foot. The crutch was just the right length. It had been fashioned from a straight branch of some kind of German tree other than pine. This branch was straight, strong, and long enough for the part that branched out and formed a "V" to fit snugly under my right arm. Not the best in the world, but I could hobble around. I put on the worn boot. It would keep me from bruising my foot as I hopped around.

"Wheeler," I said to him.

"I thank you so much. Now I can join you in your explorations of this camp. Thank you again."

As the March days warmed, Ziggy gave us permission to go into the courtyard and enjoy the sun. As the sun warmed the days, it warmed me too, and I began to thaw for the first time since I set foot in Europe.

Out in the courtyard each of us found a warm sunny spot, and sat stripped to the waist. The warm sun felt so good. We had all hoped this would get rid of at least a few of the lice and fleas, but they enjoyed the warmth as much as we. We began to pull them from their embedded locations in our flesh. When they did not break in two and we got them out whole, we killed them by squashing them between our thumbnails.

But squashing lice and fleas between our thumbnails was not the only entertainment we had while sunning. We found the ground was covered with dandelions. They had not begun to bloom and the leaves were large and very tender. We supplemented our diet with fresh dandelion greens. We didn't cook them — just ate them as we pulled them. We got three good meals of dandelions while sunning in the courtyard of Stalag XIIA.

As more and more new American POW came into the camp, we heard more and more scuttlebutt about the end of the war being near. Major Zeigler believed this very strongly — not from our scuttlebutt, but from German sources. On 25 March he and his entire staff deserted their posts and took off to Frankfurt to keep from being captured. The entire camp was without a commander. The highest-ranking American POW was Major Turner who, by military protocol, took command of American POWs. We all applauded this because we knew the food would be better, and we would be treated better in every way.

When Major Turner went to the cupboard he found it bare except for one fifty-pound sack of white flour. For breakfast on 26 March we were served what the chiefs of Stalag XIIA called "doughballs" — just what the name implied — balls of dough made by mixing flour and water, kneading, and then pulling off bits and shaping into balls. These balls were then dropped into boiling water. They came out looking like small dumplings and tasting like small dumplings without any seasoning of any kind. We all thought they were delicious — there just weren't enough of them.

For dinner, we were served potato-peeling soup and a slice of sawdust bread. Ziggy and his staff had returned and assumed command without a fight.

The scuttlebutt was that when Major Zeigler reported to his headquarters in Frankfurt, his commander became infuriated and ordered him and his staff to return to their command and to make a formal surrender of the pow camp when the American Army conquered Heppenheim. It was further said that Major Zeigler came back with a new dress uniform, new shiny boots, and new sidearms.

Tuesday, 27 March, soon after we were served breakfast, all hell broke loose. A 20mm rifle bullet crashed through the window by Marvin's bunk and into the wall on the other side of the room, making quite a splash. All of us who could, got down on the floor pronto. Marvin was hysterical. We did what we could to calm him. I could understand how he felt, just lying there and unable to do anything for himself.

Someone said a unit of the American Seventh Army, 14th Armored Division, had pulled up to the gates of the front courtyard and parked a Sherman tank with its guns pointed at the front door of the camp. All who could made a dash for the room across the hall to watch the surrender of Stalag XIIA. It was indeed a show.

Before any American troops entered the courtyard, we watched Major Zeigler and his staff fall into formation. Ziggy was indeed dressed for the occasion. He was wearing his new dress uniform, which had been neatly pressed, and white, white gloves. He had on his new shiny boots, and on his left hip he carried a sword in a bright shiny scabbard, supported by a beautiful leather belt and shoulder straps. When the captain of the American troops began moving toward the gate, Major Zeigler gave the command: "Gleichschritt, Marsch!" and lead his formation with the goose-step of the Nazis toward the captain of the American troops.

He goose-stepped to within ten feet of the captain and halted. In a very precise military manner he reached over with his right hand, drew his sword, and saluted very smartly — touching the bill of his cap with the point of his sword. He then took the point of the sword in his gloved right hand, and with the blade resting on his curved left arm, and the hilt extending about twelve inches beyond the arm it was resting on, moved in close enough so the captain could take the hilt. This the captain did and returned the salute.

With this formality out of the way, the captain gave the order to his aide to put Major Zeigler into his jeep and the rest of the staff into trucks. He then ordered his troops to raise the flag of the United States of America.

As Old Glory ascended the mast, the soft, spring breeze caused her to ripple, and the red, white, and blue were bright as she waved in that early morning sunlight, serving notice to the world:

"This territory captured and held by American troops."

And the voices of the prisoners from within the walls of this prison compound swelled into a mighty anthem that cascaded into a thunderous crescendo, causing the words, "Oh, Say Can You See. . ." to bounce across the treetops of Heppenheim and the Black Forest of Germany.

With the flag at the top of the mast, the captain gave this order:

"Move in and see what you can find!"

A wall of troops moved across the courtyard and into the hospital. Inside they fanned out and covered the place like oil covering a pond of water. This was very emotional to all of us who were prisoners of the Germans. We were no longer their prisoners of war. We had been returned to control of the U.S. Army. How glorious it was! How glorious!

Each soldier greeted every ex–POW. They grabbed and hugged us — gave each of us candy, all kinds of rations — C, K, and D — and cigarettes, matches, paper, and pencils, and they sat and talked. They wanted to know how we had been treated. We, too, talked and asked questions:

"What's going on in the world? Is the war about over? How did you cross the Rhine? How did you get here?"

They answered our questions. The soldier talking to me said:

"Very early yesterday morning, 26 March, our Army, the Seventh Army, crossed the Rhine on a pontoon bridge near Worms, north of Mannheim. We then moved south to Mannheim. We had to do some mopping up in and around this industrial city. Early this morning, 27 March, we moved swiftly up the Autobahn to Heppenheim. We met a little resistance as we entered the city but we have met very little resistance on our drive east. At the rate we are moving, we will meet the Russians in Berlin in less than sixty days. We were the seventh army to cross the Rhine. All are moving swiftly toward Germany's capitol city. I bet Adolf is getting nervous. There is no way he can stop us now."

I looked at him and proudly said:

"I was with the Seventh Army when I was captured. I was with the 62nd AIB, 14th Armored Division."

"Say, you guys look like hell. All of you look like you have lost a lot of weight. You all look like you could stand a bath, clean clothes, a haircut. All have that hungry, hollow, haunting look. Damn it! I don't like the way these damn Germans have treated my buddies. I'm going to hit them harder and I'm going to hit them mean. We're going to eliminate these bastards from the face of the earth. Say, buddy, is there anything else I can do for any of you guys?"

"Just keep giving them hell and get this damn war over so we can all go home and live the rest of our lives like human beings."

"There's our signal to move on. I feel honored to have been a part of bringing you guys back under U.S. Army control and out of this filthy hellhole. Well, you are free now. Keep your chin up and carry on. You'll be home soon! auf Wiedersehen, Amigo!"

They left as quickly as they had come and we were no longer prisoners of war. We were again soldiers in the U.S. Army.

I looked around and suddenly thought, "Say, who's captain of this ship? I saw Ziggy being hauled away."

It didn't take long to find out. Major Turner came in and told us our liberators had left him in charge for the rest of the day and that night. Lieutenant General Alexander M. Patch would visit the camp tomorrow and name a commander and tell us his plans to evacuate us. Major Turner went on to tell us we would not like him for doing what he had been ordered to do.

"Men, I know you are all hungry — in fact, starving. I know because I'm one of you, and I'm as hungry as any of you. I know the liberating soldiers left you all kinds of food and candy. That's great, but here's the problem: If you gorge yourselves on all that rich food and candy you will come down with acute diarrhea. I know for sure you will be evacuated the day after tomorrow. You don't want to be shipped out of here as 'shit-asses,' do you? I begged enough good, wholesome food from our liberators to serve you three good meals. They will not be big meals, but this is for your own good. In a couple of days you will be able to dive in and eat all you want.

"I will serve you dinner tonight. Tomorrow, 28 March I will serve you breakfast and dinner. Thursday, 29 March you will be shipped out of here very early and will arrive at your destination in time for breakfast.

"I am leaving as large a tub as I could find. Be good boys instead of 'shit-asses' and dump the food and candy and other things to eat that your liberators left you in this. Keep your cigarettes and smoke as many as you want. I'll send after the tub in a little while. Thank you, men."

As he turned to leave, Sergeant Holmes yelled out:

"Tenn ... *shun!*

We had all learned long ago, if you can't stand at attention, sit at attention; if you can't sit at attention, lie at attention. However we executed the order, we all got rigid. Major Turner turned and said, "Thank you, men," and left.

Sergeant Holmes then said,

"As you were, men."

Out of respect for their commanding officer, who was also one of them, the men put every bit of the food into the tub.

The major did serve a delicious meal, but as he told us, we didn't think it was enough.

After dinner, I went sound asleep and the fleas and lice didn't bother me a bit because in my dreams I heard Him say:

"Be Not Afraid, I Am with You."

Breakfast the next morning was also very good and we were served more than the night before. I guess we were getting conditioned to taking on more food, meal after meal.

I was getting some of the paper the soldiers had left me to write Ginny a letter when the door to our ward flew open and a master sergeant entered and yelled:

"Tenn ... *shun!*"

Through the door entered General Patch, his aides, some of his staff, and what looked like all the war correspondents covering the war in Europe. They began taking pictures, interviewing some of us, and interviewing some of General Patch's aides.

General Patch walked to the window beside Marvin's bed because it was a good place for him to stand and address everybody, and they could all see him. He stood first on one foot and then the other, and became more disgusted and impatient with each passing second. Time and time again he looked at his watch, and finally called out:

"Colonel, I need to see you."

The colonel let the photographers take just one more picture before seeing what the general wanted. This was a bad mistake!

When the colonel finally reported, General Patch said to him:

"Get rid of all the war correspondents and do it fast."

The colonel carried out his orders pronto and reported back to Patch, who told him:

"Colonel, this is a very important mission I am about to assign you. I want you to listen to my orders very carefully. Not under any condition do I want you to goof off. If you do you will find yourself working up the ladder again from the rank of private. It's much harder the second time around. Do you understand me, Colonel?"

"Yes, Sir."

"Then let everybody listen to me very carefully as I outline my plans for evacuation of these wounded American soldiers from this horrendous prisoner-of-war camp. These men have suffered enough and we are going to get them out of here as soon as possible."

The colonel broke in and said:

"That will be just as soon as the east-bound traffic across the Rhine has let up, won't it, General?"

"Hell no, it will be at 0100 tomorrow. I have issued orders to halt all east-bound traffic across the Rhine at Worms tomorrow at 0300. I have issued orders to have all the vehicles and drivers you need to transport these 290 wounded soldiers out of here. You will have these men loaded in these vehicles and ready to depart at 0100. You will be in the lead vehicle and proceed to the east end of the pontoon bridge crossing the Rhine at Worms. You will park your column in the west-bound lane. The last vehicle across will be my Jeep driven by my driver. He will pull up alongside you and ask for the password, which for this occasion is 'Doughballs' from an incident all of you experienced a few days ago. After you give him the password, he will turn the Jeep around and drive alongside you and say, 'Follow me.' He will lead you across the pontoon bridge and to a landing field. I have ordered enough planes and crews to fly you to the nearest Mobile Army Surgical Hospital (m*a*s*h). Here you will be examined and a determination made as to which General Hospital to evacuate you. If you require any emergency surgery, you will receive it there. You will get to this forward hospital in time for a big breakfast. Men, this is as far as I take you. I pray that God will be with you throughout the rest of your journey home. Are there any questions?"

Sergeant Holmes stood up on his right leg and said:

"Sir, I have no questions, but on behalf of all of us, thank you, Sir!"

There was ever so slight a quiver in the general's voice as he said:

"That's all, men. Dismissed."

As he turned to leave, the master sergeant yelled out,

"Tenn ... *shun!*"

When the general was out of the room he said:

"At ease."

Some of the war correspondents stayed around and took many more pictures. They interviewed me and took pictures of me. I never saw any pictures or stories published. The chaplains who came in when the general did stayed a long time and talked, and the men were all eager to talk to them.

Lee E. Davis, Chaplain U.S.A., came by my bunk and spoke to me. I asked him to sit down, and we talked for a long, long time. I had so much I wanted to talk to him about. We both seemed to get a lot out of the visit. The next day he wrote Ginny a letter (see page 158).

As Lee was leaving, he turned to me and said:

"Bruce, you are not going to like this, but while some of the men of the Seventh Army were going through Major Zeigler's office they found all the letters and postcards all of you had written home. They had never been mailed. They will be mailed today at 1800 hours by some of the men of the Seventh. If you have any more mail, they will mail that for you. I know this news upsets you, for you had thought Virginia might have heard from you and knew you were a prisoner."

                                    640th Clearing Co APO #408
                                    % Postmaster, N. Y., N. Y.
                                    March 29, 1945.

                    Zorns
Mrs Virginia M. ~~Jones~~
Brownfield, Texas.

Dear Friend,
                                        Zorns
        Yesterday I met your husband, Bruce C. ~~Jones.~~ He had the
day before come under the jurisdiction of the United States
Army by extention of our lines deep into German territory. That
day was for him the answer to a soldier's prayer.

        I understand that Bruce was captured by SS troops near
Hatton, France while serving with a unit of the Seventh Army.
(But you will be hearing from him about that.) For he wanted
nothing more than to write you. "That", he said, "has been the
hardest of all to bear--not being able to write to my wife and
her not hearing from me." And I sat there with him while he told
me a story that was a sermon--far more than I have to say.

        Bruce will be back in the bank at Brownfield and you will be
proud of him, as he is proud of you, and Thomas Bruce, too. And
I shall pray for you as I have *for* Bruce that God's blessings may
be yours to cherish and to hold.

        And may God continue to deliver us to our own.

                            Sincerely yours,

                            Lee E. Davis

                            Lee. E. Davis
                            Chaplain, USA.

Ginny received this letter from Chaplain Davis on April 13, 1945.

"Thank you, Chaplain. I'm going to write her now."

        [Words in parentheses were cut by U.S. censors.]
                                (Heppenheim,) Germany
My darling Ginny
    and Thomas Bruce:
    This is Easter week—the week of the resurrection of Christ. It is
a week I shall always remember for I feel as though I too have been
resurrected. It is a great week for all of us. Just a year ago on Palm
Sunday we christened Thomas Bruce and this year two days after
Palm Sunday on March 27, the Yanks captured this German town
and a prison hospital with (290) American prisoners. I am sure you
have read the stories in the papers regarding the conditions of this

hospital and treatment we received here. I shall give you a few of the details and elaborate on them in letters after this one.

I was wounded and captured by SS troops on January 12, 1945 while the 62nd AIB was making an attack on Hatten in Alsace France. I was hit by a German 88mm shell in the ankle of my right leg. Our battalion was forced to retreat and I was left on the field and later picked up and evacuated to a German hospital. While I was in the German hospital I received excellent care and treatment – the same as the German soldiers received. For four days the German surgeons tried to save my leg, but it was so badly smashed they were forced to amputate it about halfway between the ankle and the knee. On January 21, I was evacuated from the German hospital to the prison hospital. Here our treatment has been the worst possible. The food has been just enough to exist on – our bread ration has been ten men to the loaf for the day. Soup for dinner. We have had no heat, even through the cold winter days and nights. Lice and fleas have been abundant. But through it all my love for you and Thomas Bruce, and my determination to return to you have pulled me through in fine shape. My wounds have all healed and in a day or two I will be evacuated from this place to a hospital in France or England and from there to a general hospital in the States. So before long, possibly in less than a month – surely by our anniversary, I'll be seeing you. The American doctors say I will be able to walk again soon without even a limp. So I, or rather we, have a lifetime of happiness ahead of us.

Darling, I have never felt blue or depressed over losing my leg. Instead, I have been thankful that I came through that awful attack alive. So many of the boys did not and so many of those who did were wounded worse – far worse – than I. I hope you feel the same way about it. The worst part of it all has been my thoughts of you and the misery and torture you must have gone through these past three months after receiving notice I was missing in action. I have written you one letter and two postcards, but I have just found out these were not mailed by the Germans. They are being mailed today, along with this letter, by someone with the Seventh Army. I doubt the American Red Cross has notified you I was a prisoner of war. The Germans pay little attention to such details. I hope you have had faith in my safe deliverance.

My darling, I love you so very much. I hope your love for me has not and will not change. I do not want you to love me through pity, for I feel I am a far better man than I was before I left home. I have been through enough to truly enjoy the heaven that is ours.

For us the war is over. The homeward trip begins early tomorrow. I will be in the good old USA soon. I will have to stay in a general hospital in the U.S. I will have a reamputation of my leg. After this heals I will be fitted with an artificial one and go through training on how to use it, and when I become proficient I will be discharged from the Army. We are going to build our house when I get home and do all the things we have always planned.

Happy Easter, my darling, to you and Thomas Bruce. We are so very, very lucky. You will hear all about it when I see you and we can talk together. I love you both so very much.

Bruce

When I finished writing Ginny, I glanced around the room and noticed several of the fellows stewing around getting ready to leave. I didn't know what they had to do to get ready. I was going to wear out the same uniform I wore in, and I had this on, plus one very worn left boot, plus the lice and fleas embedded in my flesh. The rest of them I was leaving in the straw stuffing of my mattress. I wondered how hungry they would get before someone else occupied my bunk. I was proudly clutching the homemade crutch the Wheeler-Dealer had brought me. I was ready to leave!

I glanced over at Charles. He was clutching a crutch very much like mine. He told me the Wheeler-Dealer had just brought it to him. He was waving the crutch and smiling. He was ready to leave!

Someone wandered across the hall and looked out the window onto the courtyard. He yelled out,

"Say, the flag is still flying. Shouldn't it be taken down?"

"No, it is to be left up. It will be taken down after we leave," answered Sergeant Holmes.

"Before we leave, why don't we pledge our allegiance to this flag we have missed so long?"

"Yeah," everyone responded.

"You lead us in it, Sergeant."

"Men, every time I see someone misuse our flag I am convinced he does not know what our flag stands for and what these things have cost over the years. Every time I hear the Pledge of Allegiance being presented in a sloppy, messy, slovenly, slushy, or muddy manner by some group of people in a meeting putting on their patriotic front, it convinces me they know not what the flag means. We all know what the flag means. We are all proud of the flag and we pledge it proudly as follows:

"Please face the flag. Ten . . . *shun!* Hand . . . *salute!* Repeat along with me:

"I pledge allegiance to the flag of the United States of America
And to the Republic for which it stands,
One nation indivisible,
With liberty and justice for all."

"*Hut!*"

(Note: "Under God" was added by Congress in 1954 under the urging of President Dwight D. Eisenhower.)

"That's great, just great, Sergeant," said Marvin.

"That sent chills up and down my spine — made me even more proud of our flag."

The time was well past midnight. Time to get moving. And then whistles began blowing. Some GI from the evacuation team stuck his head through the doorway and said we were fixing to leave — the stretcher cases would be moved out first.

Charles and I looked over at Marvin who was radiant in anticipation of beginning his trip home. I said to him:

"Marvin, you are going first, but we will be close behind you. Good luck, my friend, and may God go with you all the way." He smiled, one of the few smiles we had seen on his face, and said to Charles and me:

"I want to thank you guys for all you have done for me. If it had not been for the little boosts you gave me those times when I needed help the most, I would not be going home now. We'll meet again down the line. Goodbye for now."

Soon after Marvin was carried out, the same GI stuck his head through the doorway again and yelled:

"Fall out! Assemble at vehicles for loading."

This was what we had been waiting for. The fact that we were beginning our journey home stunned my mind, and in this condition it failed to recognize that my right leg had been amputated. It sent out signals to my muscles to get in a hurry and go down the steps two at a time. My muscles responded and those that controlled the movement of my right leg told it to take two steps at a time. My right leg stepped out and I tumbled head over heels to the bottom of the stairwell. I sat up and moved around a bit. Miraculously I was not hurt. I got up ready to move out.

Charles and I managed to get into one of the uncovered trucks that had bench seats down two sides. We wanted to see all we could of Germany as we left.

Promptly at 0100 the colonel, who was in the lead Jeep, got out and stepped into the middle of the drive so the entire column could see him and yelled:

"Forward ... *haarch!*"

As the column began its journey west to the Rhine, the early morning was lit by a brilliant moon that had been a full moon a few days before. As we began our drive down the Autobahn, we could see the outline of trees that made up the Black Forest. We drove through the forest and on to the rolling hills. We traveled very fast over this super highway and were soon in the flat land bordering the river.

In the early morning moonlight the Rhine River sparkled like a jewel. Its banks were lined with tall, stately trees that appeared to be reaching for the heavens. The colonel parked his Jeep in the west-bound land of the access to the pontoon bridge. The time was 0230. For the next thirty minutes we stared in disbelief at the monumental amount of men, material, and equipment the Seventh Army was moving east into Germany. We looked across the river at the column that had halted, and further than we could see was more and more equipment, men, and material. This was just one army. Six others were already across and heading for Berlin and a meeting with the Russians—these were the American First, Third, and Ninth, the Canadian First, the British Second, and the French First. None of the Armies was meeting any significant resistance. The German air force had been destroyed; their artillery was silent, so moving east was just like driving to grandmother's house. It was apparent that the end of Hitler's Third Reich was imminent.

We saw a Jeep pull alongside the colonel's, drive away, turn around, and pause again at the colonel's Jeep. And the whole column began to move, first across the pontoon bridge—a single-lane structure. On the other side we followed the first Jeep, which was stirring up quite a cloud of dust, across mile after mile of open fields beyond the bridge. We finally came to an airstrip where there were two large C-47s parked with their doors open. The men jumped out of their vehicles and ran to the planes and scrambled into their cargo bays. Charles and I were able to climb out of the truck and slowly hop along, with the aid of our crutches, to the planes and very tediously pull ourselves into one, onto a bench, and fasten our safety belts.

After about forty-five minutes in the air, the planes landed on another dirt airstrip. In front of us were row after row of tents. This was a Mobile Army Surgical Hospital. As its name implied, it could be moved as close to the front lines as was safe. Wounded men from the front line battlefields were sent here for emergency surgery and other medical needs and when they were more stable, transferred to a general hospital far back of the front lines. These hospitals, because they were always close to where the fighting was, saved many a wounded GI.

Hospital personnel met our planes and directed us to the tent we were to occupy. Inside were rows of folding cots, made up with sheets and blankets. Each man was assigned a cot. The floor was the natural terrain, the latrine (or latrines) were behind our tents — rows of the two-holers. You could use these if you could get to them under your own power; otherwise it was bedpan and urinal for you.

We had just gotten settled when our breakfast was served. What a meal! Bacon, scrambled eggs, three hotcakes, syrup, biscuits, jelly, hot coffee, orange juice — all we could eat. Yeah! Things were getting better all the time.

We had gotten the idea we would be bathed, de-loused, and issued clean uniforms but this would come at the general hospital where we were assigned. Doctors came around and made quick examinations and noted the type of wounds we were suffering from. They told us we would be flown out early in the morning, and we would be told where we were going just prior to boarding.

We were up early and were served another big breakfast. Afterward, we were handed slips of paper. Mine read:

Plane No. 1
Paris — 48th General Hospital

I was going to spend part of April in Paris!

Chapter Ten

April in Paris

When our plane from the Mobile Army Surgical Hospital (m*a*s*h) landed in Paris, there were ample vehicles waiting to take us wherever we were supposed to go. At first I was loaded into an ambulance. Then I realized I wouldn't be able to see any of Paris from inside this enclosed vehicle. I wanted to see as much of Paris as I could — opportunities to do this didn't happen very often to me. I yelled as loudly as I could and I think all the attendants heard me because they all came running to my ambulance.

"What's the matter?" one of them asked.

"I want to see Paris. Load me in the truck over there with the benches. It's not covered. I'm strong enough to ride in it."

"Okay, but you are a hell of a lot of trouble."

"Quit your bitching and get me moved out of this jail."

As the convoy began to drive through the streets of Paris, I could tell she had been badly wounded. I recalled one of the popular songs of the time, *The Last Time I Saw Paris.*

Her heart was not young and gay today but old and sad. I would never have believed this had happened to Paris if I were not riding through her scars and wounds. The war was still being bitterly fought. Blackouts were required.

By the time Major General LeClerc's forces liberated Paris on 25 August 1944, Parisians had been depleted of everything — food, clothing, coal, and nearly everything else. The shortage of coal had turned the "City of Lights" into a city of darkness and from a warm city to a freezing city.

The convoy stopped at a street crossing. One of the Parisians paused and greeted us. I asked him:

"What has happened to the city's gaiety?"

"You should have come when you were not here," he replied as he continued across the street.

Although Paris had been spared total destruction, the convoy had to wind around and take streets that had not been blocked by the barricades the French Forces of the Interior (F.F.I.) had built to bottle up the Germans in the center of the city. Suddenly we turned a corner and there she was!

With all her beauty and splendor glowing in the bright Paris sun, it was not hard to see why the world considered her one of its most famous Gothic cathedrals — the cathedral of contrasts — Notre-Dame of Paris!

In my study of architecture, one of my assignments had been to make a freehand sketch of Notre-Dame. This was a delicate and time-consuming project. I had to sketch the three rose windows, with all their delicate lead tracery, that decorated her facade. The stained glass in these windows dated back to A.D. 1100. In contrast to these beautiful windows were the grotesque gargoyles. Supporting the high walls of her sanctuary with its vaulted ceilings were the graceful flying buttresses. She was truly a beautiful and inspiring structure that at one time had been two separate basilicas.

As we drove past her, I turned and looked at her until she was out of sight. What a surprising and exhilarating experience — to see Notre-Dame in the bright sunshine of this once-beautiful city! Paris would be beautiful again when this was was over.

Not even when I was making my freehand sketch of the delicate and intricate rose windows did I dare dream of ever seeing this masterpiece of Gothic architecture! How wonderful she was!

After a short time, the convoy pulled close to a very large, multistory building and the attendants began unloading patients. Charles and I had been riding together. We very tediously climbed out of the truck. With our homemade crutches, we began hobbling toward the entry.

I noticed a high-ranking officer — I could not tell his rank — standing over to one side, observing the unloading. He noticed Charles and me and yelled out to the attendants:

"Some of you lazy bastards get a stretcher for each of these two men and carry them in," and he pointed to us.

Before we knew what was going on we were on stretchers.

"Take these men to this entry." He pointed to a side entry that had a double set of doors.

"I want you to strip them of all their clothing, stand them against the east eall, and spray them heavily with powdered DDT. Take all their clothing and burn it."

When the spraying began, fleas and lice began to fall and almost instantly we could see an unbelievable number on the floor. They were good and fat. We were told to stand there for a little while – to assure a thorough kill, we assumed. Then a doctor had us put back onto the stretchers, carried to a bathroom, and put into a tub of hot water. Hot water, I said! How wonderful it felt! While I was soaking I asked the doctor what this place was.

"This is the Army's 48th General Hospital – one of its finest. Men wounded in combat are cleared through our Mobile Army Surgical Hospitals, and some of them are sent here and some to other general hospitals. Here they receive treatment to get them strong enough to be shipped to a general hospital in the States which will care for them until they are discharged.

"When I get you cleaned up, I'm going to send you to the barber for a haircut. We've got to shampoo this tangled mass of hair first. How long has it been since you had it cut?"

"It's been over six months."

"When you get dried, I want you to get up on that table. I want to do some work on that stump."

A couple of orderlies helped me finish bathing, shampooing, drying off, and then onto the table. I noticed the doctor had a stiff brush – very much like the ones we used to groom horses – and a large bar of brown soap.

"Is that lye soap?" I asked him.

"So you've lived on the farm and your mother made lye soap from some of the grease rendered from pork skin. No, this is not lye soap but an antiseptic soap the Army uses. It's good stuff. You've had a guillotine-type amputation; it's been badly infected; pus and blood have caked and formed an ugly looking scab. I'm going to scrub all this off."

"Is it going to hurt?"

"When I get all of this crud cleaned down to the flesh, you will be able to feel the brush. I'll be careful not to hurt you. It's got to be cleaned. I don't see how you kept from getting a serious infection and dying while you were in that filthy prisoner-of-war hospital. Someone must have been watching over you."

"Indeed He was; all the way."

The orderlies brought me a pair of pajamas, a robe, and a house shoe for my left foot. They put me on my stretcher, carried me to the barber shop, and set the stretcher on the floor. When my time came, I got up and hopped to the chair. This cut took a little longer than the one I got before I was shipped out. This one was a good haircut. When he got through, the barber put on some tonic and

Brylcreem and massaged it well. When he got through combing it, he shaved me and put on a good-smelling lotion. It felt so good! He held up a mirror for me to see the front, then held it so I could see the reflection of the back in the mirror above the back bar. I liked what I saw very much. How good to be back in civilization again. When I paid him, I gave him a tip.

I was lousy with money, having been paid my back pay for three months in French francs. It was a pile of paper and it took a whole lot to pay for anything.

On the way back to the ward, I had the orderlies stop at the PX where I bought a comb and brush, toothbrush and paste, a small tube of Brylcreem, a small bottle of tonic, a small bottle of after-shave lotion, safety razor and blades, shaving cream, a small bottle of Listerine, and a little carrying case to put it all in. I was back in the business of complying with what was expected of me by society in order to enjoy the niceties of life.

The orderlies took me into a ward that had about fifty men in it. There was an abundance of French nurses, supervised by an American RN with the rank of captain. The ward was very well equipped. I found out all new incoming patients were put in this ward the first few days for observation. The captain assigned my bunk. Sure enough, it was across the aisle from Marvin and Charles.

The nurses didn't fool around getting down to business. I had barely gotten settled when one of them came at me with a needle. She told me it was penicillin and I was to get a shot every two hours, twenty-four hours a day.

"That's a lot of shots. How long do I have to take them?" I asked her.

"About ten days," she replied.

"How can I get any sleep?"

"Just go to sleep. Don't worry about waking up. We'll give the shots when they are due whether you are awake or asleep."

After the shot, she handed me a great big pill.

"You take one of these every four hours. You'll have to wake up to take this; it's awfully hard to swallow."

"What is it?"

"Sulfanilamide."

"We carried this in our first-aid kits. It was in powder form and we sprinkled it on the open wound to prevent infections."

"It's a sulfur-containing organic compound used in the treatment and prevention of various infections. The penicillin is an antibiotic produced by a green mold and is used against various bacteria. It is referred to as the 'miracle drug' and is credited with saving the lives of many American soldiers. I think your country is the only one able to produce it at this time. I'll be seeing you in two hours," and she prissied off to the nurses' station.

I looked over to Marvin and Charles. They were clean; their hair had been cut and combed; they were shaved; they had on clean robes, pajamas, and house shoes. They didn't look like the ex–POWs I'd been with this morning. The doctors had taken off Marvin's cast. He did, indeed, look like a different man and he was smiling and joking all the time. To look at him now made me feel warm all over.

Marvin needed to call a nurse so he yelled out,

"Fur-line."

I admonished him:

"Marvin, we're in France, not Germany. Besides, in Germany they are called Fräulein, not fur-line. In France they are called 'mademoiselle.' Most Americans call them mam'zelles."

"I can't say any of those fancy names you want me to call them. Oh, Fur-line!"

One of the mam'zelles finally came to his bed. He asked her for a duck. When he got it, he put it under the cover and proceeded to urinate into it.

That wasn't for me. Even though they took my homemade crutch from me, I was going to the latrine. I could easily hop that far. I got up and began hopping toward the latrine. I didn't get very far before one of the mam'zelles stopped me and wanted to know where I was going.

"To the latrine," I answered in a disgusted voice because I didn't think it was any of her business.

"What for?"

"Now look, mam'zelle, that's my business."

"Why are you going to the latrine?" she asked again.

In exasperation I answered her very plainly:

"Mam'zelle, I'm going to the latrine to take a much-needed piss. Do you want to come along and watch me?"

She screamed:

"No, no, you can't do that. No, no."

The captain heard all this shouting and came to see what was going on. The mam'zelle, in her excited French, told her and the captain said:

"That's all, Nurse; I'll handle it from here."

When the mam'zelle was gone, the captain said to me:

"I'm sorry you were caught up in this information mixup. Someone should have told you we collect all urine in this ward. Here's the story: The French pharmaceutical houses have not discovered the secrets of manufacturing penicillin. Our American pharmaceutical houses do not produce enough to supply our needs and to sell any to the French, but the French have discovered that penicillin given a patient is used by the patient's body to kill bacteria attacking it. The kidneys then filter the penicillin from the blood stream and discharge it into the urine. The French have developed a process of distilling this urine and recovering a very high percentage of the penicillin given the patient. This is also a very high quality penicillin. This is the French Army's only supply of this wonder drug. They have suffered heavy casualties — many, many wounded — and this is their only source of supply. Now be a good boy and help us help them."

"I don't like the French, but to help you I will comply. Thank you, Captain."

I climbed into my bed and asked the mam'zelle for a duck. When she returned with it, I saw that it did, indeed, look like a duck with no head.

With this day, and all of its wondrous happenings on my mind, I drifted off into the sublime sleep of one who had everything going his way.

Marvin and Charles woke me fairly early the next morning, wanting to tell me something. When I got wide awake, I looked across the aisle and Marvin said to me:

"The doctor you had yesterday stopped by. He didn't want to wake you, so he asked if we would give you the message that 'your tests indicate a serious problem with your stump that will require at least thirty more days of treatment before you will be able to return to the States.' Well, that's the message."

"What did he tell you guys about your going home?"

"As scheduled, within the next week or ten days."

"They are going to ship you two out without me? That's a crock of shit!" I began to rant and rave, and kept it up for about ten minutes before Marvin broke in:

"*April fool*, Bruce!" and he laughed and laughed.

"Today is April first and here we are in Paris. Do either of you guys know the song, *April in Paris*, written before the war?"

They both shook their heads.

"I didn't much think you would. Before the war, spending April in Paris was the 'in thing' to do. Paris was a city of lights, of romance, of fine wine, of excellent cuisine, of luxury hotels, of everything that's light and gay. The words to this beautiful song tell the story.

"The RN told me that now 'April in Paris' is spent under harsh wartime conditions." She told me:

"Heavy black drapes are drawn at night to block the light from shining outside. Outside the city is in total darkness. There are no tables under the trees. People cower in their blacked-out houses and listen for the air raid sirens. Their houses are cold and they, the people, are cold, and they are sad, and they are hungry.

"But when the sun rises in the morning and sends out its light and its heat, the city changes. The people are warmed by the rays of the sun. The people become gay and happy and the city takes on a form of gaiety, something that has made Paris famous for years. And the chestnut trees bloom because of these rays, but the people are still hungry.

"Yes, it's 'April in Paris,' and the people who were sad at night in their blacked-out houses are happy again in the bright spring sun. Now when this war is over and the thick, dark drapes can be taken down to let the light pour out and coal can be used to generate electricity for heat and lights, Paris will once again become the 'City of Lights and Gaiety'; the people will no longer be hungry — we will be feeding them."

Charles remarked:

"I remember well the liberation of Paris. The Allies were rushing toward the Seine River. Ike and Bradley hoped they could bypass Paris and let the Germans go on feeding the city's four million inhabitants for a while longer. But they had not reckoned with the explosive mood of the French Forces of the Interior — the resistance organization — in Paris. By 19 August, these partisans were openly shooting at German soldiers, and the German Commandant threatened to carry out Hitler's order and completely destroy the city before the Allies arrived. The Swedish Consul General, Raoul Nording, had a plan he hoped would save the city, as well as many French and German lives. With the full cooperation of General Dietrich von Cholitz, the German commandant, Nording sent several representatives through the German and American lines to Bradley's headquarters asking for an immediate Allied advance on

Paris so the German staff could surrender to regular enemy troops rather than the F.F.I. General Bradley, thoughtfully taking French national pride into consideration, ordered the French 2nd Armored Division, under the command of Major General Jacques LeClerc, to move in. This unit was followed by an American Division, the 4th Infantry Division, of the First Army. The German garrison surrendered after very little resistance and Paris was again a free city.

"My Army, the Third, was located south of the First Army, and I heard many stories of the things the Germans did to Paris and her people.

"The occupation was oppressive in every region of the country. Germans searched houses, arrested innocent civilians, rationed food and fuel, carted off valuables, and deployed young men to work in Germany. An occupation force of more than 30,000 administrative and security troops took over 500 of the finest hotels, hung huge swastikas from public buildings and statues, reserved the finest restaurants for their officers, set aside cinemas and brothels for their soldiers, named streets after German heroes, and melted down more than 200 of Paris's statues for the bronze.

"The 160,000 Jewish residents of Paris were subjected to the brutal excesses of Hitler's racial policies. They were forced to wear yellow stars on their clothes; they were banned from restaurants, markets, parks, and phone booths. More than 30,000 were deported to concentration camps and very few survived.

"But the Parisians mastered the war, even though it was a desperate struggle for existence. The Germans confiscated most of the coal and the 'City of Light' was put on a schedule of rotating blackouts.

When power was cut, most businesses did the best they could. Some moved goods onto the sidewalks and traded by daylight. Barbers and manicurists took advantage of the daylight and several movie theatres kept their projectors running on current generated by sturdy bicyclists. Some housewives stuffed paper into makeshift stoves to heat water. From day to day, the people had a hard time just getting from their homes to their jobs and to the stores.

"After four years of occupation, the people of France had much frustration and hatred to get rid of. Death was the fate of many genuine collaborators; for women who had fraternized with the Nazis there were the shaved heads and the contemptuous hoots of their countrymen as they were forced to parade through town.

"I'm damn glad the Germans got run out of Paris. I hate to think of them owning such a beautiful trophy. Yes, Paris will again be Paris in a short time. The French bitches with their shaved heads will grow new hair and 'Paris in wartime' will be quickly forgotten and once again her heart will be young and gay."

The following day we were moved out of this large ward into semi-private rooms (two men to a room). Marvin and I were put in the same room. This pleased me very much because I had become very attached to the little fellow. He had more guts than anyone I had run into in a long time.

About one hour before dinnertime one of the men from the dining room detail came into our room carrying a tray with two jiggers of something on it. My first thought was that it was some kind of medicine. He very professionally set one beside me and the other beside Marvin and said:

"This is some of France's finest brandy. Our orders are to serve each of you one jigger before each meal to increase your appetite so you will eat more and gain weight faster. The commander of this hospital wants you to look good when you ship out of here. I will see you guys one hour before each meal until you ship out to the States. This brandy is strong. Happy sailing."

This I could not believe. A jigger of the finest French brandy before each meal. This was going to make us all feel good. How great things were going for us, the ex–POWs of Stalag XIIA. I picked up my jigger and looked over at Marvin:

"Let's drink a toast to our good fortune."

"Bruce, I'm embarrassed. I don't drink. I never have. It's a family belief and I don't think I should violate it."

"Marvin, don't be ashamed of any family belief if you think it's right. I admire you for taking this strong stand."

"Bruce, you shared your bread with me when I was hungry. I will never forget it. I would like you to have my brandy. This is not the same as sharing your bread, but this is all I have now."

"If this is what you want. You know I love to have a drink. To be able to drink all day through is really going to be something. I'll be flying high the next few days before we ship out. How great it is! Marvin, you pretend you are drinking these when any one from the hospital comes around. If they get any idea you aren't drinking them they will quit bringing them. Okay?"

"I'll do anything necessary. I really want you to have these, Bruce."

It wasn't long before we were served dinner, and what a dinner it was — roast beef, brown gravy, mashed potatoes, green beans, fresh asparagus with cheese sauce, hot dinner rolls, coffee, and for dessert a large piece of German chocolate cake. There was more of anything we wanted. After the two jiggers of French brandy, I asked for seconds of everything. I really put the grub away and how wonderful it was. After dinner, Marvin and I talked for a while but even before it was good and dark I got sleepy. I called for a mam'zelle, asked for a duck, took care of my chores, and fell sound asleep, oblivious to anything around me.

The cocktail waiter was in early the next morning bringing us two jiggers of brandy. After he left, Marvin handed me his and I downed the two of them in a hurry. We had barely finished dressing when breakfast was served — and what a breakfast! With this meal we began to see a little French cuisine enter the menu. We were served crepe suzettes along with the traditional American breakfast of scrambled eggs, sausage, biscuits, gravy, jam, and jelly. The flaming crepes did indeed add the French flavor and atmosphere.

Later the "Pink Ladies" called on Marvin and me. These ladies were members of an organization whose membership consisted of wives, sisters, and mothers of American servicemen stationed in Paris, and Parisians who wanted to work to express their appreciation to the Americans for the work they did in getting rid of the German domination of France and particularly of Paris.

These gals were doing a great job working with the wounded American soldier. They came and visited him every day — counseled with him about his problems, wrote letters for him if he was unable to write, ran errands for him, purchased presents for him to take home, and did things he could not do for himself. They really made the wounded man maintain a high regard for himself and to see his importance to his God, his country, his mother and father, his wife, his children, and his home. They helped in so many ways I simply cannot recall them all.

I began talking to these ladies about what I should take home to Ginny from the war. I told them about the little book I'd found in the Siegfried Line, *Sonnets from the Portuguese*, which Hans was going to give someone but in his haste to retreat left in one of the concrete shelters. I was going to give this to Ginny but I too had lost it. I went on to tell them about my P-38 which General Patton took away from me. I was going to give this to her but it had gotten away also. One of the Pink Ladies spoke up:

"What a shame! Those would have been wonderful souvenirs, but they are gone from you forever. How about some perfume from Paris? Paris and perfume are synonymous. Paris is famous for its sensuous perfumes and the most sensuous of all are in the Chanel line. How about a bottle of Chanel No. 5? It is famous around the world and it's manufactured here in Paris just a short distance from here. The main office is located close by and sales are made there. They will gift wrap it for you too."

"Chanel No. 5 is not Ginny's favorite perfume, but as you say, it's famous around the world and is manufactured and sold here. I guess it would be a great buy. Okay, would one of you do my shopping for me and buy a bottle of Chanel No. 5 to take back to Texas as a souvenir of this war and a present for my wife?"

One of the women volunteered and said:

"I'll go by the office on my way here tomorrow morning. If you will let me have $30, I'll purchase a bottle and have it gift wrapped and bring it to you in the morning. All right?"

"That's very nice of you. Thanks," I responded and handed her a pillowcase full of French francs — enough to be worth 30 American dollars. This is what the Pink Lady told me it would cost.

The next day we were told to assemble in the open gallery in the east wing on the third floor — that is, all who were assigned to be flown out of Paris at 1700 hours, 12 April 1945.

When everyone had assembled, we noticed Charles present, as was his roommate wheeler-dealer. All who were in our ward at Stalag XIIA were here. We were all going to fly home together. The officer in charge of this meeting, the purpose of which was to pass out information on emergency procedures to be followed in the event our aircraft was involved in an over-water accident, began by asking:

"Do any of you men object to being flown home in a C-54 aircraft? If not, I would like you to sign this form which states that you have no objections. Men, all of you assembled here are to be evacuated from this hospital by trucks and ambulances to the Paris Airport at 1600 hours, 12 April 1945. Here you will be loaded into a C-54 aircraft which has been equipped with stretcher hangers, three deep, down both sides of the cabin. Each of you will go as a stretcher patient. There will be one registered nurse with the rank of captain and three nurses' aides to take care of your needs. They will serve you meals every twelve hours — not the fancy ones you have been getting, but adequate. Your destination is New York's La

Guardia Airport. Your route will be as follows: Leave Paris 1700, 12 April 1945, arrive Azores 0200, 13 April 1945; leave Azores 0300, 13 April 1945, arrive Gander Airport, Newfoundland, 1200, 13 April 1945; leave Gander Airport, Newfoundland, 1300, 13 April 1945, arrive La Guardia Airport, New York, 2100, 13 April 1945.

"Your aircraft will fly with radar on and all lights blacked out. There's still a war going on. We don't think the enemy can get to us but we are not taking any chances.

"There will be a wounded soldier aboard with a serious lung injury. His doctor has stipulated that the plane will not fly over 4,000 feet all the way. It will be a rough ride across the large expanse of the Atlantic. It seems to me that waves get over 4,000 feet high when the wind is up over the Atlantic. They will be lapping the bottom of your plane. Now let me talk to you about emergency equipment carried on overseas flights: your registered nurse will point out the equipment I am discussing. First, there is the life raft. The crew will deploy these if it becomes necessary. Inside this aircraft they are deflated. They are inflated by the crew when they are deployed by simply pressing this button to activate the ingredients that manufacture the gas that will inflate the raft.

"Each of these rafts is equipped with emergency supplies which include food and water and necessary equipment. Should a raft have to be used in the water, it will be commanded by one of the crew who has had extensive training in survival and rescue of passengers of an aircraft involved in an accident over or on water.

"The nurse is now holding up the life belt which will be issued to you when you board. You will put it on and wear it all the time through the entire trip. It is not inflated either, and is inflated like the rafts by pressing a button. The nurse will demonstrate the proper procedure. Please pay close attention while she demonstrates how this is done. This belt will not be uncomfortable at all. You will inflate it as you are being evacuated from the plane.

"Men, this is all I have. On behalf of all of us at the 48th General Hospital, Paris, France, I wish you 'bon voyage.' It is a thrill to all of us to have been able to get you in shape so we could ship you off of this war-torn continent of Europe to the good ol' United States of America. Dismissed."

And they loaded us onto our stretchers and carried us to our rooms. The next few days were spent taking shots and pills, drinking French brandy, and eating the superb food the French chefs prepared for the patients of the hospital — excellent cuisine.

About the middle of the afternoon on the day we left, the evacuation team came in with stretchers and began carrying us out and loading us into ambulances. Promptly at 1600 the convoy pulled away from the 48th General and headed for the Paris Airport. We arrived there about 1630 and were immediately loaded on the plane. Stretcher hangers had already been installed so all there was to getting us loaded was slipping the handles of the stretchers into the hangers and securing them. At about 1650 the captain started the motors, and at 1700 the C-54 climbed from the runway, circled, and headed west into the afternoon sun. We flew over the northwestern half of France and left the coast of the war-torn continent of Europe at Brest. We were following the sun, but we couldn't keep up with it. As it outdistanced us darkness, darker than any we had ever seen, enveloped us and we bounced up and down on what seemed to be the top of the waves of the Atlantic at 4,000 feet. About one hour after it got totally dark, it began to rain and it rained and rained. About all we could see on this part of the flight was darkness and rain, darkness and rain. Most of us took advantage of this and slept. I woke up and looked around. Marvin said to me:

"The captain is preparing to land."

I looked out my window, and all I could see was rain and darkness. Everything was blacked out.

"Where in the hell is he going to land?" I asked Marvin.

"He's supposed to land on one of the nine islands of the Azores. I can't see a single one of them, much less a runway, but I surely hope he can find a runway somewhere in that darkness down there. Oops! He's touched down. What a smooth landing! Not even a bounce! I've heard these old boys fly by the 'seat of their pants.' Oh well, who needs eyes when your pants can see so good?"

Chapter Eleven
"Oh! You Beautiful Doll"

The first man aboard was one of the service men dragging a large air hose to heat the plane while it was on the ground, and the motors were cut off. The first thing he said was:

"We have some very bad news for you, men."

I smarted off and asked:

"Are you going to send us back to Europe?"

"We have just received the news that our Commander in Chief, Franklin Delano Roosevelt, died last night, 12 April 1945, of a heart attack in Warm Springs, Georgia. Immediately thereafter, Vice President Harry S Truman was sworn in as the thirty-third President of the United States of America."

"What a shame!" commented Charles.

"And just before we claimed victory. He did want to see us beat the hell out of the enemy, and he did want to make the announcement that the enemy had surrendered unconditionally. His undivided attention to every detail of America's involvement in this war was too much for his frail body — just too much," continued Charles.

"I wonder if Harry knows anything. I think all he ever did was preside over the Senate and attend ceremonial functions," I added.

"That's what everybody says," remarked the man with the air hose.

"We'll just have to wait and see how he does," he concluded.

"This is a hell of a time to be breaking someone in as President of the most powerful nation on earth," observed Charles.

"I just hope our military momentum does not falter. If it doesn't, this war will all be over in Europe in another month at the most. We have Hitler hiding in his bunker now," concluded Charles.

Although it was only 0400 hours, the nurses decided this was a good time to serve our first meal of this trip. Everyone was wide awake and concerned about changing commanders near the end of the war. The meal consisted of a half-pint carton of orange juice, coffee, bacon and egg sandwich, butter, extra slice of toast, and jelly. Not bad at all.

Just as we were all finishing, the air hose man came back aboard and picked up the air hose and dragged it out in preparation for take-off.

This pilot was like the first one, that is: noncommunicative. I don't guess there was much to talk about except the Atlantic Ocean. That's all we could see, but we were getting a good close-up view of it from 4,000 feet up.

I didn't know what I expected Newfoundland to look like, but it was different from anything I had in my mind. The place was one big chunk of ice. As far as the eye could see, there was only ice, ice, ice, and more ice. We came into Gander Airport to refuel and take on a new crew.

When the new crew had gotten settled and had their maps placed where they could pull out the one needed without hunting for it, the captain came back and introduced himself:

"I'm Captain Mohr. I'll be your pilot on this last leg of your trip from Paris to New York. I am very proud to have this opportunity to help you guys on your homeward journey. You have done a great job, and I thank you. Now, to keep all of you from getting bored, I'm going to play a little game with you. I will give you all the information about our flight from Gander to La Guardia — the distance, the air speed, the altitude — we will continue at 4,000 feet — the headwind we will be bucking, the departure time, and any other information necessary. Now I want you guys to get out your slide-rules and figure our ETA — Estimated Time of Arrival. The man that comes the closest wins this."

He held up a one-quart bottle of J&B Scotch whiskey and all of our tongues fell out of our mouths. None of us had tasted even a drop of this beautiful nectar since we left the United States. How wonderful it would be to win this! We were all determined to do our very best. Captain Mohr then passed each man a little square of paper to write our answer on and a pencil to write it with. We would fold the paper, sign it, and drop it in his cap when he passed it around.

Everybody was out to win because they all got busy scratching their heads and figuring. But with all of this effort, it was still a big guess to come up with the right answer. But, nevertheless, we all worked real hard on this problem. While we were all trying to figure the winning answer, Captain Mohr said:

"When this war is all over and we get all the wounded flown back from Europe, I have a good job waiting for me. I am going to be a tour guide for this very large travel agency in New York. I will be narrating all of the tours I am guiding. If you don't mind, I would like to practice on you fellows during the rest of this trip. I have studied my geography lesson and I will do you a good job."

"This pilot is different from the other two. He wants to talk and they didn't. I think this is great. I have always wanted to know something about what I am seeing. I think this is an excellent idea. What do you others think?" I looked around at the rest and they all nodded their approval.

"Looking forward to hearing about what we are seeing, Captain. It's all yours."

"That's fine. I won't let you down, thank you. We will be taking off in just a little while, say 1300 hours. We will fly south and a little west out of this Canadian island, across the northern tip of Nova Scotia, across Prince Edward Island, down the coast of the U.S.A. We will follow Maine's coastline to Portland and then take a more southerly course to Boston, continue over Massachusetts, Rhode Island, and right smack into New York. I've got to get back to the cockpit. You men relax and take it easy. Look out of the plane, because we will be flying over some very beautiful landscape. From time to time I will come on the intercom and tell you where we are and what we are seeing."

The nurses decided this was about the only time we could eat our second meal so they passed it to us. It had been packed in a plastic box—another sandwich, a slice of chocolate cake, and they handed us each a carton of milk. None of us were very hungry—too excited to eat.

Marvin seemed to be making it OK. He was a different person since he was freed from the POW camp and was cleaned up and the casts removed at the 48th General Hospital. He was on his way home to his mother and some of her cheesecake. I was happy for him. His was such a pathetic case when we first saw him.

Sergeant Holmes was relaxed and enjoying life now that he was out from under old B and G. He got the right bedroom slipper. The orderly at the 48th was concerned about what he would do with one right slipper when he issued me the left.

Captain Mohr came on over the intercom:

"During some of our flight to Maine, we can see the bleakness of Quebec, the eastern part of the great Canadian Shield—a granite plateau rising to some 6,200 feet above sea level and covering some 1.8 million square miles, nearly one-half of Canada's land area.

"We are now passing some of the shield. Off to our right you can see some of the oldest landscape in the world — this great Canadian Shield — some of its rocks date back 600 million years. In just a few minutes you will see the eastern edge of the Boreal Forest. This unbroken belt of forest covers Canada from east coast to west coast. It is Canada's greatest renewable resource. We will be hitting the northern end of the coastline of Maine. You will see the beautiful scenery of Maine — the forest-covered mountains, blue lakes, rivers. How would you like to come here hunting and fishing? Nice, isn't it? We have quite a bit of flying just getting down Maine's shore. Relax and enjoy it. Our next town of any size is Augusta. I'll point it out to you."

"I can hardly believe I'm nearly home!" Marvin exclaimed.

"The first thing I'm going to do when I get to New York is call Mother. I bet she thinks I'm dead. She has not heard anything about me since I was wounded and captured. Major Zeigler did not mail any of those cards and letters we wrote in the POW camp. She will start cooking and baking. The first thing she will bake will be my favorite — cheesecake with cherry topping. Oh, she will be so happy and so will I!"

We were all so happy for the little guy. His case had been so pathetic, but he had made a remarkable recovery and was doing great. He was going to live and would, in time, recover completely. He was on his way home — that was all he ever wanted.

The little guy had set an example. Everyone on the plane began to talk at once and each was telling what he was going to do when he reached New York. Everyone was talking loudly and it was impossible to hear what anyone was saying.

Captain Mohr came on the intercom:

"If you look to your right, you will see the capitol of Maine — Augusta. Next is Portland."

"Charles, where will the Army send us from New York?" I asked the sergeant.

"I've been told they will send us to the Army General Hospital that specializes in treating our type injury that's closest to our home town. You and I will probably go to a hospital that specializes in the treatment of amputations, the fitting of prosthetic appliances, training to properly use them, and therapy to build the muscles used in wearing these prosthetic gadgets. You and I will probably be sent to the same hospital. They told me in Paris the best Army hospital specializing in the needs of amputees is in Texas — McCloskey General in Temple. Do you know where Temple is?"

"Do I know where Temple is! Do I know right from left? Of course I know where Temple is! I took my basic training at Camp Hood and Temple is the closest town. Well, it looks like I am going to wind up where I started — a 360-degree circle, but a lot has happened as I traveled around its circumference."

Captain Mohr came on:

"We are flying over Portland. I am going to change my course to a little more south. We will pick up a bit more of the Atlantic, but we will be on a straight line to Boston. You may be able to see Cape Cod out of the left windows. It will be a little east of our line of flight. We will fly over Boston in just a little while. When we get past, keep your eyes open for the Statue of Liberty. We will fly right over her."

"The Statue of Liberty!" I exclaimed.

"Captain, can you bring this plane down and fly 360 degrees around the Statue? When I left New York on the USS *LeJeune*, I could not get a good view of the Lady — she was too far away and there was a heavy fog. I have never seen her up close."

"Now look men, I can't fly this plane just anywhere I want, as I have been doing. When I get close to Boston I'll be under control of Boston's air traffic controllers; as I near New York I will come under control of New York's. Tell you guys what I am willing to do. I will contact New York's controllers and ask if I can bring this plane down and circle the Statue of Liberty. Stand by, I'll let you know what they say."

"You know, they just may let him do it," observed the sergeant.

"I hope they do; I would like to see her up close," I replied.

The captain came in over the intercom:

"Guess what?"

"*What!*" we all yelled.

"The Tower gave me permission to come down to 1,000 feet and circle the Lady. They are going to track me and tell me when to begin circling. They are also going to bring me out of the circle on a tangent that will make me straight into La Guardia — I will not have to get back in the pattern."

"Did they give you any trouble?" we all asked.

"No, they were extremely nice. They asked me to tell all of you that New York's Air Traffic Controllers welcome you home and they are proud of the job all of you have done. You are some of the first POW's to be returned to the States. It will be a few minutes before we begin this maneuver, so I'm going to briefly tell you about the statue:

"The statue was given to the people of the United States by the people of France after the Civil War. Funds were contributed for this project by the people of France. No funds of any kind from the government of France were used. The statue is made of copper sheets hammered into shape by hand and assembled over a gigantic steel framework. In 1885 the statue was disassembled and shipped to New York City. She was reassembled on a pedestal that had been built within the walls of Fort Wood on Bedloe's Island. She was dedicated by President Cleveland on 28 October 1886.

"There is a plaque at the entrance of the pedestal. On this is engraved a sonnet by Emma Lazarus, written in 1883 to help raise funds for the construction of the pedestal. It is entitled *The New Colossus* and it reads:

> Not like the brazen giant of Greek fame,
> With conquering limbs astride from land to land;
> Here at our sea-washed, sunset gates shall stand
> A mighty woman with a torch, whose flame
> Is the imprisoned lightning, and her name
> Mother of Exiles. From her beacon-hand
> Glows world-wide welcome; her mild eyes command
> The air-bridged harbor that twin cities frame.
> "Keep, ancient lands, your storied pomp!" cries she
> With silent lips. "Give me your tired, your poor,
> Your huddled masses yearning to breathe free,
> The wretched refuse of your teeming shore.
> Send these, the homeless, tempest-tost to me,
> I lift my lamp beside the golden door!"

"In her right hand the Lady holds high the torch of freedom and in her left she holds a tablet with the date of freedom, July 4, 1776.

"The copilot is bringing her down. I'd better get back to the cockpit."

The captain barely had time to get out of the cabin when Marvin cried out:

"I see her! I see the Lady! We're home! We're home! Oh, thank you, God! We're home!"

Sergeant Holmes looked out and he saw her. He laid back down and with his strong, booming, baritone voice sang the words to *Oh! You Beautiful Doll* . . . . And every man in the cabin joined him in singing this beautiful song.

The singing stopped as suddenly as it began. This planeload of seasoned combat soldiers, all of whom had fought in the most bitter engagements in Europe, all of whom had been wounded, and most of whom had been prisoners of war, began to cry unashamedly like babies. Their eyes overflowed with tears of joy and their voices choked. Captain Mohr came back in and the emotions were so tense he began to cry too. When he calmed down some, he said:

"We are beginning to circle the statue. This has got to be a most emotional occasion. This is my first trip around. I'm going to see and feel things I have never felt or seen about this gift from the French people. Those of you on the right can just look down a little for a gorgeous view of this beautiful doll. Those across the aisle will have a good view too, because the plane will be tilted a little as we bank while we are making our 360 degree circle. You won't get many chances to experience this adventure so take a good look and enjoy it."

Every man became submerged in his own feelings, but each man inhaled deeply the sweet, exhilarating breath of freedom as he looked down on this symbol of freedom with freedom's torch in one hand and freedom's date in the other.

What a sight to see! The sun was beginning to set over New York Harbor, and as it did, she sent out the colors of her spectrum with the longest wavelength — the reds, the oranges, the yellows, and the greens. The oranges and yellows blended into gold, and as we circled, constantly changing our direction, the red and gold rays danced around on the statue forming a continuously changing pattern of shades and shadows. As these patterns changed, they created the illusion of movement, and I could see her waving her torch to welcome me home. What a welcome!

The plane became level and took off in a straight line. The voice of the captain came in over the intercom:

"We are headed straight for La Guardia with clearance to land. We will be on the ground in fifteen minutes. Hang on."

He set the plane down as smoothly as the pilot did on the runway of one of the islands of the Azores, but that poor pilot did not have any lights. La Guardia was brilliantly lit and so was the entire city of New York. She sparkled like a many-faceted diamond. What a contrast we had experienced in less than thirty hours. We had left the blacked out, war-torn continent of Europe and had flown into the brilliance of New York City and the United States.

Captain Mohr came to the door of the cabin and said:

"We have just landed at New York's La Guardia Airport. This is the termination of your flight originating in Paris, France. You will deplane here and be taken into the medical center of the Army's post here on the field. By the way, Zorns won the bottle of Scotch. He didn't come very close, but closer than the rest of you. We touched down at 2046 hours Eastern War Time. Be sure you gather up everything you brought aboard. I'm going in with you guys. Here, pass this back to Zorns."

Before anyone left, I said:

"There's not enough whiskey to serve everyone on this plane, fellows, sorry about that. All of you from the same ward I was in at Stalag XIIA get together on the inside. We'll have a farewell party. We will probably never meet again."

I gathered up all of my belongings. This didn't take long. I got my shaving kit with all of its toilet articles, my bottle of Chanel No. 5, and the bottle of J&B Scotch I had just won. I laid them neatly on my chest and carefully covered them with my hands so they didn't fall off. I was ready to deplane.

A crew from the Army post began unloading the plane. I was fairly close to the front; so were all of my ward mates from the POW camp. By the time we had gotten out of the plane, a line had formed and we were forced to wait. A customs officer walked up to my stretcher, looked down at the things I had and grabbed my bottle of J&B Scotch and said:

"You can't bring this into the United States."

I reached up just as fast as he had reached down and grabbed the Scotch and said:

"The hell I can't. I won this on this trip."

"You can't bring this in," and he grabbed at it again, but I wouldn't let him have it. We were doing a lot of loud talking and Captain Mohr heard us and came over to see what was going on. After the customs officer told him, Captain Mohr took him aside and they talked for a little while. Captain Mohr got back to my stretcher about the time the line began to move and said:

"I had to pay him tax on that Scotch, I bought it in a free port. I think I had better walk along with you and keep you out of any more trouble."

About this time, we entered the building. We hadn't gone more than ten feet before the orderly, another one of those insulting, stupid, corporals stopped us, reached down, and grabbed my bottle of Scotch.

"Don't you know you can't bring alcoholic beverages on to a military base?"

"The hell I can't," and I reached up and jerked it out of his hands.

The captain looked around and asked:

"What's going on?"

"Captain, this soldier is trying to bring a bottle of whiskey onto this base. You know this is against regulations."

"It's a long story, Corporal, so why don't you just get lost."

"But Sir, it's against Army regulations to . . ."

"Corporal, get me your commanding officer."

"Yes Sir, I'm going."

"Where?"

"To get lost, Sir, as you suggested."

I was carried to the end of the hall without further interruptions. The double doors were opened, and projected from within came the lyrics to a very popular song of the time. These lyrics were projected like the flies a baseball coach belts to an outfielder. Only one person from Broadway could belt the lyrics so loudly — Ethel Merman. She continued to sing, *Rum and Coca Cola.*

She looked up and saw us.

"Hello there! Everybody come on in and have a seat. I have a welcome for you from the Mayor. Mayor La Guardia wanted to be here so badly and greet you on your arrival. On account of President Roosevelt's funeral tomorrow, 14 April, he could not make it. He asked me to fill in for him.

"I'm Ethel Merman, and speaking for the entire City of New York, I welcome you to our city on your way home from the war. I understand all of you were wounded during this conflict and all of you were prisoners of war. You are among the first prisoners of war to be returned from Europe. New York wants to show her appreciation.

"Mayor La Guardia asked me to tell you the City of New York, in appreciation of your sacrifices and contributions toward winning this great war, will pay for your telephone call home anywhere in these United States.

"I notice some of you brought in some refreshments. The nurses are setting you a table over there. They will bring you ice and mixes.

You men relax and enjoy this occasion. When you have finished your drinks, please go to the bed the nurse has assigned you. You will be served dinner, and afterward your nurse will bring you a phone and you may call home.

"Those of you not having refreshments will be served now.

"Throughout dinner, I will sing a medley composed of a part of the following: *America the Beautiful, You're a Grand Ole Flag, Yankee Doodle Dandy,* and *The Star-Spangled Banner.* I hope you enjoy the medley."

Her accompanist began running his fingers up and down the keyboard of the piano and he finally settled them down to playing the stirring march by John Philip Sousa *The Stars and Stripes Forever.* He finally blended in the music of *America the Beautiful* and after the introduction, Ethel Merman sang the words.

She sang this song twice and her accompanist blended this into the introduction of *You're a Grand Ole Flag.* She threw her head back and with all the patriotic emotion Mr. Cohan wrote into this great song of World War I days, she sang the words.

There were no great patriotic songs to come out of World War II, but then there were no George M. Cohan's either. But the World War II years had Ethel Merman to belt out the songs of Cohan and others as they had never been belted out before and she gave them a greater meaning — the equivalent of a new song. She really took out after *Yankee Doodle Dandy.*

She sang this over three times, each time getting louder, and each time our applause was louder too.

It didn't take the eleven of us from the same ward in Stalag XIIA long to finish off the fifth of J&B Scotch, but we had a good time doing it, and we had a chance to tell each other goodbye. We knew we would never see each other again — we were all fixing to call home and we would become involved again in life as it was before the war — that would take all of our time and energy. There were twelve of us at first, but one died just before we were liberated and the cannibalistic syndrome that engulfed us at that time was something to be forgotten.

I headed over to my bed when she began to sing *The Star-Spangled Banner.*

And every man came to attention. Those that could, saluted.

Miss Merman was just finishing her show when I got to my bed and what a show it had been! We gave her a thunderous round of applause. She gracefully curtsied and said:

"Thank you, thank you. Again, I extend you a welcome from all of the people of New York. We are so very proud of all of you. May God be with you the rest of your journey home. Good night". And she stepped out into the night.

One of the nurses brought my dinner on a tray and set it on the table beside the bed. It looked good and it had been a long time since I had anything to eat. But the thrill and excitement of calling Ginny killed any appetite I had. I asked the nurse to take my tray and bring me a phone. She looked like she understood the way I felt. She brought a phone and plugged it into a jack beside the bed. I placed my call immediately.

"Operator . . . operator . . . this is Bruce Zorns. . . . I'm calling from the medical center of the Army base at La Guardia. . . . I understand I may call home and the City of New York will pay for the call . . . is this correct? . . . It is? . . . then I want to place a call to Virginia M. Zorns at number 3302 in Brownfield, Texas . . . what's that? . . . oh . . . you want to know where Brownfield, Texas, is . . . . I thought you might want to know . . . operator . . . if you will route this call through Dallas, the operator there will complete the call . . . you are placing it as I suggested? . . . thank you . . . you say it will take a few minutes? . . . I'll hang on . . . you have her! . . . operator, you did this in record time . . . thank you . . . hello, Ginny? . . . Ginny . . . oh, there you are . . . hello, darling . . . I'm home."

"Bruce, oh, Bruce is this you? I just can't believe you are home. Oh, darling, I'm so happy. What a day this has been. Everything happened. This morning about ten o'clock, the postmaster called Big Boy and told him there was some mail that appeared to be from you. They wanted him to come check it and tell them if it would be alright to deliver it. They didn't want to deliver me something that would upset me any more than I was. Big Boy could tell the letters were from you . . . there was one from Chaplain Davis . . . Big Boy could tell one of the letters from you was of a current date. He knew you were alive. This was the first we had heard since you were reported 'Missing in Action.' The post office delivered them right up . . . three letters written while you were a prisoner of war . . . one written on the day you were liberated . . . one from Chaplain Davis. How happy these made me. I have been reading them over and over all day long. When anybody came by, I read these to them. Everybody is happy. Oh, I just can't believe it has happened . . . for me to find out you are alive . . . then you call me . . . I just can't believe it. . . . I wait for months and months. . . . I hear nothing. . . then in one day, bingo! and I hit the jackpot. Darling, where are you?"

"I'm in New York at the medical center of the Army base at La Guardia."

"Oh, I'm so happy. I'm going to Lubbock and catch a plane and fly there to see you. I'll see you in a few hours."

"Now wait a minute. I want to see you just as badly as you want to see me, but I'm still in the Army, and I have to do what they tell me. They tell me they are going to fly all of us out of here early in the morning. Here they are breaking us up. Some will go one way, the rest another. They won't tell us where we are going. Tomorrow we fly to somewhere and spend the night. They say they will tell us then where we are headed. So, maybe, tomorrow night I can call you and tell you where to fly to. OK?"

"I want to see you so badly tonight, but if you think best, I'll wait and talk to you tomorrow. . . . No, it's not OK. . . I want to see you tonight."

"Is Thomas Bruce there?. . .OK. . .let me talk to him."

"Hi, there Thomas Bruce. How are you?. . .oh, you want to come to New York and see me tonight. . .you come to see me when Ginny does. . .probably day after tomorrow. . .you like that. . .I'll see you day after tomorrow. . .good night. . .I love you."

He was talking a blue streak when he handed the phone to Ginny.

"Bruce, do you think you will know where they are sending you by tomorrow?"

"I think so. . .anyhow, I'll call you tomorrow. . .I love you so much."

"Here, I am still telling you goodbye. I'll be expecting a call tomorrow. Maybe after that, there will be no more goodbyes. . . . Big Boy and Granny said hello."

We had just finished eating breakfast on the morning of 14 April when the loading detail, with their stretchers, began carrying us out and loading us on our assigned planes. We didn't know which plane we were assigned, but apparently the men of the loading detail did. They had lists of who would go in what plane and where that plane was going. Marvin was loaded into a plane that took off first. Charles and I did not get to tell him goodbye or to even find out where he was going. I did not ever hear from the little fellow again. We each went our way and got caught up in the act of living our lives day by day, doing what was expected of us by society.

Another plane loaded. Charles was on this one. I did get to tell him goodbye, but he did not know at the time where he was going. And, as it was with Marvin, I never heard from him again.

I was loaded on the third plane. It took off and headed south and a little west. Finally, I asked one of the crew:

"Where will this plane take me?"

"We will fly into Atlanta, Georgia, and spend the night. The following day you will be transferred, along with five others, to a smaller plane and flown to McCloskey General Hospital, Temple, Texas. You will stay there until you are discharged in about six months. How does this sound?"

"Very good. I took basic training at Camp Hood and it is twenty-eight miles from Temple. My wife and baby can join me and stay with me until I am discharged, and then we can go home together — civilians again."

We landed at Atlanta about 4:00 P.M. and were taken into a medical center at this field. I immediately called Ginny.

"Hello, darling. . . . Here I am in a medical center at Atlanta Airport, Georgia. . . . Guess where I am going. . . . You don't know? . . . Would you like to see me tomorrow? . . . Oh, you would. . . . Well, get you and Thomas Bruce some clothes packed and head out for Temple. . . . Get a room at the Kyle Hotel for a few days. . . . I will arive at McCloskey Hospital about 4:00 P.M. . . . I am so anxious to see you and Thomas Bruce. . . . Plan to stay until I am discharged some time in September. . . . Can you make it?"

"Oh, Bruce, I am so happy. I just can't believe it is all happening. Yes, I can make it. I'll be waiting for your plane to land at Temple Airport. Darling, I'm so excited. Bye, I've got to go get ready. See you tomorrow when your plane lands at Temple."

"Goodnight, darling, see you tomorrow, McCloskey General Hospital, Temple, Texas."

Chapter Twelve

"The Strife Is O'er, the Battle Done, the Victory of Life Is Won; the Song of Triumph Has Begun. Alleluia"*

I was looking out of the window when the pilot began descending for the landing. I looked all around. The landscape didn't look right. This didn't look like the terrain around the little airport at Temple. Something must be wrong. Maybe the pilot had to make an emergency landing before he got to Temple. When one of the crew came by I asked him:

"What's wrong? This isn't Temple."

"No, this is the landing strip at Camp Hood. Ambulances will meet us and haul you fellows into McCloskey. It doesn't make any difference. You'll get there about the same time."

I thought to myself:

"The hell it doesn't make any difference. It damn sure does! Virginia is to meet this flight at Temple Airport. She doesn't know anything about this landing strip. I thought we had our reunion planned perfectly. Now it's all screwed up. Damn it! Damn it! There's no use getting mad. I am nearly there. She will find me somehow. I just hate for her to have to go to all that extra trouble. She's going to be tired anyway."

The ambulances took us straight to our ward. We had been admitted and ward 42 had been assigned to us before we left Atlanta. We didn't have to check in at the main office or the admissions office. The orderlies had a list with our name, serial number, and rank. They had assigned each of us a bunk and had laid out a pair of pajamas, robe, and house shoes for each of us.

*Giovanni Pierluigi da Palestrina, Italian composer 1588, translated from the Latin 1861 by W. H. Monk.

190

They checked us in and told us to bathe and clean up, that dinner would be ready to be served about the time we got through. One of the orderlies handed each of us a pair of wooden, adjustable crutches and said:

"Let's see how you get around on these."

Most of us took off and did real good. I had wanted a pair of crutches ever since my leg was amputated, but I was just now getting one. I could walk real well with the crutches. The orderly told us:

"I'm glad to see you get around so well on these. You will go wherever you're to go on them. We don't like to use wheel chairs. You don't get any exercise with them. By using crutches, you get a lot of good exercise which will go a long way toward building your muscles so you can wear a prothesis."

I bathed, shaved, and spruced myself up. Our dinner trays were brought to us just as I was finishing. Dinner was delicious. After eating, I got on my crutches and walked around our ward getting acquainted. Ward 42 was large. Fabric partitions could be drawn to produce a hallway with eight semi-private wards on either side. By pulling other partitions these could be made private. Two large baths were in the center, one on either side of the hallway, with a dressing area in front of each bath. The four double front-wards and the four double rear-wards on the right side of the hallway would use the bath on the right side and those on the left would use the bath on the left. This all made for a very efficient use of space.

I walked to the doorway leading into ward 42 from the hallway. I wanted to watch for Virginia. I thought to myself:

"It's 7:30 P.M. and she hasn't shown up yet. She's bound to have had a very rough time trying to find me. She's going to be very tired and Thomas Bruce will be sleepy. I hate the mix-up, but there is nothing I can do—just have to wait and let her find me." I continued to stand at the doorway because I wanted to see their reaction when they first saw me standing on my one leg. I thought to myself:

"How will they feel? Will they feel sorry for me or will they abhor me? Will they feel sympathy, compassion, tenderness, kindness, or love, or will they dislike me and avoid me? Will they see me as a cripple they will have to care for the rest of my life? Will they have a feeling of antipathy and enmity toward me? Will they be overprotective and want to do everything for me—open doors, pick up things, carry things, not let me help them?

"No! I don't want this overprotection. I want to be as normal as possible. I can't do this with everybody treating me like a baby. I may not be able to do all the things I want to do, but I want to try."

I dreaded seeing them — afraid of their verdict. But I knew Ginny. I knew she would do the right thing. She was serious when she said:

"I do," when the preacher asked her the questions in our wedding vow:

"...for better or for worse, for richer or for poorer, in sickness and in health, and forsaking all others keep you solely unto him, until death do you part...."

She answered affirmatively all of the questions of her own accord. I knew she would accept my condition as though nothing had happened.

I saw her enter the far end of the hall. She was walking along with her head bowed. She must have a problem bothering her. Thomas Bruce was not with her. She walked to within one hundred feet of me before she raised her head, and when she did she saw me. She let out a yell:

"*Bruce...!*" threw her arms up and out and began running toward me. She embraced me tightly and my crutches fell to the floor with a bang. I hugged her so very tight. We stood there in the hall for a long time — I was standing on one leg — she had both legs firmly planted keeping me from falling — we both were in heaven. What a joyous reunion! Finally we broke and I asked her:

"Where is Thomas Bruce?"

"I left him in bed at the hotel. I hired one of the hotel's babysitters to stay with him. He is one sick little boy."

"What is the matter with him?"

"He has a severe case of diarrhea. He was sick this morning when we left Brownfield. I chartered a flight from Brownfield to Temple from Pete Harris. Big Boy didn't think I should make the long drive by myself and with Thomas Bruce. He also thought I would not have time to drive to Temple and meet your plane which you said would arrive about 4:00 p.m. As it turned out we barely made it to the Temple Airport by that time. What a day this has been!

"I told you Thomas Bruce was sick when we took off from Brownfield — he had been sick all night, but he seemed much improved by the time we left. Pete thought he would be all right once we got in the air. Everything went along fine until we got nearly to

Waco. Then this diarrhea hit him again and he let go and messed himself up. He was beyond being cleaned while the plane was flying and besides the plane needed cleaning too. Pete got on the radio and got permission to land. He cleaned the plane, and I went into the restroom and cleaned Thomas Bruce. Thank goodness I had brought everything I needed. We loaded up and took off and came on about thirty minutes before your plane was supposed to land. Pete was really a lot of help to me. He took me into the office to check the schedule of incoming flights. Here they told him they did not have any listing of any Army flights to land today, nor did they have any for any other day. They suggested I try the train and bus depots.

"Pete suggested he help me rent a car for a few days — it began to appear I had a lot of running around to do — too much to depend on cabs. He got me a good clean Ford for a week. He wanted to stay and help me check into the hotel and get Thomas Bruce settled, but I told him I could handle everything else. He took off to Brownfield; I took off to the Kyle Hotel. I was going to get the baby settled before I began hunting you.

"The personnel at the hotel were real nice. Some of them remembered me from Camp Hood days. They gave me a real nice room and called a lady who was on call for them to work as babysitter. She came to the hotel in just a little while. She was middle aged, clean, and attractive. She helped me bathe Thomas Bruce and put him to bed. He was asleep before we got him covered up. I told the babysitter I did not know how long I would be. She told me she could stay until I got back. And I left to go hunting for you.

"You mixed me up good this time. I checked with the buses and trains. I didn't think it would do any good and sure enough they both told me they never carried wounded troops. Then I came to the hospital. I checked at the admittance office, and they told me they had not admitted anyone and they were not expecting anyone today. I checked at the main office, and they didn't have you registered. I thought to myself:

"Was Bruce just playing a trick on me when he told me he would get here at 4:00 P.M. today? Did the Army change its mind and send him somewhere else? Could the plane he was riding in have had trouble and crashed? These questions and hundreds more kept running through my mind. I became confused; I didn't know what to do. I was about ready to go back to the hotel and call home when a soldier stopped me as I was leaving the main office."

"Pardon me, ma'am, I overheard you asking about your husband being sent here from Atlanta. I apologize for listening and this is really none of my business. You looked so distraught I thought what I saw earlier this afternoon might be of some help to you. About 4:00 P.M. I saw several ambulances unloading men on stretchers. I overheard one of the drivers say, 'Take all of these men to ward 42.' I don't know where ward 42 is, but we can step over here to the desk and find out."

The man at the desk was very nice. He took us to the door and pointed out the building ward 42 was in.

"Just go in the side door you can see from here. You will enter a very long hallway that leads straight to ward 42. I hope you find your husband."

"We thanked him and the soldier walked me to the car. He wanted to know if he could be of any further help. I thanked him for what he had already done. He walked on down the street, and I drove to the side door that had been pointed out to me. I began the long walk down the hall, and here I am in your arms.

"What caused all of this mix-up? Why didn't you check in at admissions? Why didn't the business office show you as registered?"

"It's a long story. Let's go in the ward. I want to introduce you to the fellows. OK?" Most of the men looked up as we entered.

"Hey, you guys, I want all of you to meet my wife, Virginia."

"We're so happy to know you, Virginia. We will be pleased to have you visit Bruce any time. If we can be of help any time, please call on us."

Virginia replied:

"Thank all of you. You are so nice."

We walked out onto the patio and sat on one of the couches — very close together — and I began to explain:

"I didn't know what was going on until after it had happened. We were assigned ward 42 before we left Atlanta. For some reason we landed on the airstrip at Camp Hood and ambulances brought us here. We were not told we were going to land at Camp Hood instead of Temple. I didn't have any way to let you know of these changes. I knew you would have a lot of trouble finding me and I knew you would be tired, but I didn't know of all the trouble you had with Thomas Bruce — you must be really tired. Anyway, I knew I could depend on you to work things out.

"Well, things are going to change. The war is over. I'm going home with you. I'm going to work things out from now on — thank you for handling them during the war.

"Because we were registered and assigned to ward 42 before we left Atlanta, we did not have to check into admissions. All of the papers have not reached the main office so they do not show me registered. It's all a comedy of errors or Murphy's Law — 'anything that can happen will happen' — and it did happen."

I reached in the pocket of my robe and got the gift I bought her.

"Here's a little gift I brought you from Paris. I know it's not your favorite brand of perfume, but it's made in Paris and it is world famous. I bought it from the company's Paris office."

"I didn't expect you to bring me anything, but I had hoped if you did, it would be something from some of the places you had been. I will treasure this very much. I will wear it with my black lace nightgown. I understand Chanel No. 5 is a very sensuous perfume. Thank you, darling."

"Don't we need to begin looking for a place to live — a furnished apartment. A few days after my operation, I'll be getting leaves, and I can come in and spend the nights with you. I expect we will have company drop by too."

"Oh, yes, Big Boy and Granny want to come and visit us as soon as we get settled. Say, Bruce, we're going to need to buy a car. I've saved over $5,000 since you've been gone — from your salary the bank continued to pay you, from your life insurance renewals, from farm rents. I have paid all of our debts and have this much in the bank. I think we can buy a good used car for about $1,500. The auto companies have not made any new cars for a long time and no one knows when they will begin. I can ask Big Boy to find us a good one and write a check to pay for it and drive it here when they come. What do you think?"

"I think you are one hell of a good money manager. You've done better than I ever did. I never realized you had saved this much money. Sure, let's get us a car. We really do need one now — particularly since you have Thomas Bruce. You need one to hunt for an apartment, go shopping, run to and from the hospital, and to haul me around from place to place. Yes, we really do need a car. Do you suppose Big Boy will do this for us?"

"I know he will. He likes to do things for people. Just before I left home this morning, he asked me if there was anything he could do for us. I told him I couldn't think of anything — he said just call him if we thought of anything. He really wants to help. I'll call him when I get to the hotel."

One of the orderlies came out and told us it was nearly time for lights out. He asked me if I would like for him to walk Virginia to her car. I didn't realize it was so late. I told him I would appreciate him walking her to her car. I asked him to wait a minute.

I turned to Virginia and said:

"Darling, we didn't get much talking done tonight. I didn't realize it was so late. We'll get an earlier start tomorrow. Since it's Sunday, you can come to see me anytime after lunch. Be sure and bring Thomas Bruce. Good night, darling, I love you so very much."

And we kissed, and kissed, goodnight.

Monday morning, 16 April, all of us from ward 42 walked to the mess hall. It was a long way, but we made it on our crutches. When we finished breakfast, we were led outside to an exercise field. We sat on the ground. Our leader was on a platform at the front of the field. He put us through an hour of exercises which were strenuous, even though we were sitting on the ground. We had calisthenics every morning, Monday through Friday, unless we were excused by a doctor's order.

After our exercises, I was sent to Captain Jones's office. He wanted to examine my stump and arrange a date for the re-amputation. He was very surprised when he discovered the doctor in the German military hospital had left plenty of flesh and skin to close the end of the stump without having to shorten the stump. He told me this would not be a serious operation, but I would be confined to bed for a week. He set a date of 23 April at 8:00 A.M. for the operation.

I did not have any other appointments, and I thought I was through for the day — this was foolish thinking. I was fixing to lie down for a nap when this orderly brought in an armload of ace bandages and told me to get all of them rolled today. I rolled and I rolled. I took off for lunch and finished rolling just before dinner.

Virginia came in a short time after I had returned from dinner. She was elated. She had found an apartment, "first rattle out of the box," this morning.

"Don't expect too much, Bruce. We will be fairly comfortable. It is two story with the living room, kitchen-dining room, and bath on the first floor, and a large bedroom upstairs. It is furnished and the furniture is good. I will have to arrange for a baby bed for Thomas Bruce. I think I'll buy one and we can take it home with us.

We will need it there. The rent is $50 per month and I rented it for five months. I am going to move in tomorrow. Big Boy and Granny are coming to visit the day after tomorrow. They are going to stay two days and return home on the third day. Big Boy is buying us a car, and he is driving it here loaded with some things I asked Granny to bring me. I am getting them reservations at the Kyle Hotel. Everything has worked out perfectly."

"I went to see Captain Jones this morning. He's the doctor who is going to do the operation on my leg. He has scheduled the operation for 8:00 A.M. on Monday, 23 April — that's a week from today. I need to be at the hospital one day before the operation. I'm going to get a four-day leave beginning Wednesday, 19 April, the day Big Boy and Granny get here and ending Saturday, 22 April. That will give me one full day before the operation. How does that sound?"

"That sounds fine to me."

"I talked to Captain Jones about how long it would take for my leg to heal enough so I can be fitted with a prosthesis. He said it would take about four months for the leg to heal and to be shrunk so it could be fitted with an artificial limb, and then it would take about two months to manufacture and fit the limb so I could use it in all of those physical therapy programs the Army has outlined for me. He said it would be about six months before I could expect to be discharged. We can look forward to one-half year more of Army life. Say, where is Thomas Bruce?"

"Some soldier wanted to take him to the PX for an ice cream cone. He will be here in just a minute. That's all right, isn't it?"

"Oh, sure, that's fine. I was just asking because I'm so anxious to see him — it's been over six months. I bet he has grown a lot."

"He has. He is talking more and much better. Don't talk baby talk to him. He's trying to talk grown-up talk — and doing a good job of it.

"I think I see him coming. That's one of the guys from ward 42. It's nice of him to buy Thomas Bruce a cone."

He looked up and saw me and came running to me yelling:

"Daddy, Daddy, I'm glad you are home from the war and you were not killed." I picked him up and kissed him and told him,

"My, you have grown a whole lot and you talk like a big boy."

"Daddy, this is Sergeant Baker. He is a nice soldier. He took me and bought me this ice cream cone."

I looked over at the Sergeant and said:

"Hello, Baker, thanks for buying the boy an ice cream cone. You have made a friend forever."

Virginia and I talked and talked. We had so much to talk about. Time ran out on us and the orderly came and walked Virginia and Thomas Bruce to the car.

On Tuesday, 18 April, I talked to Captain Jones about a leave beginning tomorrow at 0800 and ending Saturday, 22 April, at 1700. He thought this would be good and granted it, but told me to be sure and get back Saturday night because he had ordered some tests to be run before the operation.

Virginia picked me up promptly at 8:00 A.M. Wednesday morning. She was in a good mood. She had gotten moved and had the apartment looking real cute. Yesterday, when she checked out of the Kyle Hotel, she left detailed instructions for Big Boy, or anyone hunting us, on how to find us.

When we got to the apartment, she fixed us breakfast. When lunchtime rolled around, we went out to a restaurant that served Mexican food. We all loved this. I said to Ginny:

"Isn't it nice for all of us to be eating together again?"

"You bet it is," she replied.

We sat there and talked until it was a little after 3:00 P.M. She jumped up exclaiming:

"We had better get back to the apartment. Big Boy and Granny will be coming in just any minute now."

We had just gotten back, washed our hands and faces, when they drove up. Granny was driving Big Boy's car, and he was driving a nice looking Chevrolet two-door coupe. It was a light blue color and had good-looking white sidewall tires. It was a perfect car for the three of us. We could put Thomas Bruce in the back seat and he would have to stay there until we let him out.

We went to the door and yelled:

"Get out and come in."

The greetings were very warm. They treated me like I had just returned from the dead. They were happy to see Virginia although Thomas Bruce got most of the attention — but this is as it should be. Finally Big Boy said:

"Come out and let me show you the car I bought for you. I think I got a good buy. I paid $1,550 for it and wrote a check on you guys to pay for it. It has low mileage — about 40,000. It's a real good car except for one thing — it came from the coastal area of Texas, and the salt has badly rusted the bottom side. It has a long way to go before the fenders begin to fall off. It will last you until you are able to buy a new one. Well, what do you think?"

"Daddy, I think it's great. Thank you for going to the trouble of finding it for us and driving it to Temple."

I asked:

"Did you check for us and buy some insurance on it?"

"Yes, I did. I bought it from Robert L. Noble Company. It's fully covered. They will mail you the policy in a few days. Here's your temporary coverage. The insurance was pretty high, but you have to have it. Your being in the service made it run a little higher. Don't ask me why. Mr. Noble told me to tell you to notify him when you are discharged. You will be entitled to a refund of the additional premium you are paying for being in the service."

"We sure do thank you, Mr. May." I always called him Mr. May instead of Big Boy.

We went back in the apartment and began to talk. I wanted to know what had taken place in Brownfield since I had been gone and they wanted me to tell them about my experiences. We talked and we talked and dinnertime rolled around. Mr. May said he knew a place where excellent steaks were served and he wanted to take us out for dinner. This invitation was accepted unanimously.

It was indeed an elegant steak house. Mr. May and I ordered beer while the steaks were cooking. Virginia wanted a beer so badly, but she did not drink in front of her folks. I kept telling her how good the beer was, and that she ought to order one. She looked at me like she could kill me.

The steaks were served, and they were delicious. I hadn't had a steak since I shipped out for Europe. You just don't find anything like this anywhere except in the United Sates.

After dinner we were all so full we wanted to go to bed, so the goodbyes were short. They drove us to our apartment, and as we were walking to the door Big Boy yelled to us:

"See you about seven o'clock in the morning for breakfast."

Virginia had invited them to breakfast. She told me she was going to serve orange juice, toast, ham and scrambled eggs, and coffee. I said that would be fine.

Then came bedtime. I had looked forward to this time and this night for over six months. When she came upstairs from the bathroom, she looked lovely. She was wearing her black lace nightgown, and she had doused herself with her Chanel No. 5. Her beauty and the aroma of the sensuous French perfume made her voluptuous. We were swallowed by exhilarating sensations. And then came morning and our heaven of the night vanished into ham and eggs of the new day.

Breakfast was delightful. The food was excellent and the conversation enlightening. We talked and talked. For lunch, we ordered hamburgers and continued to talk until 7:00 P.M. The Mays wanted to go to the hotel and order dinner in their rooms. They were tired, and they wanted to get an early start for their return home. They seemed to have enjoyed their visit. They were pleased Virginia, Thomas Bruce, and I were reunited, and we were going to return to Brownfield. I was going to work for the bank, and in a few months we were going to build our house. We enjoyed their visit so much.

This second night was as exciting with Virginia as the first. We must have been made for each other. We were going to sleep until Thomas Bruce woke us, but he had gotten to where he slept later than we. At 10:00 A.M. the doorbell rang. I got up to answer it. Standing in the doorway was my sister, Leila May, and her husband, Herman Arthur Swan. They lived in Abilene and had come to Temple to visit us. They had first gone to McCloskey and inquired about me and were told I was on leave, but we lived at the Kyle Hotel. The Kyle furnished them with our current address and here they were. This was indeed a delightful surprise. We got dressed in a hurry; visited a lot with them; skipped breakfast, and took them out for lunch. After lunch we continued to talk until about 4:00 P.M. They said goodbye—they had to drive back to Abilene.

Time passed so quickly. Before we knew what was going on, it was Saturday and the clock said 4:00 P.M. It was time for me to return to McCloskey. I had to prepare for my operation Monday at 8:00 A.M. Virginia drove me to the hospital in the car Big Boy brought us. It was just right for the three of us. She told me she would return the rented one first thing Monday and then come to the hospital.

Sunday they ran all kinds of tests on me. After a very light dinner, I was told I could not have anything to eat or drink from midnight until after the operation. At 7:30 A.M. I was wheeled into the operating room. There Captain Davis and those assisting began to prepare me for the operation. They told me I would be given a "spinal block."

"What's that?" I asked.

An aide replied:

"We will stick a needle into your spine and inject the fluid in the syringe into your spinal column. This will cause anesthesia in the lower part of your body. The upper part will not be affected. You can see, hear, talk, feel, and smell the same as you could before the injection."

"Can I watch the operation?"

"You could, but Captain Davis won't allow it. He claims it makes some patients nauseated. We'll stretch a curtain across your abdomen so you can't see. You will hear everything that's going on. Any other questions?"

"Will the spinal block make me nauseated?"

"Not likely. Well, here goes. I'm going to bend you double to inject this needle. You will feel a little sting. It won't last long. How's that? Did it hurt much? You didn't know I had done it? Well, it's done. Captain Davis will begin the operation just anytime. Tune in on it and listen. You'll find it interesting."

In just a little while I heard the Captain:

"Zorns, how are you feeling? Can you feel it as I cut your stump open? OK, that's good. I'm signing off now. You continue to listen as we talk about the operation."

I could hear them as they talked to one another about what they were doing, and what they were going to do. I didn't know what it all meant so I dozed off to sleep. When he was finished, Captain Davis shook me and woke me up.

"This must have been very boring for you to go to sleep during the operation. Well, we're finished. It turned out better than we expected. Now you have a good stump that is six inches long below the knee. We didn't have to shorten it very much to acquire skin and flesh to close the end. Your doctor in Germany knew what he was doing. You will feel some pain when the anesthetic wears off. I have prescribed medication for the pain. Just call an orderly when you begin to hurt. You made a good patient. I'll be checking on you two times a day. I am moving you out of ward 42 into a semi-private room just a short distance from 42. For the next week, I want you to stay in bed and not move around. I'll see you this evening."

They wheeled me out of the operating room and to my semi-private room. There was Virginia waiting for me.

"How did it all go?" she asked me.

"Fine," I replied.

"Bruce, this is a nice room they have assigned you. I have met your roommate. His name is Slim. He's tall, good-looking, and very personable. I like him a lot, and I know you will. He has his left leg off above the knee — way above, but he gets around good on his crutches. Oh, here he comes now."

I watched him as he came down the hall. He really moved fast on his crutches. He was so tall his crutches had to be extra long, and when he stepped out he covered a lot of territory in just one step. He came into the room, spoke to Virginia, and looked down at me. Virginia introduced us.

"Slim, this is my husband, Bruce. You two will be rooming together for a while."

"Hi there, Bruce. All Virginia talks about is you. Glad to know you. We'll see a lot of each other during the next few days. You'll have to stay in bed for the next week. I can move around. If I can do anything for you, let me know."

I noticed from the insignia on his uniform he was a staff sergeant.

"Glad to know you, Sergeant. Where did you serve?"

"I was with the Tenth Army in the Pacific. I was wounded 1 April 1945, during the invasion of Okinawa. That battle is still going on."

About that time, Thomas Bruce walked into the room and said to the sergeant: "Hi, Sergeant Slim."

And it was Sergeant Slim from then on.

It was getting about lunch-time and the sergeant said:

"They will be bringing you lunch in a few minutes. You don't mind if I take Virginia and Thomas Bruce and buy them lunch?"

"I think that would be great. You guys come straight back."

They brought me a big lunch and it was good. I ate it all. I hadn't had anything to eat since supper. I was a little weary and I dropped off to sleep. Thomas Bruce woke me when they returned. We talked, and we talked. About 4:00 P.M. Captain Davis came by with an aide. The aide took the bandage off so the doctor could take a look at my stump. He asked Virginia, Thomas Bruce, and Slim to take a look. Thomas Bruce observed:

"Daddy, it looks like the way they sew the cover on a baseball."

"That's the way it looks," said Sergeant Slim.

"They have taken the long skin the doctor gained by shortening the stump a little, and turned this piece of skin and flesh back over the bone at the end of his stump and sutured it to the back of the leg. It looks just like the cover of a baseball."

"Zorns, you've been through a lot today. I'm going to have my aide give you a shot for pain and give you a pill for sleep. I want you to get some rest tonight. Everything looks good at this time. See you in the morning. Goodnight all."

"I think that's an invitation for us to leave," said Virginia. Thomas Bruce kissed me goodnight. Virginia bent down, kissed me, and said:

"I'm glad that's over for you. You are just that much closer to being out of the Army. Goodnight, darling, I'll see you tomorrow afternoon. I love you so much." She told Slim goodbye, and she and Thomas Bruce left.

Slim went to his bed and turned on his radio. I looked over to my nightstand and saw that Virginia had brought me mine. I said:

"Sergeant, you fought in the Pacific and I fought in Europe. The war is still being fought in both theatres. You and I believe all of our enemies are whipped. Why don't you keep up with what is going on in the Pacific and I'll keep up with what is happening in Europe. I have a feeling the ending of this great conflict is going to be as explosive as the beginning."

"I think you are right. That's a great idea. We will both be here for several more months before we are discharged. Every day we can get together and summarize just what is going on in our theatre."

"How are we doing in the Pacific at this time, Sergeant?"

"We are just beating the hell out of them in every engagement. The end of Japan is near. I have seen hundreds of pale Japanese soldiers just waiting for their glorious end and nothing more. They hope, somehow, their magnificent ancestors will come to their aid and turn the tide of battle in their favor.

"The biggest blow to Japan began in February 1945 when General Curtis Le May employed the napalm bomb (jellied gasoline and magnesium). He loaded these into our massive B-29s and sent wave after wave of them to drop these bombs on factories, docks, urban areas, and even Tokyo itself. Japan, with jerry-built houses and over-concentrated industrial centers, was particularly vulnerable to incendiary bombing.

"In mid–March General Le May dispatched 334 B-29s from Guam, Saipan, and Taiwan on the most destructive bombing mission ever recorded. Taiwan became a massive super-fortress base from which the B-29s would destroy Japan."

"Sergeant Slim, I'm getting sleepy. Let's continue this tomorrow."

"I'm getting sleepy too, goodnight, Zorns."

Captain Davis made his rounds next morning before breakfast was served. He came into the room in a happy mood. He jauntily spoke to Slim and then addressed me:

"How did you fare last night?"

"Fine," I replied.

"I didn't wake up a single time. I feel good. Can I get up and walk around on my crutches?"

"No, I don't want you moving around any this week. When you walk around on crutches your blood rushes to your legs. This extra pressure on your stump could cause bleeding. We don't want this. Stay down the rest of this week, and then you can run around all you want to."

Soon after he left, Virginia and Thomas Bruce came by. Slim took them to lunch, and after they returned we all sat around and talked until about 4:00 P.M. when they had to leave. They had not been gone long when Captain Davis made his evening rounds. He examined my stump, had his aide change the bandage, and left with the following admonition:

"Stay in bed and don't get up on your crutches."

That night, I gave a summary on the war in Europe.

"Slim, President Roosevelt was the first head of a major warring country to die. On 12 April a tired and prematurely old Franklin Roosevelt was resting at Warm Springs, Georgia, when suddenly he complained:

'I have a terrific headache.' Two hours later he was dead of a massive cerebral hemorrhage.

"Roosevelt died at Warm Springs, which was for him a tranquil haven. He knew at the time of his death his cause had won.

"Roosevelt knew, too, he was loved by the American people. This letter I am quoting indicates the deep feeling the average American felt for him. It was written by one of my mother's sisters to another.

Thurs. April 12

Dear Sis,

News has been coming in tonight of so much emotion, I can't go to sleep. No doubt you have listened to many beautiful tributes to the President. His death seems to be one of those things we just did not think would happen. These are the things that hit hard because we fence our reason against them. I bet the nation really wept, each at his own radio, over the news. We hope others may be strong, as the need will be great.

Now, for the better news — Bruce has been heard from. He is alive
and coming home....

Love, Nat

"Sis, Mrs. Emily May Tandy, listened to the funeral of President Roosevelt as it was broadcast worldwide. On the back of the letter from Nat she wrote the following very brief, but beautiful account of these services.

Salute...
The garden acres at Hyde Park...
The grass...the trees...the old red barn...
The muffled drums...
The flag-draped casket carried by privates in the army, navy and
    marine corps wearing G.I. issue clothes...
The song of a bird...
The flag folded and placed in Mrs. R's lap...
The short Episcopal sermon beginning:...
    'I am the resurrection and the life...'
The closing prayer...
The bark of a lonely little dog...
Taps...

"Upon hearing of the news of Roosevelt's death, the eyes of men and women in the streets of Moscow filled with tears. But such was not to be the fate of the Axis dictators.

"Mussolini was the first of them to go. Few men in the twentieth century had risen to such heights as Benito Mussolini — or had fallen so hard. He was Italy's dictator for twenty-one years. He ruled with an iron fist. When he spoke from his balcony in Rome, oceans of worshipful admirers roared their approval. At his command, armies were launched into Ethiopia, Greece, and Yugoslavia. Through his career, scarcely a word of criticism was tolerated.

"But then in the summer of 1943, while Sicily was being overrun by Allied armies and Italy's economy was crumbling, his supporters turned on him and King Victor Emmanuel III divested him of his powers and had him arrested.

"After his arrest, he was taken to a ski resort in the Apennine mountains about seventy-five miles northwest of Rome.

"German intelligence agents learned of Mussolini's whereabouts and at Hitler's direction a rescue mission was organized. In a very daring and daredevil attempt, which almost failed, the rescue team reached Mussolini without a shot being fired. The old dictator said:

'I knew my old friend Adolf Hitler would not desert me.'

"The Germans took him to Rome, then on to Vienna, and then to Hitler's headquarters at Rastenburg in East Prussia. Hitler met him with tears in his eyes. He was bent on restoring the Duce to power, but Mussolini had not only lost power, but had lost his health and his mental ability. Benito talked only of retiring and Hitler was aghast.

"The two talked for three days and Hitler finally had his way. On 15 September Mussolini approached Hitler and said bitterly:

'I have come for my instructions.'

"The instructions were brutal: A new Fascist republic would be established in northern Italy under Mussolini, but the Germans would call all of the important shots.

"The Duce listened humbly to the man he had once considered his protégé, and on 27 September he flew to the village of Gargnano and established the headquarters of his new republic in German-occupied northern Italy and became Hitler's puppet dictator.

"His time was running out. His health continued to decline; the people had deserted him. The Allies were penetrating deeper into Italy.

"As the Allied forces moved into northern Italy in April 1945, Mussolini fled toward Switzerland, but his truck convoy was ambushed by partisans. Mussolini was wearing a German soldier's greatcoat and a German steel helmet as a disguise. He nearly got by, but one of the partisans happened to notice his expensive leather boots and grabbed him. He was taken to a farmhouse where he was joined by his mistress, Claretta Petacci, who had begged to be reunited with him. The next day, the partisans drove them to a nearby villa where they were ordered out of the car. They shot Claretta first, then Mussolini.

"The following day, the partisans dumped their bodies in front of a garage in Milan. Crowds gathered around. Some laughed, some shouted obscenities. One woman fired a pistol five times at Mussolini to 'avenge her five dead sons.' Finally, the mutilated bodies were hung upside down for all to see. For hours the crowds jeered and spat on them. Finally, as the bodies began to bloat and stink, they were taken down. The body of Mussolini was buried in the family tomb in the village of Predappino.

"Slim, that's not a very glorious end for one of the world's most powerful men. He did not have the love and respect of his people that President Roosevelt had.

"I'm going to see if I can get passes to go to town and spend some nights with Virginia and Thomas Bruce. From the news, it appears that Germany could fall any minute. I will keep up with what's going on and give you a summary in a day or two."

I had stayed in bed for a week after my operation. The date was 30 April 1945. All I had to do was wrap my stump with ace bandages every night and every morning to prevent swelling and to induce shrinkage. I asked Captain Davis about my getting a pass every night and all day Saturday and Sunday to spend with Virginia and Thomas Bruce. He said he did not have any objections if I would promise to wrap my stump every morning and night as I had been instructed. This I promised. I began requesting passes from my orderly.

Virginia and I began exploring Temple's eating establishments. The first nightly exploration was to the Kyle Hotel dining room. We had heard they were offering a very delicious special — fried chicken giblets. This consisted of chicken livers and gizzards breaded and then deep fried to a golden brown and served with cream gravy, baked potato, mixed green salad with blue cheese dressing, hot biscuits and honey, and a choice of drinks, including beer. For dessert there was lemon pie topped with whipped cream. What a meal!

I began watching the headlines of my papers to keep up with what was happening in Germany. On 2 May all papers carried this bold headline:

Berlin Falls!

The radio stations were all broadcasting this news and everywhere I turned I could hear individual radios loudly blaring:

"Berlin Falls!"

Disconnected fragments of information as to Hitler's whereabouts thrashed about in the news for a few days. Finally the following account of Hitler's last days was released by American Intelligence. It was generally accepted by all nations except Russia. Stalin kept insisting that Hitler was not dead but he was hiding somewhere. Stalin suggested Hitler had escaped to a U-boat and this was done with the connivance of Switzerland.

The intelligence report stated that Hitler's suicide was witnessed by Joseph Goebbels, Martin Bormann, and Generals Burgdorf and Krebs. Hitler's valet testified he had poured gasoline on the corpse and Hitler's surgeon had ignited it. Later his body was positively identified by his dentist's assistant from his teeth. This identification was made early in May 1945.

On 3 May I got together with Slim and gave him a summary off the intelligence report on Hitler's last days.

"Slim, when Hitler heard of the degenerate deaths of Benito and Claretta, he knew his and Eva's turn had come. The Battle of Berlin was raging all around him although his chancellery was still defended against the Russians. On 29 April he dictated his personal will and his political testament.

"1. He named Martin Bormann, the number two Nazi, his executor,
   2. He expelled Göring and Himmler from the party because of their disloyalty to his frenzied last-minute commands.
   3. He appointed Grand Admiral Karl Dönitz President of the Reich and Supreme Commander of the Armed Forces.
   4. He made a last appeal against 'International Jewry.'
   5. He concluded: 'I, myself and my wife — in order to escape the shame of overthrow or capitulation — choose death.'

"His wife was the plump Eva Braun, whom he had married the day before in a wedding ceremony in the chancellery, attended by only a very few of their closest friends. There was a very short reception, complete with wine and cake.

"Early in the morning of 30 April he shook hands with the remaining members of his entourage and retired with his wife, Goebbels, Bormann, Generals Burgdorf and Krebs, his valet, and his surgeon to his underground bunker deep below the streets of Berlin, which were being heavily bombarded by Russian artillery and American aircraft.

"Slim, a few other Nazi bosses were left behind to send the final telegrams.

"About 3:15 that afternoon, Hitler took a silver box from his pocket and opened it. He handed Eva Braun, his wife, one of the large cyanide capsules and he set the other one on the table in front of him. He pulled open the drawer of the table in front of him and got a pistol and set it beside the capsule. Eva was sitting on a sofa in front of him. She placed the pill in her mouth. Then Hitler did, then he immediately placed the pistol in his mouth. When he saw her swallow, he swallowed and pulled the trigger.

"The corpses were taken into the chancellery garden by Bormann, Hitler's valet, and a surgeon. Russian shells were falling all over the garden and the three had to dodge them. When they finally got through the Russian fire, they placed the corpses in one of the shell holes, doused them with gasoline, and ignited them. The blaze was as bright as the exploding shells. Goebbels had an SS orderly shoot him and his wife after she had poisoned their six children. Bormann disappeared without a trace.

"Slim, although Berlin fell 2 May, the actual surrender of Germany came at 2:41 A.M. 7 May 1945, in a modest schoolhouse at Rheims.

"Admiral Hans von Friedeburg, Field Marshall Alfred Gustav Jodl, and his aide, Major General Wilhelm Oxenius, signed the terms. Eisenhower refused to attend in person. Instead he sent British, French, and American emissaries to accept unconditional surrender of all German forces to both the Western Allies and the Soviet Union, together and simultaneously. When the brief ceremony ended, Jodl said with much difficulty:

'With this signature, the German people and armed forces are, for better or worse, delivered into the victor's hands.'

"The Allied representatives made no comment.

"The Germans were then conducted to Eisenhower's office and asked if they understood what they had signed.

'Ja,' said Jodl.

"The next day, to symbolize unity among the victors, the ceremony was repeated in Berlin, where Zhukov signed for the Soviet Union.

"May 8 became the historic V-E day.

"And the entire world, except Japan, rejoiced at the news. But nowhere were the demonstrations more wild than in Moscow. The announcement came long before dawn, and thousands of people poured into the streets wearing everything from pajamas to fur coats. The crowds stayed on and grew larger. Everywhere the Red Hammer and Sickle hung beside the Stars and Stripes. Roars went up:

'Long live Truman!

'Long live Roosevelt's memory!

'Long live the great Americans!'

"Slim, this is my summary of the end of the war in Europe. I gained this information by listening to the radio as it happened and by reading about it the next day in the newspapers. Nothing, Slim, has sent chills up and down my spine as much as have the events of the last eighteen days of the mammoth conflict, and as I look back on them now, they seem to have been a wild dream.

"Now it's up to you to summarize the ending of the war with Japan."

Virginia and I had dinner at a different restaurant in Temple every night until we had tried them all. Then we went back to those we liked the best. This took money and driving around took gasoline.

One afternoon we stopped at a Magnolia station for gas. We stopped at a Magnolia station because Big Boy was consignee for Magnolia in Brownfield.

Here we met Todd Stewart. He waited on us, and I introduced myself. I told him I was a patient at McCloskey — had been wounded in Germany — worked in a bank before I was drafted — my father-in-law was an agent for Magnolia in Brownfield. I explained I needed to buy gasoline on my Magnolia credit card, and from time to time I needed to cash a personal check on my bank in Brownfield. I further told him I could not go to the local bank for this because I was on duty when the bank was open. I stood there scared to death while I waited for Todd to respond.

"No problem. I'll be happy to handle this for you."

And I breathed a big sigh of relief. This began a very close relationship. Todd took us under his wing and went out of his way to be nice to us the rest of the time we were in Temple. He introduced us to his lovely wife Eva Jo. They invited us to their home for dinner several times. We invited them to have dinner with us at some of the better restaurants. They would take Thomas Bruce home with them to spend the night. He really enjoyed these occasions. These last ninety-odd days we spent in Temple were very enjoyable.

One day, while I was enjoying their hospitality, I thought back to other days and other times and other places and other people being nice to me. It had happened to me all over the United States. I thought back to the pass I got to go into Washington D.C., while I was stationed at Fort Meade, Maryland. I thought of the unbelievable incident of Mr. and Mrs. Oscar W. Gearheart stopping their car as my friend and I were just walking down the street trying to figure a way to see Washington and asking us if we would like for them to show us the Capitol. What a time they showed us!

And I thought back to the time I spent at Camp Campbell, Kentucky. I thought of C. W. (Bill) Bailey and his lovely wife, and the lovable Mrs. Day. These people made the last few days before I was shipped overseas the happiest of Virginia's and my lifetime.

Now, here at McCloskey General Hospital, Todd and Eva Jo Stewart were making the three of us feel right at home, and this made the time fly.

All of these were great American patriots fighting the war on the home front and doing as much to win as any other essential industry. I salute all of them. They deserve a medal.

I was called into the artificial limb shop about the middle of June. I was measured for my prosthesis. The Army manufactured the limbs for their patients. Although they had trained technicians and good equipment, the finished product was still crude looking and very bulky and heavy. It took these technicians a long time to finish a prosthesis, but in their defense I will say they did have to wait, in most cases, for the patient's stump to stop swelling and for it to shrink as much as it was going to.

It was quite interesting to observe the manufacturing process. First, they took a piece of willow-log and began to carve and saw on it. It began to take the shape of the leg below the knee. The foot came pre-manufactured — they selected the right size. The inside of this limb was carved out so a bucket could be inserted. This was sometimes called an insert. This was made out of leather and was made to fit the stump. The stump fitted into this bucket. Stump, bucket, and all slipped into the hollowed out piece of willow. A brace hinge was fastened to either side of the limb. These extended about fourteen inches above the knee. A leather corset was bradded to the brace hinges so the corset would lace in the center. We spent many an hour working with the technician to get this thing to fit as comfortably as possible.

Sergeant Slim was having his prosthesis manufactured the same time I was. His amputation was above the knee and his prosthesis was much more complicated and much harder to make than mine. We were spending a lot of time together in the shop, waiting for the technician to make some changes so we could try it on again.

On 25 July he began to give me his summary of the war in the Pacific from his last report to date.

"Bruce, you remember I told you I was wounded 1 April in the invasion of Okinawa. It took eighty-two days to conquer this island. 110,000 Japanese were killed and 11,000 surrendered; and 11,000 Americans were killed. It was the Japanese determined defense of this island that caused President Truman and the Joint

Chiefs of Staff to conclude the only way to get Japan to agree to an unconditional surrender was to invade the main island.

"This, they estimated, would cost each side one million men and extend the fighting two years.

"Japan had lost all of its strategic island bastions. Japan's navy and air arm had been shattered and Major General Curtis E. Le May's 21st Bomber Command was fire-bombing vast sections of the main island on a daily basis. A naval blockade had severed many of Japan's vital supply lines. The Japanese were starving, yet they gave no concrete signs of capitulating. This reluctance to lay down arms stemmed from two reasons — their belief that to surrender was a disgrace and their concern for the future of their Emperor, Hirohito, whom they venerated as a descendent of the gods.

"Bruce, this is all I have to report at this time. I'll stay tuned-in and report again just as soon as something happens. OK?"

"That's fine, Slim. We're both going to be around for a good while longer. When you have something new, let me know."

During the late afternoon of 6 August, he came running into the shop all excited and out of breath.

"Have you heard the news?"

"What news?" I replied.

"This morning the fire-bombing raids on Tokyo planned by General Le May were cancelled. Instead of a large number of our B-29's, one lonely B-29, the *Enola Gay*, piloted by Colonel Paul W. Tibbets, Jr., with a specially trained crew took off and headed toward Japan accompanied by three or four other planes. This plane was named *Enola Gay* on instructions from Colonel Tibbets. This was his mother's name and he wanted to honor her because she encouraged him to learn to fly.

"At 8:15 A.M. Colonel Tibbets released over Hiroshima a uranium bomb of the type called 'Little Boy.'

"On his return he reported:

'As far as I was concerned it was a perfect operation.'"

Slim continued his report:

"It will be hours before the mushroom clouds, smoke, and flames have sufficiently blown away to permit adequate photo-reconnaissance. I'll give you a report tomorrow as the news comes in."

Slim was even more excited the following day.

"All radio stations and all newspapers have been reporting the bombing of Hiroshima. More information about the atomic bomb was contained in the press release covering the explosion of the first atomic device. That release reported:

"At 5:30 A.M. 16 July, in a remote New Mexico desert the very first atomic device was placed upon a steel tower near Alamogordo Air Base and detonated. Under the direction of Dr. J. Robert Oppenheimer, a theoretical physicist from the University of California, the 16 July test was successfully staged, producing what an official War Department release later described as 'a revolutionary weapon destined to change war as we know it, or which may even be the instrumentality to end all wars.'

"So secret was the development of this project only a handful of persons were aware of its existence. Not even Vice President Truman knew until the day after Roosevelt died and he had been sworn in as President. It remained for Truman to decide if, how, where, and when this fantastic weapon should be employed.

"When this device was exploded, and immediately upon the burst of flames, Dr. Oppenheimer thought of two passages from a Hindu epic.

"One went: 'If the radiance of a thousand suns were to burst into the sky, that would be the splendor of the Mighty One.'

"The second was: 'I am become death, the shatter of worlds.'

"This tremendous blast rushed out across the desert, and above it rose the first of those awful mushroom-shaped clouds.

"Even after Colonel Tibbets, Jr., dropped the bomb on Hiroshima and the Japanese had time to survey the damage, even after the demand to accept unconditional surrender or face complete destruction, the Japanese did not indicate any willingness to accept the terms of the Potsdam Declaration. I will report back to you when the Japanese make a move."

Slim came running into the shop during the afternoon of 9 August.

"A plutonium bomb known as 'Fat Boy' was dropped on Nagasaki today. The destruction exceeded the most careful estimation of scientists.

"It is impossible to convey the full meaning of these twin detonations. The casualty toll was staggering, and of course, fails to suggest the indescribable suffering incurred. Estimates claim — no one knows for certain — the following casualties:

"Seventy thousand to 80,000 killed in Hiroshima with a like number injured; 40,000 killed in Nagasaki with 60,000 injured."

Slim made the following observation:

"As terrible as those casualty figures are, the bombs did not cost nearly as much as an invasion would have cost."

On 10 August Slim heard the following:

"Tokyo has sued for peace on the basis of the Allies' Potsdam Declaration, but requested that Hirohito be retained as Emperor. Truman, acting on the advice of his top advisers, has come to the decision that this stipulation is in the best interest of the United States."

Actual surrender came on 15 August, and this brutal war was over.

I told Slim the next time we were talking:

"You and I heard the end of the war over the radio. I heard the beginning on radio, too. Here is that story:

"It was ten o'clock in Berlin, Friday, 1 September 1939, when Hitler announced to the Reichstag and the German nation he had ordered German troops to invade Poland.

"This announcement was carried around the world by radio, and yet few capitols in Western Europe paid much attention to it. These Europeans did not want to give up the last few days of their summer holidays.

"But on Sunday, 3 September 1939, at 11:15 A.M. Prime Minister Neville Chamberlain announced over BBC:

'This country is at war with Germany,' Londoners experienced their first air-raid alert.

"That Sunday, the alarms were false; no bombs were dropped anywhere in the West. But no one could deny summer was over and war had begun.

"I heard the frenzied announcement by Hitler — probably the most frenzied of his career — while I was in bed in my apartment, Brownfield, Texas, 4:00 A.M. Friday, 1 September 1939. The news media had carried information that Hitler would address the Reichstag, and this address would be carried by radio around the world. I had purposely gotten up early to hear it. I was single at the time — three years out of college — in excellent health — just right for military service. This address disturbed me, and yet I did not realize I had been listening to the beginning of the most devastating war in the history of mankind."

On 1 September 1945, at 11:15 A.M., our time, six years after Hitler ordered German troops to invade Poland, I listened to the ceremony that officially ended this barbarous conflict. It was broadcast by radio around the world and the world listened intently. I listened to this dramatic occasion from my bed in ward 42, Mc-Closkey General Hospital in Temple, Texas.

This event took place on the deck of the battleship *Missouri* anchored in Tokyo Bay. The ship flew the same flag that flew over the Capitol in Washington the day Pearl Harbor was bombed by the naval and air forces of the Empire of Japan.

Seventeen days before this ceremony, Japan had surrendered. On 15 August 1945, Emperor Horohito had issued the following statement:

"We, the Emperor, have ordered the Imperial Government to notify the four countries: the United States, Great Britain, China, and the Soviet Union that We accept their Joint Declaration. . . ."

And at 7:00 P.M. on that same day, President Truman read the following statement to White House correspondents gathered in his office:

> I have received the following message from the Japanese Government in reply to the message forwarded to that Government by the Secretary of State on August 11. I deem this reply full acceptance of the Potsdam Declaration which specifies the unconditional surrender of Japan. . . .

The war was over!!! The guns were silent and the victors celebrated wildly.

Even though the Emperor had surrendered his nation on 15 August 1945, such things had to be done officially and formally.

The formal ceremony took place at 1:00 P.M. 2 September 1945, Japanese time, and was presided over by General MacArthur, Supreme Commander of Allied Forces in the Southwest Pacific.

Jammed together on the deck of the *Missouri* was a mass of correspondents from all warring powers and Allied officers: British and Australians with scarlet bands on their caps and collars; Gaullist French with vivid decorations; Dutch with gold-looped emblems; Chinese in olive drab; Russians in stiff shoulderboards, and Americans simply garbed in plain suntans.

Representing Japan was the one-legged foreign minister, Mamoru Shigemitsu, wearing striped pants and top hat. He limped aboard the *Missouri* from a gig flying the Stars and Stripes. Accompanying him was General Yoshijiro Umezu, representing the general staff.

Jammed above the deck, wherever they could find a place to stand, were hundreds of the crew of the *Missouri* in their white uniforms anxious to witness this monumental occasion which was not likely to be duplicated again.

MacArthur opened the ceremony with a brief and generous address. Now Shigemitsu limped forward and with great dignity signed two copies — one in Japanese and the other in English. He was followed by Umezu. MacArthur stepped forward, and with him were two high-ranking officers who had been rescued from Japanese prisoner-of-war camps: Lieutenant General Jonathan M. Wainwright, who he was forced to leave behind in Corregidor, and Lieutenant General Sir Arthur Percival, the loser of Singapore. MacArthur then signed and he was followed by Admiral Nimitz. Now the Allied delegates stepped forward one at a time in prearranged order and signed two copies. The last delegate signed and *it was done.*

General MacArthur concluded this ceremony with this short statement:

> We are gathered here, representatives of the major warring powers, to conclude a solemn agreement whereby peace may be restored. The issues, involving divergent ideals and ideologies, have been determined on the battlefields of the world and, hence, are not for our discussion or debate. Nor is it for us here to meet, representing as we do a majority of the people of the earth, in a spirit of distrust, malice, or hatred. But, rather it is for us, both victors and vanquished, to serve, committing all our peoples unreservedly to faithful compliance with the understandings they are here formally to assume. It is my earnest hope . . . that from this solemn occasion a better world shall emerge . . . a world dedicated to the dignity of man . . . . Let us pray that peace be now restored to the world, and that God will preserve it always. These proceedings are closed.

With this ceremony and the statement by General MacArthur,

"The strife is o'er, the battle done, the victory of life is won, the song of triumph has begun. Alleluia!"

I sat there on the side of my bed in ward 42 and turned the radio off and contemplated what I had just heard. I was in a daze. I could hardly bring myself to believe the war was over. Yet everyone had expected it. Look how many times Virginia and I said to each other:

"This war will surely be over some time!" But now it's over, and it's hard to believe. It seems like we are all in a vacuum, just milling around not knowing what to do or how to do it.

The war may have been over, but I was still in the Army. That afternoon Staff Sergeant Bill Lewis, our physical therapy director, took us out to ride horses and to walk down steep inclines.

This may sound like we were wasting our time on the trivial, but mounting a horse is very difficult for an amputee without expert instruction on the proper procedure. When it came to mounting horses, I was lucky my right leg was amputated instead of my left. Most horses are trained to be mounted from the left side. All I had to do was go to the left side of the horse, put my left foot in the stirrup, swing my right leg over the saddle, and put my right foot in the right stirrup. I was ready to ride. This was easy for me because I still had my left leg and mounting was the same as it had always been.

The soldier with his left leg amputated had a problem. He needed a horse trained to be mounted on the right side, or he needed to be strong enough so he could mount the left side of the horse by grabbing the saddle-horn and swinging himself into the saddle. Very few could do this.

Every GI had his own problem. There was nearly every type amputation in this group today: below knee right, below knee left, above knee right, above knee left, AK right and left, BK right and left.

These double amputations seemed impossible, but Sergeant Lewis had the answers and he went about patiently instructing each individual how to mount a horse. In less than thirty minutes he had everyone mounted and he headed us west across the pastures of Central Texas.

We rode for about twenty minutes and he halted us at the top of a little hill and had us dismount. This presented problems, as did mounting, but the sergeant had the answers and got everyone off. He led us across the plateau of the hill to the other side, and we saw why we had stopped. From the plateau of the hill, the side sloped down about thirty degrees to another level. This slope was about twelve feet long. Sergeant Lewis walked over to the slope and began his lecture on "Slopes."

"Slopes are very difficult for the amputee to navigate. It's easier for him to climb stairs or curbs. Here's why: the foot of your prosthesis does not have a movable ankle. When this foot is attached to the leg of your prosthesis, the entire unit is rigid. There is no bending the foot up or down. If you were to begin walking down the slope as you did before you lost your limb, you would tumble head

over foot to the bottom. You can go up and down slopes safely.
Here's how: When you get to the beginning of a slope turn sideways
facing in a direction that puts your prosthesis next to the slope. Now
step down with your prosthesis the distance of a medium step. Now
bring your natural leg down to this level. Keep repeating this until
you are at the bottom of the slope. You are actually walking down
the slope sideways. Not very graceful, but you can get down the
slope without falling. Are there any questions? How are you going
to climb the slope?"

Someone yelled out:

"The same way we came down."

"I should let you try it. You climb it in reverse order. You take
your first step with your natural leg. You step up and out. When this
leg is planted, raise your body with this leg and bring your prosthesis up beside it. Repeat until you are at the top. Let's all start
climbing. When you get to the top, mount your horse. We need to
get back to the hospital."

The sergeant got everyone to the top of the plateau, mounted
and he headed us toward the hospital. On the way back, he gave us
our assignments for tomorrow.

"Tomorrow morning, we are going swimming. Everyone meet
at poolside at 0900 hours. Go by the leg shop and pick up your prosthesis before you come. After swimming, we are going to play eighteen holes of golf on the municipal course."

The hospital had a beautiful Olympic-size swimming pool. We
had been swimming a lot since we first arrived at McCloskey. They
continue to encourage swimming. This is the best form of exercise
for amputees. Most can develop a style of swimming and excel in
it. Most amputees enjoy this sport. I did. But this was short-lived.
I went swimming with Ginny and Thomas Bruce one Sunday in the
municipal pool. It was crowded, but we were enjoying it until one
of the very young children – a boy about two years old – yelled to
his mother:

"Look mommy, that man just has one leg," and he kept pointing
at me.

I have never been swimming since.

Golf is an ideal sport for the amputee. Sergeant Lewis had told
us he would get us some carts. I could just picture us riding around
the course in a three-wheel electric cart. Here the pro-shop came
with the carts. We each fastened our clubs to the cart given us and
walked and pulled our clubs around the course. Before we started,

we each got a hamburger and Coke. All who started made it around the course, except two. They were the two double amputees in our group. I was surprised at what they had already accomplished today.

Golf is a sport you can enjoy playing for a lifetime. Its big drawback is its cost. That eliminates many.

The leg shop continued making adjustments on our prosthesis. Every day, when we finished the project assigned us, we would go by the shop and talk to the technician about points of pressure that developed during the day which caused the prosthesis to pain the stump. We left it in the shop overnight. I had never worn mine home. Day by day we were getting closer to a comfortable fit.

On 9 September I received notice to pick up my prosthesis at the leg shop, put it on and wear it and report to the office of Captain John Somers, Assistant Post Personnel Officer, at 0900 hours, 10 September 1945.

Virginia took me by the leg shop and on around to Captain Somers's office. I walked to the door and knocked. I heard him say:

"Come in."

I opened the door, stepped inside, came to attention, saluted, and said:

"Private First Class Bruce C. Zorns reporting as ordered, Sir."

"At ease, Private. I would like for you to walk across this room a couple of times. I want to see how you walk."

I made the two trips across the office and paused. He said:

"That's very good. You are as good a walker as we have turned out. Sergeant Lewis has told me you have done a lot of good going and visiting amputees who are depressed over losing one or more limbs. He said your visits, in every case, cheered them and they began to apply themselves to solving their problems and trying to learn how to live a good life with their handicaps. I want to thank you, too.

"Say, how would you like to become a civilian?"

"You mean, to be discharged?"

"Yes."

"When?"

"Right now. I have yours prepared and signed by Lieutenant Colonel Charley H. Freeman, our Post Executive Officer. I will need to get your thumb print on the lower left-hand corner of the back, you will need to sign under this, and I will need to sign it in the lower right-hand corner. There are other documents we have to execute."

The way I was feeling, I would sign anything — even a deed to the south forty — if it would help get me out of the Army. We signed and signed, and finally the captain said:

"Well, that's it. Here's your discharge and here is your muster out pay of $300." I jumped up and came to attention and saluted the captain. He said:

"Zorns, your saluting days are over. You are a civilian now. I suggest that you get out of that uniform just as soon as you get some civilian clothes."

I reached my hand across the desk and shook his hand and said:

"Thank you, Captain," and I turned and literally bolted out of his office in a dead run toward the car and Virginia. Before I could stick my head inside one of the windows, Virginia yelled out to me:

"Bruce, what on earth is the matter with you? You're acting like a mad man."

"I am a civilian and I am rich," I told her.

"You're what?"

"I'm a civilian and I'm rich," and I handed her my discharge and the $300 cash.

"Oh, you are already discharged from the Army. This is the moment we have been waiting for. We'll never be separated again — never say any more of those sad goodbyes. Bruce, this is wonderful. Let's go home today. It's not too late to start. It won't take me very long to pack. Do you need to go by ward 42 and pick up anything?"

"I have a few clothes there and some of my shaving stuff. Drop me by and I'll run in and get whatever is there. I'll be right back." I ran into the ward; gathered what I thought was there; said goodbye to the fellows there, including Sergeant Slim. As I was leaving, I noticed my radio, disconnected it, put it under my arm, and said goodbye to ward 42 and McCloskey General Hospital. I will be eternally grateful to this great institution — it did a lot toward rehabilitating me, as it did for thousands of other Army soldiers.

As I climbed into the car I said:

"Let's go."

Virginia pulled up alongside the curb when she reached the apartment. I had thought to get my cane and crutches as I left ward

42. I reached in the back seat and got my cane. When I opened the door I heard music. I asked Virginia if she knew where it was coming from. She told me:

"There's a little church in the middle of the next block, just down the street from where we are parked. Their choir practices for the next Sunday's services once or twice a week. In the summer they raise the windows to the choir room. If the breeze is soft enough and from the right direction, the music carries a little past our apartment. I have heard it several times since I've lived here. It's a good choir—I've enjoyed listening to them."

"Ginny, do you remember my telling you about the portable church service the 14th Armored Division brought to the 62nd Armored Infantry Battalion the day before we were committed to battle?

"You do?

"This song we hear was the closing hymn of that service.

"I also told you during the singing of this great hymn I saw God and He saw me. I can never forget this service."

I climbed out of the car with my cane and began to walk to our apartment. I was doing pretty well with my walking. About half way there, I saw Thomas Bruce run out of the apartment. He was crying over and over again:

"Daddy, daddy, you can walk again! Oh, daddy, I'm so happy! You can walk again!" He was sobbing and crying with joy. His emotions were uncontrollable. He ran to me and held up his arms. I picked him up and held him ever so tight and said:

"Yes, yes, my son, I can walk again." He was sobbing and crying with joy. I could not retain my composure, and my eyes filled with tears. I had heard Virginia admonish him just a few days ago:

"Brave soldiers never cry."

I didn't want him to see me with tears in my eyes, so I put him down and turned away from him. I looked up into the blue sky of central Texas. I looked and I looked, but I could not see into the infinity of space as I had done in my Forest Cathedral at Epinal, France. I would like to talk to Him and have Him talk to me. I know He's there, so I'll talk to Him. I stood at attention and said:

"Oh, God, the great war is over...the guns are silent...peace has been restored to Your world. ... I have returned safely...I have been reunited with my family...I have been discharged...we are returning home...I can walk again. ... Oh, Father you told me in my Forest Cathedral at Epinal, 'Be Not Afraid, I Will Be with You.' Oh, God, you were indeed with me — *all of the way.* "

I snapped to attention and saluted Him and said:

"Thank you, *Sir.*"

I waited for a minute. I thought He might speak to me. Well, anyway, I knew He heard me. I turned to go to the car, and as I did I heard the combined choir as their voices reached a mighty crescendo as they sang the last verse of *God Will Take Care of You,* and I was able to filter out the voice of God as He sang to me:

"I Will Take Care of You."